How to Improve Profitability Through More Effective Planning

WILEY SERIES ON SYSTEMS AND CONTROLS FOR FINANCIAL
MANAGEMENT

Edited by Robert L. Shultis and Frank M. Mastromano

EDP Systems for Credit Management
Conan D. Whiteside

Profile for Profitability: Using Cost Control and Profitability Analysis
Thomas S. Dudick

Zero-Base Budgeting: A Practical Management Tool for Evaluating Expenses
Peter A. Pyhrr

Forecasting Methods for Management
Steven C. Wheelwright and Spyros Makridakis

Direct Cost and Contribution Accounting: An Integrated Management Accounting
System
Germain Boer

The Corporate Memory: A Profitable and Practical Approach to Information
Management and Retention Systems
Barbara N. Weaver and Wiley L. Bishop

Pricing Techniques for the Financial Executive
John C. Lere

The Strategy of Cash: A Liquidity Approach to Maximizing the Company's Profits
S. D. Slater

Fringe Benefits—The Depreciation, Obsolescence, and Transience of Man
Stanley M. Babson, Jr.

Competing for Capital—A Financial Relations Approach
Bruce W. Marcus

How to Improve Profitability Through More Effective Planning
Thomas S. Dudick

CONTRIBUTORS

Ralph M. De Biasi, Vice President of Finance, Leviton Manufacturing Company

Leo G. Blatz, Vice President and Controller, Consumer Products Operations, The Singer Company

Thomas S. Dudick, Manager, Ernst & Ernst

Paul H. Elicker, President, SCM Corporation

Charles S. Ferris, Chief Engineer, Southern Bell Telephone Company

Sam R. Goodman, Vice President and Chief Financial Officer, Ampex Corporation

Richard M. Hexter, Executive Vice President, Donaldson, Lufkin & Jenrette, Inc.

George Ingram, Jr., President, Reed-Ingram Corporation

Leonard Kamsky, Vice President, W. R. Grace & Company

James W. McKee, Jr., President and Chief Executive Officer, CPC International, Inc.

Paul Maranka, Manager, Materials, Automation & Measurement Division, Bendix Corporation

D. Larry Moore, Manager of Materials, Sperry Flight Systems Division, Phoenix, Arizona

Ralph P. Moore, Vice President, Liggett & Myers, Inc.

Richard M. Osgood, Vice President, GTE Sylvania, Inc.

Peter A. Pyhrr, Vice President—Finance, Alpha Wire Corporation

John E. Rhodes, Chairman, Finance Committee, Schlumberger, Ltd.

Joel L. Roth, President, Industrial Distributors of America, Inc.

Robert M. Schaeberle, Chairman of the Board, Nabisco, Inc.

William W. Simmons, Consultant, W. W. Simmons, Inc.

Frank J. Tanzola, Senior Vice-President and Corporate Controller, U.S. Industries, Inc.

Richard J. Tersine, Associate Professor, Old Dominion University

Michael R. Tyran, Chief, Controller Systems Planning, General Dynamics Corp.

To
my sister and brother-in-law
Stella and Bill Cullen

FOREWORD

The increasing complexity of corporate affairs demands that an organized and anticipative approach be taken to decision making. Although other names are sometimes used to give emphasis to the special objectives of particular corporations, such an approach is commonly referred to as *business planning*. The body of knowledge pertinent to business planning has now reached significant proportions. The specialized techniques contained in those writings provide many useful professional insights, but care must be taken to avoid being trapped in a maze of methodology. No technique can effectively substitute for a realistic and incisive consideration of a firm's resources, objectives, and accomplishments.

The primary requirement for effective profit planning reflects the Greek adage, "Know thyself." It is essential that a corporation give full consideration to its available resources and its controlling limitations before it begins its process of profit planning. A failure to give such consideration may lead to an unattainable tabulation of hopes and dreams that are poorly rooted in the soil of economic reality. In pursuing this introspective examination, it is as important to identify the limitations of an economic enterprise as it is to identify its traditional strengths, since an awareness of limitation may subsequently direct the employment of resources toward the most effective areas.

In a quantitative sense much of the essential data needed as a prelude to business planning can be derived from the official accounting records of the corporation. To the extent that such data is comparative, audited, and subject to detailed analysis, the accounting records can usefully clarify historic circumstances. However it is also important to insist that a qualitative consideration be given to the available resources, and this may mean the development of specialized data banks that transcend the materials normally made available to shareholders. Foreign cash is not necessarily a resource if a foreign government has placed a limitation on remittance or use. Receivable balances may not represent potential cash if collection is in doubt. Inventories may not lead to profitable sale if they represent obsolescent stocks. The quality of resources is an important part of the assessment process.

The fast-moving pace of today's economic world may also make it necessary to dissect and to restate the customary financial facts of an operation to identify specialized influences. The elimination of foreign exchange influences, price level changes, or escalated interest rate assumptions from the operating data may significantly clarify the true economic consequences of historic corporate action. Similarly, explicit data dealing with market size, product characteristics, the economic and political environment, and other data may also be usefully presented as an element of the corporation's tabulation of resources and limitations. The business plan should not be allowed to suffer from the ills that limit conventional accounting.

The planning process begins with a knowledge of a corporation's strengths and weaknesses. It can proceed intelligently, however, only if it assists the evolution of those factors into the achievement of a specific set of goals and objectives. The goals may be purely economic or they may extend to cover such social issues as pollution, safety, training, product quality, and employment. Obviously to be effective the goals must be mutually compatible and, in certain cases, priority rankings must be established. In short, the objectives established for the planning process must represent in business terms the corporate philosophy and, in turn, that philosophy must become the lodestar against which subsequent progress may be evaluated.

Obviously a strategic plan must concern itself with both a near-term and a more distant view of economic probabilities. It must result from a judicious consideration of various patterns of operation and a review of the available alternatives that may be used in response to actions taken by the competitors, the markets, the political world, the weather, and many other things. Having identified both the timing and the alternatives, the plan should weld the corporate people into an integrated weapon that mirrors the objectives of the executive group and permits an intelligent and coordinate search for optimization and security.

The advantages of the business planning process are many, but one should not forget that one of the most valuable contributions of a planning approach is the opportunity that it affords for subsequent measurement. In this connection, the profit plan should not be considered as complete until the goals identified in the program have actually been accomplished. Identification of plans is a useful but sterile exercise unless energized. The organizational approach and financial discipline of a corporation should emphasize a monitoring of the planned achievement so that an awareness of a deviation from expectations can come quickly to the attention of the executive group.

In sophisticated planning systems, performance monitoring can employ various mathematical appraisal techniques. Whether measured with complex data systems or by quantitative models or by simple manual methods, it is essential that aberrational conditions and results be isolated and dealt with promptly. In some cases a change in circumstances may automatically put contingency programs into action. Only if the profit plan constitutes a continuous operating technique, will it play its full role in the achievement of the corporate objectives.

Whether employed as a project discipline or as the program for a total corporate enterprise, effective profit planning represents the means of integrating an organization's quantitative and qualitative objectives with its environment and with its method of operation. If clearly and professionally expressed, profit planning can preclude Pavlovian reactions to events by substituting realistic awareness and conscious decision making. If carried out with vigor and intensity, it represents a very strong stimulus to executive action. Although a professionally executed plan demands a sizable commitment of time and money, it also goes a long way toward making operational achievement a foregone conclusion.

This book constitutes an intriguing commentary on many of the profit planning attitudes and techniques that a distinguished group of perceptive business personalities have found to be of value. It does not seek to be a textbook for the business planning expert, but it does isolate a host of significant guideposts for executive review. It offers something useful to each reader, and I enthusiastically recommend it to your attention.

HERBERT C. KNORTZ
Executive Vice President
and Comptroller,
International Telephone
and Telegraph Corporation

June 1975

SERIES PREFACE

No one needs to tell the reader that the world is changing. He sees it all too clearly. The immutable, the constant, the unchanging of a decade or two ago no longer represent the latest thinking—on *any* subject, whether morals, medicine, politics, economics, or religion. Change has always been with us, but the pace has been accelerating, especially in the postwar years.

Business, particularly with the advent of the electronic computer some 20 years ago, has also undergone change. New disciplines have sprung up. New professions are born. New skills are in demand. And the need is ever greater to blend the new skills with those of the older professions to meet the demands of modern business.

The accounting and financial functions certainly are no exception. The constancy of change is as pervasive in these fields as it is in any other. Industry is moving toward an integration of many of the information gathering, processing, and analyzing functions under the impetus of the so-called systems approach. Such corporate territory has been, traditionally, the responsibility of the accountant and the financial man. It still is, to a large extent—but times are changing.

Does this, then spell the early demise of the accountant as we know him today? Does it augur a lessening of influence for the financial specialists in today's corporate hierarchy? We think not. We maintain, however, that it is incumbent upon today's accountant and today's financial man to learn *today's* thinking and to *use today's* skills. It is for this reason the Wiley Series on Systems and Controls for Financial Management is being developed.

Recognizing the broad spectrum of interests and activities that the series title encompasses, we plan a number of volumes, each representing the latest thinking, written by a recognized authority, on a particular facet of the financial man's responsibilities. The subjects contemplated for discussion within the series range from production accounting systems to planning, to corporate records, to control of cash. Each book is an in-depth study of one subject within this group. Each is intended to be a practical, working tool for the businessman in general and the financial man and accountant in particular.

ROBERT L. SHULTIS
FRANK M. MASTROMANO

PREFACE

Every executive has his special area of expertise. When asked to speak or write, he does best in the area that he knows best. It is with this in mind that *How to Improve Profitability through More Effective Planning* was written. Executives who were known to have something important to say on subjects related to improving profits were asked to contribute to this book.

The first chapter points out that while the potential problem areas increase mathematically, the related *challenges to the executive* responsible for profits multiply geometrically. On this highly realistic note the author discusses various methods of dealing with the problems, and he cautions against setting unattainable goals.

Another chapter underscores the importance of *employee participation*; an informed employee who feels that he is participating is a motivated employee.

A triumvirate of top level executives contributes its opinions as to what constitutes *practical profit planning*. Three of the opinions expressed are:

- Coordinate, guide, present, question, challenge, and *innovate.*
- Avoid being entranced with looking at tomorrow and forgetting that today's problems must be solved to get to tomorrow.
- Don't avoid risks. Identify them so they may be profitably and prudently exploited.

What to expect from executives responsible for improving profits is underscored through the development of the following points:

- Exercise mature business judgment.
- Speak out forcefully.
- Exercise good follow-up procedures to assure that the plan will be met.

Although several authors deal with the organization as a whole, one of them stresses the *importance of the marketing function* as providing a great potential for improving profits. In fact, it is suggested that marketing should be looked at as the hub of the organization and that all other functions should be considered as services providing support for the marketing effort. This author is critical of the average financial executive because of the tendency to concentrate on past history rather than to look aggressively at the future.

Ironic though it may seem, another author criticizes cost control as an inadequate means of improving profits. He points out that *cost reduction will achieve greater savings* because it goes beyond the goals established through budgets and seeks to reduce costs beyond the levels established by the budgets and standards.

The importance of taking a systematic approach to capital controls is illustrated by the example wherein some companies will obtain approval for an expansion involving building and equipment, and then a year later will seek another appropriation to meet the related requirements for utility services. The author recommends *capital appropriations by program*—in which all phases of an investment in new facilities will be collected in a single program—permitting an evaluation of the return on each program.

For companies in which installment selling is a factor, *receivables can be reduced even with increased sales,* thus providing another avenue to improving return on investment. A case history of a well-known company is illustrated.

Another author criticizes the mere development of a profit plan as passive management if positive steps are not taken to quantify the results and to *monitor progress against the profit plan.* A method followed by a well-known company is illustrated with specific examples of a novel system in which performance is given visibility through points awarded each quarter and the results widely publicized within the company.

Other related subjects are also developed in the book. These deal with common pitfalls in making acquisitions and expanding from within. The *Ten Commandments for Assuring Profitable Expansion* are summarized in one of these chapters. How an investment banker can assist in *minimizing the overall costs of long-term capital* is also covered in another chapter.

Although the book is heavily flavored with the philosophy and experience of practical business men, it includes a good balance of the theoretical—dealing with the Delphi technique, the changes in our modern society and how they affect business and profits, and the multinational trends affecting modern business.

No single author could possibly write expertly on the range of topics covered in this book. For this reason, selection of the authors was critical in the development of the various techniques for improving profits. It is the opinion of the editor that the authors have done their work well.

THOMAS S. DUDICK

Middletown, New Jersey
June 1975

ACKNOWLEDGMENTS

The chapters of this book are adapted from speeches given to members of the Planning Executives Institute, audiocassettes of a conference on corporate planning jointly sponsored by Advanced Management Research and the Planning Executives Institute, as well as from material solicited by the author from various experts in their fields. Some of these speeches subsequently became the bases for articles published in *Financial Executive,* a publication of the Financial Executives Institute; *Management Adviser,* a publication of the American Institute of Certified Public Accountants; and *Managerial Planning,* a publication of the Planning Executives Institute.

Permission to reprint, in modified form, the following papers is gratefully acknowledged:

Chapter 1. "Challenge to Profits," by Paul H. Elicker, *Managerial Planning,* copyright 1972 by the Planning Executives Institute.

Chapter 3. "Systems Theory in Modern Organizations," by Richard J. Tersine, *Managerial Planning,* copyright 1972 by the Planning Executives Institute.

Chapter 4. "The People Factor In Profitability," by Ralph M. De Biasi, reprinted by permission of *Management Adviser,* November-December 1972, copyright 1972 by the American Institute of Certified Public Accountants, Inc.

Chapter 6. "What Is Practical Profit Planning?" by Robert M. Schaeberle, James W. McKee, Jr., and Ralph P. Moore, *Managerial Planning,* copyright 1972 by the Planning Executives Institute.

Chapter 7. "Strategic Profit Planning," by Richard M. Osgood, *Managerial Planning,* copyright 1972 by the Planning Executives Institute.

Chapter 9. "The Zero-Base Budget Process," by Peter A. Pyhrr, Chapter 3 in *Zero-Base Budgeting* by Peter A. Pyhrr, copyright 1972 by John Wiley & Sons.

Chapter 11. "Pressures on the Professional Manager for Profits," by Thomas S. Dudick, Chapter 13 in *Profile for Profitability* by Thomas S. Dudick, copyright 1972 by John Wiley & Sons.

Chapter 12. "A Computerized Decision-Simulator Model," by Michael R. Tyran, *Management Accounting,* March 1971, copyright 1971 by the National Association of Accountants.

Chapter 13. "Cost Analysis for Improved Return on Investment," by Leonard Kamsky, *NACA Bulletin,* July 1965, copyright 1965 by the National Association of Accountants.

Chapter 14. "How an Investment Banker Looks at Return on Investment," by Richard M. Hexter, *Managerial Planning,* copyright 1972 by the Planning Executives Institute.

Chapter 16. "How to Make Capital Controls Work," by John E. Rhodes, *NACA Bulletin,* September 1955, copyright 1955 by the National Association of Accountants.

Chapter 17. "Reducing Receivables to Maximize Return on Investment," by Leo G. Blatz, *Management Advisor,* November-December 1973.

Chapter 18. "Information System for Materials Management," by D. Larry Moore, *Production & Inventory Management,* 1st Quarter, 1972, copyright 1972 by American Production & Inventory Control Society, Inc.

Chapter 19. "Your New Materials Management System—Let's Get the Systems User and the Computer Together," by Paul Maranka, *Production & Inventory Management,* No. 2, 1972, copyright 1972 by American Production & Inventory Control Society, Inc.

Chapter 21. "A Backward Look at Forward Planning," by Thomas S. Dudick, Chapter 5 in *Profile for Profitability* by Thomas S. Dudick, copyright 1972 by John Wiley & Sons.

Chapter 22. "Measuring Divisional Performance," by Frank J. Tanzola, *Financial Executive,* March 1975, copyright 1975 by the Financial Executives Institute.

Two other chapters were adapted from speeches. Chapter 8 is based on a speech given by Sam R. Goodman to the Association of National Advertisers, Advertising Financial Management Workshop. Certain material in Chapter 20 was adapted from a speech given by David G. Kay, First Vice President of Shearson, Hammill Company.

CONTENTS

How to Improve Profitability Through More Effective Planning

CHAPTER 1

INTRODUCTION: CHALLENGE TO PROFITS

PAUL H. ELICKER

"It would be nice if there were only one challenge to improving profitability. But as we all know, there are many challenges. If there are 25 different businesses—as there are in SCM—then the challenges to planning become more complex by a factor of 25 squared."

As executive vice president of SCM, I was in operational charge of steering the ship called SCM. After "vice" was taken out of my title and "chief" added to modify "executive," a subtle change in responsibility accompanied the change in title. Now, instead of merely steering the ship I must also decide where it is to go—this is the essence of planning for profits.

IMPACT OF GROWTH ON PROFIT PLANNING

This is not to say that suddenly, there was a responsibility for making operations profitable—that responsibility always existed. However, in the past the process of assuring profitability was simpler. The company had only one narrowly channeled product line and sales of about $37 million a year.

Our strategic business problem was how to expand that product line. We knew that if we were to survive as a company, we had to achieve a certain amount of sheer size, we had to acquire a degree of diversification, and in doing so we had to acquire technological strength.

Today, sales are well over $900 million; there are 25 separate businesses, some requiring high technological skills, and the company is acknowledged to be a skilled marketer of well-known brands of consumer products. The period of explosive growth that characterized the company during this period is un-

1

doubtedly over for a time. Now we must face the realization that the very growth we sought and achieved has made planning more complex by a factor of 25 squared.

It would be nice if, as implied in the title of this chapter, there were only one challenge to improve profitability. But as we all know, there are numerous challenges—depending upon the number and complexity of the businesses. Obviously, we cannot talk about all of these but we can discuss the general categories within which the challenge occurs. Accordingly, we will cover four.

- First, to recognize the role of the chief executive in the planning process.
- Second, the importance of balancing short-term profit improvement with the need to insure long-term growth.
- Third, there is the challenge involved in the engineering of consent among all the managers as to what the underlying objectives of the enterprise are.
- Fourth, but equal in importance to the foregoing, is the challenge of identifying basic changes in the economic, political, technical, and social climate—avoiding the threats and capitalizing on the opportunities that are implicit in those changes.

It would be surprising if the topics discussed in this chapter solved any specific problem for the reader. I do see the content as serving the role of "straight man" for the chapters that follow.

DEFINING TERMS

To begin with, a definition of terms is essential to planning itself, and equally essential to any discussion about it. In too much of the literature about planning, one man's "goal" is another man's "strategy." "Tactics" come to be confused with "short-term objectives," and so on. Agreeing on a set of definitions and then sticking to them in everything you say and write about the subject will clear away a lot of semantic underbrush in the planning process, and make finding your way much easier.

First, the term *profit planning* itself refers to the systematic examination of future opportunities and threats to a business, and also to the system of determining how best to avoid the threats and capitalize on the opportunities.

Strategic planning is the process by which the basic missions, objectives, and strategies for the company are summarized and articulated. Let's look at those three concepts.

Mission is simply shorthand for what the company's basic business or businesses are, stated in terms of what the company wants to be.

Objectives and *goals* must be differentiated. The former is simply a desired result to be achieved. the latter is also a desired result but implying a measurable time sequence and an accomplishment that can be measured in numerical terms. A goal might be to achieve a 15 percent ROI within five years, for example.

An objective, on the other hand, implies a longer time sequence and need not be measurable in numbers. As I use the term, an objective is likely to be something always just beyond a company's grasp but toward which it can continue to work regardless of intermediate achievements.

Strategy is a broad course of action—usually, a major action and usually one implying a relatively long time span. A strategy is *what* you are going to do and not *how* you are going to do it.

Finally, *tactics* refer to the "how" of implementing a strategy. If the strategy is to become a big paint marketer in South America, the tactic might be to acquire a large Brazilian paint company.

With our terms defined, we can start the planning process that is going to be our way of influencing the future. The first question that must be answered is, of course, whether there will *be* any future to influence. Just as the first rule of successful politics is to make sure you are reelected, the first rule of successful planning is to make sure you stay in business.

A crash program to ensure survival is often the first planning a company does. Sometimes the therapy is too late to revive the patient and the subsequent steps will never be taken.

Assuming you will survive, you must have an awareness and an appreciation of the intuitive planning that has always gone on. This process may not rely on formalized assessment of variables, and it may not look pretty, but it has brought many a company quite far. Among the 25 separate businesses SCM conducts, for example, about a dozen historically had some kind of formal planning and the same number had never heard of it. One of the big jobs was to integrate existing plans with new formal planning for the whole organization.

Intuitive planning has always struck me as a somewhat unsatisfying process in the absence of clearly defined strategic objectives for the overall company. The problem is that you are always vaguely concerned that there is something missing—a radically new product, an unexpected capacity increase in the industry, sudden unavailability of an important resource, or the like.

Not even the most clearly articulated strategic plan is insurance against any of those threats. Risk taking is implicit in growth. But the ability to identify and to react quickly to such surprises is much easier when you have clearly in mind what your resources are and what you are supposed to be doing with them.

Let's assume that your company is going to survive—that is, have a future, and that you're going to plan for that future on a formal basis. What are the challenges you are going to face in doing so?

ROLE OF THE CHIEF EXECUTIVE

The first challenge is to understand the role of the chief executive in the profit planning process. He is, to begin with, the head planner of the company, regardless of the numbers or the titles of those who advise him.

In the same vein, he is the chief operating officer, the ultimate director of research, the head of personnel, the chief financial officer, and the company spokesman. On rare occasions he may even tell the company's lawyers what to do. Or, if he wishes to, he may personally decide what color the napkins will be in the company dining room.

In other words, he makes decisions—some small, but frequently big ones, too.

But there are other things a chief executive does, and a surprising number of them impinge on profit planning. For example, the traditional first step of formal planning—the thorough analysis of strengths, weaknesses, and opportunities for each business within the enterprise—will not succeed unless the president makes it succeed.

He cannot simply sign a memo written by someone on his staff and forget about it. He must get down to cases with each division or group manager and keep digging until that wealth of knowledge is extracted—sometimes, it seems from their very bones. There is something to that old expression about one man forgetting more about a business than another will ever know. The answer is that he hasn't forgotten. but the information may have become so internalized that he literally can't communicate it in words and numbers. If the chief executive does not personally ramrod this basic and essential analysis, you are kidding yourself if you think the job will ever be done.

Once the analyses are complete it again falls squarely to the chief executive to correlate them into an overall strategic plan for the enterprise. This, too, means spending time, hard work, patience, and determination on the part of the president. The planning executive should understand the need for personal involvement of the chief executive and balance that need against the competing demands for his time. If he does, he can move the process forward much more rapidly than his boss can on his own.

Another task of the chief executive in which the planning executive plays a crucial role is to see that planning, review, and planning again is a continuous process. Only by constantly "nagging" all the managers to think ahead can the enterprise as a whole be kept moving in the right direction. This is an important part of the president's job.

There must be a continuing review of both strategy and tactics. Is last year's economic forecast still accurate? Are there new threats to be considered? Has there been a technology breakthrough in this or a closely-related industry? These and other questions can never be allowed to get far from the forefront of management thinking. And with all due respect to the people on the planning staff, they cannot answer these questions alone. They must be in constant touch with the operating people, and these in turn must know by direct communication from the president that this job is an important one. Without his involvement, the job will simply not be done, or, if done at all, will not be done well.

Any chief executive will tell you that one of his major problems is motivation. You could make a case for it being his single most constant and pressing problem. And it, too, is closely related to planning for profitable operations.

Naturally I have been preoccupied with this question more than with any other since I've had my present job. I've concluded that the best approach is to set standards of performance—jointly agreed upon by the operating executive and myself—and then constantly monitor the actual performance against that standard. The operating and staff executives who report to me follow the same procedure with the people who report to them. People who achieve and exceed their personal goals will be rewarded—I will see to that. And I will also see to it that there are no rewards for performance that falls short.

It is the task of the chief executive to stimulate and reward innovation in his company. He must create an atmosphere that is receptive to new ideas and is as little shackled to "the way we've always done it" as it is possible to be. In my view, to have one man who asks "why do we do it that way?" is better than to have two who simply know that it always was. It is very clear who is going to discover the *better* way.

But if you're going to encourage innovation, then you had better be prepared to accept the implicit challenge that innovators always provide. Some innovations may change the very course and nature of the enterprise. the planner must be alert to this possibility. He should be ready to work with—not against the forces that can set the ship on a different and better course. It is almost always the innovator who will exceed his budget; not the man who is afraid to change.

Most important, the planning executive can help the president create the atmosphere that fosters a spirit of innovation. Where you see examples of it, bring it personally to the president's attention. If one doesn't already exist, consider starting a program that seeks out and gives recognition to innovative people.

The final role of the chief executive that is closely allied to planning is his responsibility to provide for orderly management succession.

There's a definition of the business corporation that I rather like because of its bluff simplicity: a bunch of guys working together, trying to make a buck. If we could convince the last two or three generations of college and high school students of that—not to mention their teachers and professors—perhaps business would not have become society's all-purpose scapegoat. But the definition leaves out reference to the fact that it's going to be a different "bunch of guys" in 20 years or so.

It's very likely there is a man of 35 or so—conceivably a woman—somewhere among SCM's 30,000 people who in 20 years will be running the whole show. Planners, as well as personnel people, must be concerned with identifying that person and bringing him along. He is a long-term strategic resource of the company, and one that must not be lost sight of.

Of perhaps more immediate concern, the shareholders have a right to be reassured against the event the present chief executive gets hit by a truck or suddenly decides to open a ski resort in Montana. While the chief executive has to make this kind of decision, the planning executive must keep the line of succession clearly in mind in all of his projections. And that is true even if the planner doesn't want to get on line for the job himself!

SHORT-TERM PROFITS VERSUS LONG-TERM GROWTH

We come now to the second challenge: balancing short-term tactics with long-term strategy. Establishing short-run operating budgets that call for reasonable profit improvement but don't place in jeopardy the long-range objectives of the company is a constant challenge. And, in an economy where a company may be just turning the corner toward renewed earnings growth, the temptation to get short-run profits rapidly back to acceptable levels is almost impossible to resist. But it must be resisted if the price is one of slowing growth later on.

In other words, it is imperative that top management not become so engrossed in current problems that the long-range strategy is ignored. A conscious effort should be made not to set objectives for the first year or two of the five-year cycle that are attainable only by borrowing from the future. For example, there is no sense in clamping the lid on capital asset expansion in order to help current operating results if all indications are that the industry will be straining capacity three or four years from now. Resist the tendency to insist on quarter-to-quarter earnings improvement as the *sine qua non* of being considered successful executives.

Not a few companies who publicly adhered to the motto: "ever higher" found the memory of Wall Street to be no longer than the period that stretches between your last and your next quarterly earnings report. We had a kind of growth mania in this country which, on reflection, just could not be satisfied.

Obviously, you can err by going too far in the other direction, as well. It is at least equally dangerous to orient your thinking and planning entirely toward the future and be "at the mercy of the puddles in the road." Those resources you carefully listed in your analyses of strengths and weaknesses—the ones you were banking on to produce big earnings in five year's time—may prove illusory.

The new factory you persuaded the board to approve is almost bound to come on stream the same week everyone else's factory does. Prices plummet in the face of sudden new capacity and everyone looks around in amazement as your profit forecast goes out the window. Adequate industry intelligence—in the CIA sense of the word—can help avoid this kind of situation. For example, if Company A knows that Company B has broken ground on a new plant that will expand industry capacity by 10 percent, Company A might defer its own plans to do the same, or redirect those assets to another business. The obvious corollary is that it is clearly to Company B's advantage to make public announcement of its plans so that Company A can make its decision in full knowledge of the future competitive environment.

ENGINEERING OF CONSENT

Once you have agreed on what the overall strategy will be, and have balanced in your own mind the present against the future, you are ready to address yourself to the third challenge which is to elicit agreement among members of management as to the objectives of the enterprise.

The planning executive is the key to gaining support of the line and staff executives for the strategic plan; he is the communications link. His awareness of current operating problems and short-term tactics and their relation to the long-term strategy is of critical importance in management communications. To fulfill this role, the planning executive must have, in addition to the full confidence of top management, a close relationship with the key operating people. And that relationship must be founded on mutual respect for the other's role in the enterprise, otherwise the relationship will fracture, because it is one subjected to many strains over the course of a year.

There is an intuitive kind of planning operating people do every day. The planning executive must not only be aware of this phenomenon, he must be able to make it complementary to the formal planning program. This means the planning executive must be intimately familiar with day-to-day operating problems of the business.

If operating people don't understand the plan for their business, they will scuttle it. When a manager is confronted with a goal in whose development he had no part, his reaction might be to fudge his figures to conform with what he thinks "corporate" wants, or, more likely, simply to ignore it. In some cases, he will proceed with goals known but to him and to God, guided solely by his own intuition and personal knowledge that the goals set by corporate are simply not attainable.

If this happens not only is the planning effort unproductive, but also it is downright harmful. Once the manager is permitted to become frustrated with the planning concept, he loses all respect for the profit planning process.

One surefire way of making this happen is to overload a line manager with forms. I will be the first to agree that forms are needed in planning, but they can be absolute perils if allowed to become an end in themselves. Let's look at it from the chief executive's point of view.

What is needed is a terse articulation by the line manager of his best thoughts on the future of his participation. Obviously this can't be obtained verbally from a form—even though face-to-face meetings are an important part of the process. The next best thing is a brief, written narrative.

If you ask a certain type of manager to write a brief dissertation on the strengths and weaknesses of his competitors and of his own operation, how he expects to take advantage of his own strengths while minimizing the effect of his weaknesses in, for example, his marketing planning and allocations of capital—you will receive a blank look. On the other hand, a well-designed form can serve to isolate and organize the issues that the manager must deal with. No matter how good the form is, however, you are well advised to leave a large block of space for "other comments." That is where he will write the brief essay to explain why the simple numbers and cold facts and projections you have requested don't begin to tell the whole story of the intricate business in which he is engaged.

Accounting or budget forms don't usually work for long-range planning. This is because business groups in many companies are in reality a collection of allegedly compatible products. Take the example of a single manager of two products, one of which is profitable and the other in trouble. A standard budget form will tend to jumble them together. The real decision may be how to expand the good business and extricate yourself from the loser.

An overall plan or strategy is mandatory. Having a clear idea of where the company is going provides a way of looking at events and developments and quickly deciding whether they pose threats, opportunities, or neither. At the same time, if the planning executive has successfully communicated that overall concept to the line managers, they can relate everything that happens to their business against that concept, including those actions they undertake themselves.

An overall strategy, in short, makes it possible for line managers to see their operations as part of a larger enterprise. If they do they will be less likely to simply struggle with each other for capital and bonus money. If that is permitted to occur, you are back to the situation where you place too much stress on short-run profits.

Having an overall strategy, however, can create problems of its own. One of the most sensitive is the case of the mature business. You might define a mature business as one growing at less than 10 percent a year and in which the company has less than a leadership position. How do you explain to the manager of that operation that his most productive role in the future may be to provide cash for investment in another business where the return may be greater? No one likes to be told that the best function of his business is to be milked for proceeds to be invested by another elsewhere. An even more basic question is whether his consent should be sought at all. Acceptance of the decision that a product has run its cycle or that a business has become mature, or even senile, runs the grave risk of becoming a self-fulfilling prophecy.

If the overall strategy selected for a company is the appropriate one for that company, there is no reason why its elements should not be visible in current plans. It follows that there must be a close linkage between top management objectives for the whole company and the sub-objectives put together by the line managers with the advice and counsel of the planning executive.

It is a key challenge to the planning executive, as it has been since the inception of the art, to see to it that both line and staff executives completely understand the process. Above all, managers must know what it will and will not do for the company and for their own operations. Line managers in particular must know their key role in the process and that planning is more than just another idea dreamed up by a staff man at Headquarters.

As said before, the plan for a man's operation must be his own more than any other single person's. If it isn't, all of the "reach" so carefully inserted in it becomes completely academic. As for motivation, working his own plan is far more of a motivation for a manager than working someone else's.

The line manager should also be made to understand that planning for the future occasionally involves spending current dollars with expectation of no current return. A college recruiting program, for example, is logically a division expense in a current period, though the benefits, if any, may be years away. It falls in part to the planning executive to explain the essential nature of the investment. This problem can be eased by a system enabling you to segregate such long-term investments in strategy in a special section of the current operating budget. But, again, it's essential that the operating man knows *why* it is done, as well as how.

Finally, the line manager should know there are at least two compelling personal reasons why his full involvement in and cooperation with the planning process is required. First, the better he understands the information that comes to the surface in the planning sessions, the more useful it will be to him. The reinforcement theory in education applies to things we learn in business as well as in the classroom.

Second, for the man's bonus to accurately reflect his contribution to the company's performance, it must be tied to his performance against his long-range goals as well as to the short-term profit picture.

THE CLIMATE

After establishing an overall strategy involving the chief executive, proper balancing of short-term profits and long-term growth, and winning the consent and understanding of all concerned, the planning executive might be shocked to learn that there is still a major challenge—the economic, political, technical, and social climate.

There are definite and rapid changes going on that affect every facet of our business climate. I for one see very little "shock" in our confrontation with the future, contrary to the thesis of a book that is more widely known than read.

The ability of American businessmen to continue to move this nation and to help maintain its unique position of leadership in the world community is a point of major importance in describing our society. That they have continued to do it, despite generations of detractors from Veblem to Galbraith to Reich, is one reason that business is more challenging than a career in either government or education. To borrow a cliché, business is where it's happening in this country, no matter what the millions of people who have never been in a large organization have been led to believe. Nevertheless, the fact of change—rapid change—remains and some observations are in order.

Professor George A. Steiner in a recent article in *Managerial Planning*[1] observed, "The major opportunities to a company, and the most dangerous threats it will face in the future, lay in the business climate rather than within the enterprise." Putting it another way, having a viable business, one based on the soundest economic principles, is simply not enough anymore. In addition to serving your customers, if you want to be in the big time you have to be able to say, as does a well known steel company in Pittsburgh, "We're involved." You might go further and say, "We want to be useful . . . and even interesting," It would be well for some company to do a major advertising campaign that says, "We're relevant!"

I am not going to try to resolve the issue of whether making a profit is the primary, secondary, or tertiary objective of a business, but I venture to predict this will be a source of increasingly lively debate for the balance of this decade.

The second part of Professor Steiner's observation is equally thought provoking. He said that companies able to detect underlying changes in the eco-

---

[1] *Managerial Planning* is a bimonthly magazine published by the Planning Executives Institute.

nomic, political, technical, and social climate will have a competitive advantage over companies without that ability. The rapidly changing conditions will require a tremendous innovative spur within companies to assure their growth and survival.

Changes in the business environment can lead, perhaps unwittingly, to direct conflicts with national policies. As an example, SCM is one of five or six large companies in the paint business. It has excellent marketing know-how and advanced technology. After those five or six companies with nation-wide marketing, there are over a thousand relatively small, regional suppliers of paint. Oversimplifying a bit, the small companies compete successfully, partly in terms of price (and partly not), primarily because paint is very heavy and bulky and transportation costs are high. Because of the absence of economies of scale, it is not surprising that the small regional companies do not have the technology of DuPont, PPG, or SCM's Glidden operation. Note therefore, that the paint business is almost a model of competition, the avowed policy of the Government.

But note, too, that the Government has a strong policy of controlling the amount of lead in the environment. Most modern paints use lead not as a pigment but as a drying agent. It's the ingredient that makes it possible for you to paint your dining room in the afternoon and serve dinner the same evening.

Under the new Government policy, lead drying agents, despite the fact they constitute well under 1 percent by weight of most paints, must be phased out. Talk about a spur to innovation! Every paint laboratory in the country is scurrying about trying to find something that will make paint dry as fast as a lead drying agent. it is very unlikely that one of the thousand small paint companies will come up with that substance.

When the substitute for lead is found, and assuming the law is uniformly enforced (a rather large assumption!), the rate of attrition of the smaller companies seems almost certain to accelerate. The big companies will expand to fill the needs of the consumers and the traditional shape of a basic industry will be altered. The Government's policy to get rid of lead is inconsistent with the goal of maintaining competition, though that is not what either agency initially had in mind.

Even more basic, the fundamental concept of growth itself is under increasingly sharp attack—largely because economic expansion in the past has caused pollution. Mobil Oil Corporation recently spent a substantial sum to inform the public in an advertisement opposite the editorial page of the *New York Times* that, "Growth is not a four-letter word." The ad read in part,

"The greater part of the environmental problem stems not from present or future growth, but from past growth. It is largely a backlog problem—the legacy of 100 years of *unplanned* growth." The advertisement applauded those sentiments—it is interesting to note that they were expressed by a Socialist Member of Britain's Parliament.

It is also interesting to contrast those sentiments, considering the source, with remarks by Russell E. Train, Chairman of the President's Council on Environmental Quality and a member of his executive office. Mr. Train says: "The question of whether we should continue to regard growth—of population, the economy and resource use—as the primary measure of progress of our society is a very important one." He went on to call for "a national debate on the desirability of future growth."

Notwithstanding the fact that whenever anyone calls for a national debate it usually means they have made up their minds and are looking for allies, I find myself in agreement with Mr. Train as well as with the Socialist MP. There *should* be a debate, and the institution of business had better make its voice heard along with those of the institutions of government, education, and organized labor.

The foregoing are by no means isolated examples of rhetoric, and they are not confined to government officials. When Bryn Mawr College was host for a symposium on "The Limits of Growth" and the University of Texas, entertained a group studying "The Problems of the 21st Century," some interesting comments may be worthy of note.

At Austin, for example, the famed geneticist, H. Bently Glass said, "To renounce the goal of continuous growth is the price of our survival." At Bryn Mawr, the now-famous Club of Rome study, which was called, modestly enough, "The Predicament of Mankind," was under discussion. That study urges an early end to world economic expansion on the theory that the factors of population growth, agricultural production, natural resources, industrial production, and pollution "determine, and therefore limit, growth on this planet."

According to the *Times,* "Economists present at the session voiced the hope that new mathematical models, incorporating better and fuller data, would lift the awful decree of the Club of Rome." Better and fuller data . . . that is how polite economists say, "Garbage in—garbage out."

It is difficult to challenge any institution with so awesome a name as the Club of Rome to a debate. (It sounds more ominous than the Gnomes of Zurich!) But it is hard to believe that the five factors "limiting growth on this planet" are not susceptible to the creative application of technology—today's as well as tomorrow's.

Thomas Malthus, you will recall, predicted around 1800 that the world would soon run out of food unless population was held down. He made that prediction at the dawn of the Industrial Revolution—when there was no such thing as technology as we know it today. Malthus did not realize that the supply of food would grow exponentially, and faster than population. Likewise, the Club of Rome study, from what I know about it, does not admit of exponential growth of the technical ability to control the problems that growth itself must bring.

We are now at the dawn of an age in which new technology, coupled with a new social awareness, will not only prove able to cope with change, but also will guide and direct its forces for the general good.

Mr. Toffler says in his book, "Future Shock" that "Most technocratic planners and managers . . . continue to act as though the economic sector were hermetically sealed off from social and psychocultural influences." Unless the planning executives accept and meet this challenge—the challenge of detecting and responding to change in the political, social and technical as well as to the traditional challenges in the economic environment—there will *really* be a shocking future for business.

"Emphasis on unattainable goals reminds me of the quotation: "The man gazing at the stars is at the mercy of the puddles in the road."   Paul H. Elicker

PHILOSOPHICAL CONSIDERATIONS

Many writers on the subject of modern business oversimplify because they assume a highly static business community. The presumption is that a state of quiescience exists wherein each business functions in the same manner each day, irrespective of the changing demands of society.

THE REAL WORLD OF BUSINESS

This is quite contrary to the real world of business with its competitive pressures. The professional manager lives in a dynamic environment where one change follows another, sometimes with such demoralizing rapidity that the organization could virtually "self-destruct."

William Simmons comments on the rapid acceleration of technological progress in "speed of change" when he points out that while radio took 35 years to develop, television took only 12 years; the electric motor took 65 years before it could be applied as a source of power, the nuclear reactor took only 10 years.

It is not the introduction of new products that causes the management pressures—in fact, the introduction of a new product can be a relatively stimulating experience for most managers because of the creative demands of getting into production. It is after the introduction of a new product when competitors begin coming into the picture that pressures build. At this time prices begin to erode, automatic equipment is introduced to cut costs, substitute materials are used, and product designs are simplified. All this helps the consumer who benefits by an improved standard of living. This brings us to the point referred to by William Simmons as the period of affluence, when we no longer need worry about the simple things of life such as shelter, food, security, and leisure time, except, of course, in periods of depression.

THE POSTINDUSTRIAL PERIOD

He next discusses the younger generation and its apparent lack of concern for the work ethic. On the other hand, the generation has good deal of concern for such matters as the environment and social justice for those affected by the "oppression of modern society." The author comments on the three milestones of the twentieth century, which are marked by the agricultural society in the early 1900s, the industrial workers in 1940, and the knowledge workers in 1980. The author quotes Peter Drucker as his authority for viewing education as the emerging third force.

CHARACTERISTICS OF THE KNOWLEDGE EXPLOSION

The systems theory is applicable to education as it is to the other activities of man and nature. In studying the sun and its planets in terms of the solar system, it was possible for scientists to impute the existence of other planets unknown at the time. The Periodic Table in chemistry also demonstrates the usefulness of a systems theory in spotlighting areas where gaps exist in knowledge. The finding of these gaps has resulted in the discovery of new elements hitherto unknown. The application of systems theory is not limited to the natural sciences; it can be applied to man-made organizations as well. Examples are economic, social, and business organizations. Development of an organization chart for a company illustrates a system that assures management that it has covered all company functions needing to be monitored and supervised by a top level executive. Although Professor Tersine did not refer to computer systems as such, these represent another illustration of the development of the procedures to produce management reports that provide a clue to information gaps that must be filled if management is to be properly informed.

   The author does emphasize one important characteristic of the knowledge explosion: disciplines have been breaking up into subdisciplines of specialization. It should be obvious to the reader that as the number of such subdisciplines expands the likelihood of a breakdown of communications increases. Thus, as our fund of knowledge expands, the need for coordination among the various disciplines and subdisciplines becomes increasingly important.

TEST OF EXECUTIVE ABILITY

This is where executive ability is put to its fullest test. The general manager cannot pride himself with his credentials as a business school graduate. He must understand the problems of selling, manufacturing, engineering, purchasing, and scheduling. He must be able to challenge the financial statements and know the meaning of the components thereof. Frequently, a company or large division of a company will spend a half million dollars or more for the data processing system to gather information needed by the inventory control group, by the sales department, and by accounting. Since each of the disciplines has its needs and voices its demands strongly, the general manager is often cast in the role of arbiter who must see that each department has the information it needs and that such information is provided at an economical cost, without needless duplication to serve some unimportant peripheral request.

SUMMARY

The intent of this section is to provide the reader with some philosophical considerations to temper his thinking on profitability and to broaden his thinking on the concepts of managing. While the conceptual aspects are important, they are not a sufficient condition for effectively managing the business. The sections that follow delve into the other considerations that are so important for success.

CHAPTER 2

EXPLORATORY PROFIT PLANNING

WILLIAM W. SIMMONS

"We have moved from what we used to call the industrial state to the postindustrial state or society. One of the fundamental differences is that we have moved from goods producing industries into service producing businesses."

"Exploratory planning" can best be defined by saying that it is a matter of looking at the longer time frame ahead—not because anyone believes they can prophesy or conjecture about it, but because it gives us better direction in making decisions today and in doing our conventional long-range planning. When you take the longer range look today, you are really looking at a future of not just products or your business, but of your own and your family's future. You're looking at the world's future. That is one of the reasons I have enjoyed exploratory planning more than any of my other work—it is so intimately involved with all of our lives, not just our work but our whole life. I think you will see what I mean as we get further into this chapter.

I'd like to cover three areas in this chapter. First, I'd like to hammer home just a little of this idea of change—the fact that things are moving rapidly. Then, I would like to talk briefly about the techniques we use in exploratory planning. And finally, I relate these to what some businesses are actually doing. I think it's easy to be theoretical and to give long-winded dissertations about theories but you go away and wonder what you can do about it. I hope I leave you with some ideas of things you can do about longer-term planning.

SPEED OF CHANGE

Let's move to the first point, the point of rapid change. We really are in a world different from our forebears'. One of the indicators of this rapid change

Exhibit 1.   Speed of Change—Interval between Scientific
Discoveries and Their Application

Solar battery	1953–1955	2 years
Transistor	1948–1951	3 years
Nuclear reactor	1932–1942	10 years
Television	1922–1934	12 years
Radar	1925–1940	15 years
X-ray tubes	1895–1913	18 years
Vacuum tube	1884–1915	31 years
Radio	1867–1902	35 years
Telephone	1820–1876	56 years
Electric motor	1821–1886	65 years
Photography	1727–1839	112 years

is the interval between scientific discoveries and their applications. In the 1700s it took photography a 112 years before people understood the technology and began to use it. I emphasize people because this is the real indicator. Today communication has become so rapid that when something is discovered it almost immediately becomes a product. Exhibit 1 lists the interval between discovery and application for 11 products.

I was in England last year at a conference on planning. The Planning Officer for the British Atomic Energy Commission, in describing today's fast moving pace, said he heard a couple of little boys talking a week or so before. One of them said to the other "Did you see those two contraceptives in the coal scuttle?" The second little boy looked at his friend and asked "What's a coal scuttle?"

In the electronics business, we are someday going to be asking "What's a vacuum tube?" And I'm not so sure we're not also going to be asking someday, "What's corporate planning?" Planning should be an attitude and not necessarily a profession. I think all of us in management must play the role of catalyzers, educators, and promoters, because if management itself doesn't plan, there isn't going to be any planning.

THE NEW SOCIETY

The next thing I'd like to point out in connection with the speed of change is how fast our society is changing. I don't think we recognize this. Exhibit 2 shows the so-called emerging postindustrial society. Daniel Bell, who is one of the leading men in this field at Harvard University, says that we have moved from what we used to call the industrial state to the postindustrial state or society. One of the fundamental differences is that we have moved from goods producing industries into service producing industries. The chart illustrates this fact very clearly. Note that in the late 1940s the service industries exceeded the goods producing industries in terms of employment in the United States. Note the growing spread in the subsequent periods. This exhibit does not include Medical, Legal, or Counseling service industries all of which are moving up much faster than the goods producing group.

This doesn't mean we are producing less goods. Actually, we have more goods today in this country than we have ever had. But it does mean we are automating and that the goods are being produced with fewer people. It also means that people are doing more and more "people things." People are the key to the future as they always have been, and they are becoming more of the key to the world we approach. Since we are moving into a different society, let's review the appropriate techniques available for profit planning.

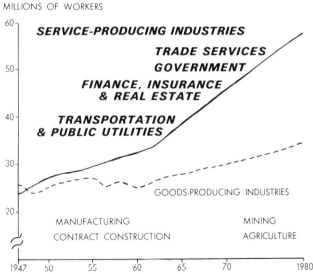

Exhibit 2.   Emerging Postindustrial Society
MILLIONS OF WORKERS

Exhibit 3.   Scenario Mode

Narrative Description
  Probable
  Possible
  Interesting
  Illustrative

Sequence of Events

Events May Be
  Simultaneous
  Sequential
  Grouped Into:
    Manufactured Story
    Case History
    Parable

TECHNIQUE 1—THE SCENARIO

The first of the three techniques is the Scenario Technique, which was made famous by the Hudson Institute and is shown in Exhibit 3. The Hudson Institute is headed up by Herman Kahn who is generally thought of as the leading futurist. Many businesses are beginning to use the Scenario Technique. How does this differ from a profit plan? As you can see from Exhibit 3, the Scenario Technique can be a lot of different things—but one thing it usually does is provide alternatives. Usually, a long-range profit plan is a single plan projecting where you are going to be sometime in the future. The Scenario Technique is a much broader approach involving two or three futures. It consists of a most likely alternative and then one that will require everthing to happen very well. It will perhaps also include an alternative that is somewhat negative.

None of the alternatives is done in the detail of the standard long-range plan. This provides greater flexibility and permits more openness because the scenario actually adopted is not revealed (see Exhibit 4.) Preparation is relatively simple because the amount of detail is small.

I'm not suggesting that the Scenario Technique replace the conventional long-range plan, but I am suggesting that it can be very helpful. General Electric Company looked at 30 or 40 scenarios. Of these, the company zeroed in on three or four and then set its immediate plans based on the most likely of these three or four. A similar approach was followed recently when IBM projected what its future might look like under several different conditions.

There are many who have turned to the Scenario Technique. Among these is The Electronics Industries Association. The theme of the conference was "Electronics 1985." In setting up the agenda a group in Glastenbury, Connecticut, called the Futures Group, prepared three different scenarios. These were distributed to the panelists and members with the message that of the three scenarios presented, they should select the one most likely to occur. Discussion at the conference centered on the various possibilities and the underlying factors influencing each.

The important lesson taught by the Scenario Technique is the need for flexibility—that no profit plan can be "cast in cement."

Time requirements to prepare a good scenario for any business would be a month with four to six people working part time. They should be people conversant with different parts of the business, since they make their own predictions. One should be thoroughly familiar with the development work and the other should be a financial man. The projection should be made very broadly. You will be amazed to find what you get out of taking those three looks at where your business might be in, say, 15 years.

Exhibit 4.   Scenario Versus Long Range Plan

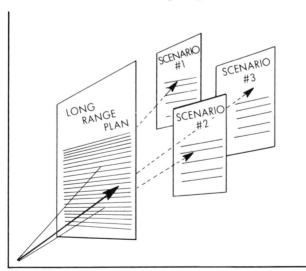

TECHNIQUE 2—DELPHI

Another technique introduced by people developing exploratory plans for the future is called the Delphi Technique. The Delphi Technique is not a forecast but a way of organizing and tabulating forecast data. It was originated at the Rand Corporation in their work for the Defense Department. Most of our major U.S. Defense projects, such as the Polaris submarine, early warning systems, and missile systems were designed or sponsored by Rand studies. The name Delphi was taken from the famous oracle at Delphi, which gave prognostications for the early Greeks.

The Delphi Technique, as Exhibit 5 indicates, is done by mailing questionnaires for opinion gathering. Any time we talk about the future there is only one way of finding out anything about it: out of people's minds. There is no future data. It just doesn't exist yet. Consequently, the way to do this is to get people together—and that's what has been done traditionally. This is what happened at the oracle at Delphi. People talked with the priest who told them what was going to happen. It's what happens in most businesses today; get-

Exhibit 5. Delphi Technique

NOT A FORECAST, BUT A WAY OF
ORGANIZING AND TABULATING
FORECASTS.

MAILED QUESTIONNAIRES FOR
OPINION GATHERING.

RESULTS SUMMARIZED AND
FED BACK. EXTREMES ASKED
TO GIVE REASONS.

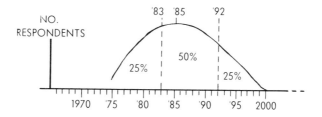

ting people together, having a meeting, having a task force, and trying to guess what the future is going to be. This is all right, but it has some drawbacks, one of which is the difficulty of gathering all of the people who are the most knowledgeable in terms of forecasting or thinking about the future. Not only is it expensive, but also a problem of logistics is presented unless a high priority is assigned in getting, 30, 40, or 50 individuals at one place at a given time.

The Delphi method eliminates the problem of people gathering because it utilizes a mailed questionnaire. You pick the best people, and you write to ask them if they will serve on a Delphi Panel. You'll be surprised to find how many have served on Delphi Panels. There are over a thousand Delphi studies going on in the United States at all times, the average such study involving anywhere from 50 to 100 people.

It might be well, at this point, to explain how a study is made under the Delphi Technique. Assume that you want to look at the ABC Company. You pick the people you think are most knowledgeable about the possibilities of the future. You don't necessarily go to the top executives. You pick someone in engineering with a good imagination, someone in marketing with a similar bent, someone in production, and finance. You may also want to utilize the services of community experts familiar with the Delphi Technique, or you may want to engage an outside service. The first questionnaire given to this panel usually asks, "What do you think is the most significant event of the next 15 years that will affect the ABC Company?" "What kinds of things will happen that will affect us the most?" You do give them a few simple ground rules. You say, for example, "Exclude the possibility of a nuclear holocaust." "Do not figure that we will be bought by another company, or that we will acquire an entirely different business."

Now list the happenings that are suggested. You will be quite interested in the responses that you get. Of the invitations to serve on the average Delphi Panel, 60 to 80 percent agree to serve. People in the business are surprisingly eager to participate. It's a real motivator, and when they agree to serve the work is taken seriously. Questionnaires are usually spaced about a month apart; the entire cycle taking four to six months. Some respondents will respond very briefly with one page, with four, five, or ten events. Others may send in 10 or 15 pages, with varying numbers of events.

This data is then turned over to a very small group for summarizing and analysis. The responses should be segregated into two groups; those containing a unanimity on a standard type of event and those that tend to be technical in nature. Such an analysis will yield 40 to 60 common events that people have suggested or ones that obviously would have a big effect.

Now you take this consolidated list, and send it back to these members of the panel. They are asked such questions as: "When do you think this will occur?" "How much of an impact do you think this could have?" "What is the likelihood of such an event occurring?" When the responses come back, they are summarized in the curved form shown in Exhibit 5. This curve answers the question "when do you think the event will take place?" In this case a few people thought 1975, most thought 1985, and some projected to the year 2000.

If you take that bell-shaped curve and cut off the quartiles, you will have the consensus of 50 percent of the panelists. That gives you three dates, in this case 1983, 1985, 1992. What that says is that the majority thought the event would happen between 1983 and 1992, the general average being 1985. You then send this information back to the panelists for every question. Each of the questions will have three dates. those who were in the first or the fourth quartile probably had reasons for believing that there would be, let's say, a minimum wage within three years instead of within five as most others thought. The questionnaire should provide space for giving the reason for selecting the year. It should also include the recommendation that if the respondent could give no reason he ought to vote with the majority. The questionnaires can cover a wide variety of questions besides the timing: "What kind of businesses will the event affect?" "Will it be good for society, or will it be harmful?" All of these provide better information about what is likely to happen in the future. There has been a lot of controversy on Delphi. Some say that it averages something you shouldn't average. I remember one engineer who said, "Suppose Thomas Edison had been asked to participate in a Delphi study." My response was, "Suppose he had, he still would have invented things; and he would have been a good participant."

"The Delphi study doesn't replace having a brilliant engineer or a scientist available. But if you can assure me that we have a Thomas Edison, I won't even talk about Delphi studies. If you have one in your company, use him. There aren't very many of them, and this sparsity forces us to resort to averaging of information. Even if averaging isn't more helpful than individual ideas, it can be used in addition to individual opinions. In other words, you can still have a think tank operation; you can still have a department head who is extremely creative; but let's also avail ourselves of a consensus, as a checkpoint.

Many companies are making use of the Delphi Technique. There is an organization called the Institute For The Future, organized under the aegis of the National Industrial Conference Board, that has become the center for Delphi studies. (Two years ago it did a very large Delphi study for the AT&T Company on the future of communications.) The Institute For The Future is composed of men who once worked at the Rand Corporation. They decided that this Delphi Technique was so powerful that it should not be limited to Rand activities because most Rand activities are done for the Defense Department and thus are secret. Everything the Institute For The Future does is made public within six months. The Delphi studies are available by writing to the Institute, which provides a list of available materials at nominal prices. Most of the studies are general enough that if you're in many different businesses you can get something out of them. You can also learn a lot about the technique by reading this material.

TECHNIQUE 3—EARLY WARNING SYSTEM

The technique that I think is gaining the most interest, and is being used extensively, is an early warning system. By that I mean a system that lets you know, before other people know, what kind of action to take. No one ever challenges the fact that things are happening in the world and that the trick is to know when. The company that is alert to taking action at the right time is the company that stays ahead; the trick is how to do it. How do you know ahead of time? In my early product planning days my company (IBM) and Eastman Kodak Company had an interchange agreement to look at each other's activities. I can remember kidding some the Eastman people one time about the fact that one of the small camera companies had come out with an automatic eye camera, a product that is universally used today.

The idea of an early warning system is to keep alert to the changes occurring around us so that our business knows when to take action. What do I mean by things that are occurring around us? This brings to mind another phrase that has come to be standard among the people who work in this field of futures, "forces for change." The things that are happening are going to make us change. A friend of mine who is a sailor, tells me that the early sailors who used the term "winds for change," understood this very well. If a sailor doesn't understand the winds, the directions they come from, and how they blow, he doesn't know how to set his sails. When he gets a change of

Exhibit 6.   Forces for Change

Changing value system
Increasing use of computers
Increase in leisure time
Burst of communications
Rising tide of education
Increasing corporate social conscience
Trend toward increasing numbers of multinational corporations
Explosive changes in biomedical field
Emphasis on long-range planning

wind he is liable to capsize. But if he understands the winds and understands how to set his sails, it doesn't matter how the wind blows; he can move fast. The same principle holds in business.

If we understand the things that are happening to us and we try to figure how to set our sails, we can move ahead. but if we don't understand the changing winds, or if we don't understand what to do when it changes, we are likely to be bowled over. I'm not going to recite the list of companies that didn't understand; there have been any number of examples. The buggy whip manufacturers and carriage manufacturers are the ones you have heard about *ad nauseam*. They have plenty of company. The trick today is to avoid being one of them. To give you a little more insight into this, I am going to run through briefly some forces for change that we used at IBM. These are fairly common to any large business.

These forces for change not only affect the business; they affect us as individuals. You'll find that companies doing work in this field will have a list of forces for change that they are trying to observe. The list that we arrived at in my work when I was in Exploratory Planning at IBM is shown in Exhibit 6. These include the changing values system, increasing use of computers, increase of leisure time, burst of communications, rising tide of education, increasing corporate social conscience trend toward increasing numbers of multinational corporations, explosive changes in the biomedical field, and the emphasis on long range planning.

THE CHANGING VALUES SYSTEM

The changing values system is the most interesting because it touches all of us; it affects us as individuals and it affects us as businessmen. Exhibit 7 shows how the character of our economy has been changing from 1944 to 1980. Note the reference to these terms used earlier—the industrial period and the postindustrial period. We moved in this country from the industrial period to the postindustrial in the late 1950s to early 1960s. I think a more pointed way of defining it is to say we moved into a period of affluence in the United States. We no longer have to worry about the simple things of life—about a house, food, security, vacation, and the ability to belong to a few organizations. Let me describe this in another vein, in terms of young people. I feel sometimes as though I lived in a laboratory because I have a 17-year-old daughter who is quite typical of the postindustrial society.

I contrast her with my own position when I graduated from college. She is just entering college. I graduated back in the thirties. I had only one objective in life. And that was to make money. That was not because I loved money.

Exhibit 7.   Changing Value System

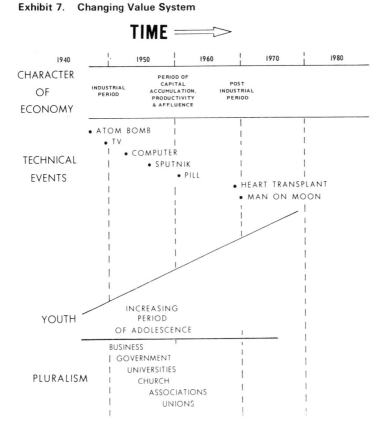

It's because money represented to me all the things I just talked about, a home, a family, education, vacation, and insurance. The young people today don't think that way; they assume they are going to get all that. In some ways this is good, they're more concerned about why we have these things and other people don't. Why don't underdeveloped countries have more? Why are there sections of our country where the wealth is distributed unfairly? They worry, "What's it all about? What is the true value of life?"

They see aunts, uncles, neighbors, and maybe even their own parents seeming to work beyond belief and not achieving any kind of happiness. So they're asking all kinds of questions. I agree they get into some trouble by going too far in their quest for life. They may get involved with drugs and other vices to which I certainly don't subscribe.

But I do understand it, and I'm sometimes amused when my friends, who have been very much of the old school, get quite upset with the young people. I ask them, "Why did you work so hard in the industrial period? Why did we get up in the morning and go to work before most young people today think about getting up? And why did we try so hard?" We did it so our families would have more. Now this has happened and you are upset. Instead of being upset let's try to understand it. Let's try to make sure that this freedom we have attained is appreciated.

This is one of the impacts of the change from the industrial to postindustrial society. Other items in the list of technical advances are the atom bomb, television, instant communication, computers, Sputnik, the pill, heart transplants, and the man on the moon. What did these events do to us? Why did it change our value system? This is a series of technical advances with real philosophical significance. What do I mean by philosophical significance? With the atom bomb, for the first time we could destroy the world.

The computer changed the whole concept of knowledge by levering the human mind. Sputnik, the first exploration in space, opened new horizons. The pill changed the role of women. Heart transplants were man's newest and most daring adventure in medicine. And finally, when the first men landed on the moon, more than 50 percent of the developed world witnessed the landing and envisaged the possibility of living in space. Some of the younger members of society will, no doubt, see colonies in space.

All of this has given people a different outlook and given our young people a different view of the world. Reflecting this view, in one of our IBM management schools a few years ago, a young controller from one of our divisions said, "You know, there is no question but people are changing. I have recently been interviewing some business school graduates, and I had one young fellow come in to see me. I talked to him along the lines that I talk to a young applicant. I told him we expect hard work out of a man. Sometimes we work long hours. Sometimes we have to work over holidays." But he continued, "There's a reward, if you work hard in our business you can get to be an executive; you can be controller, treasurer, or even division president. The young man started to laugh. I'm not a damned bit interested in being a treasurer or controller. What I want to know is how I will be able to express myself working for your company? How will I make myself felt? And what kind of good will I be doing for the world?'" This controller said, "If I had this interview two or three years ago, I'd have written on the bottom of that application blank, 'This guy is some kind of nut!' But in the light of what I know of the world today, we hired him and he's a fine guy."

The Stanford Research Institute made a film several years ago, *The Voices of Tomorrow*. It indicated how the youth on the Stanford campus were looking on life in a quite different way from the average businessman and the average factory manager. They have sold literally dozens and dozens of prints of that film to be shown in plants and factories to make people realize how this changing value system is working. This is what we have to recognize. I have spent a lot of time on it. I think it's probably the most interesting for the change because it is at the heart of so much of what we face in this changing world.

INCREASING USE OF COMPUTERS

The increasing use of computers not only is a matter of interest to a computer manufacturer but also affects all of us. The information in the circles at the lower portion of Exhibit 8 comes from a Diebold Research Survey. It indicates that we really haven't even scratched the surface in tactical and strategic planning. the computer must be adapted to these needs. We need terminals that can be used as easily as the telephone. Perhaps when that time comes we can let the computer be an adjunct to our minds, which is where it belongs, and not something to call an interpreter to handle.

INCREASE IN LEISURE TIME

The next force for change is the increase of leisure time illustrated by Exhibit 9. Anything you read today is slanted more and more to leisure time pursuits.

Reasons are: more women getting into business, more efficiency, more productivity, and a fourth very important point—people want more leisure time. We already have long weekends, and many companies are moving toward the four-day week. I have read that before the fall of Rome, the slaves were off 165 days a year. If you make a quick calculation, you come up with the realization that we are off about 135 days a year. Does that mean we have 30 days to go before the fall of our civilization? I don't think so, but we do have to make sure that we make good use of the available leisure time.

Obviously, you can come up with some thoughts on what your company can do. There are all sorts of things to do with leisure time. You can make available for your employees material that gives them information about community activities for their participation. There are free courses for people to study at home and information on interesting vacation spots, for example.

Exhibit 8.   Increasing Use of Computers

INSTALLED COMPUTERS   U.S.

	1955	1960	1965	1970
NUMBER	244	5,400	23,200	61,000
VALUE ($ B)	.177	1.9	7.7	25.

PROGRAMMERS, SYSTEM ANALYSTS & OPERATORS

	1960	1965	1970
TOTAL PROGRAMMERS, SYSTEM ANALYSTS & OPERATORS	200,000	400,000	900,000

CHANGING ROLE OF THE COMPUTERS

ADMIN.   SUPERVISORY   TACTICAL PLANNING   STRATEGIC PLANNING

1965   1970   1975   1980

Exhibit 9.   Increase In Leisure Time. Leisure Ethic
Promoted by Affluence, Education, and the Attitude
Toward Self-actualization

IBM Holiday and Vacation Policy	1954	1969
Holidays	6	10
Vacation	(1 yr) 2 wk	(1 yr) 2 wk
	(10 yr) 3 wk	(5 yr) 3 wk
	(25 yr) 4 wk	(15 yr) 4 wk
		(25 yr) 5 wk

Projection by Kahn

By the year 2000 the United States can double GNP
per capita with 25% fewer work hours for a population
150% as large as today's.

One company converted an old landing strip on its property into softball
diamonds. It was gratifying to see all eight diamonds fully utilized each day
by many employees who might otherwise follow sedentary pursuits.

BURST OF COMMUNICATIONS

When we started with these forces of change, we referred to some of the
learned people. One of the educators, speaking on communications, said, "If
I were looking for good innovative ideas, I would check the science fiction
writers." In the early 1900s if you had gone to the American Academy of
Arts and Science, the French Academy, the British Academy, or Harvard,
you would have learned little about the world today. But if you had read Jules
Verne or H. G. Wells, you would have gotten some pretty good pictures of
what's happening today. As I'm sure you know, it was Jules Verne's *Flight
To The Moon* that correctly spelled out the basic requirements for reaching
the moon. He recommended the right kind of propulsion and the right place
for landing. There is another science fiction writer by the name of Arthur
Clarke, who is also a great scientist. When the first communications satellite
was launched there was a great deal of controversy as to whether we should
have three satellites circling the earth—which would have been quite expen-

Exhibit 10.   The Burst of Communication

AVERAGE DAILY U.S. TELEPHONE CALLS (MILLIONS)

	1950	1960	1970
LOCAL	155	270	430
LONG DISTANCE	7	11	25

TOTAL U.S. AIR MILES (BILLIONS)

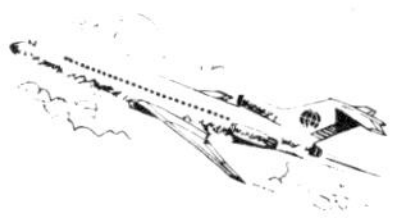

	1950	1960	1970
PASSENGER	8.5	32	70
REVENUE TON	1.3	4.8	20

INSTALLED U.S. TV SETS

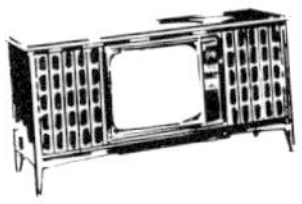

	1950	1960	1970
U.S. HOUSEHOLD	12%	88%	95%

"The Media is the Message"
MARSHALL McLUHAN

sive—or whether to have one fixed satellite over a particular area to serve certain areas of the world, the United States for example. Clarke stood alone against all the other scientists and said that the fixed satellite was the answer. The group all agreed, with the resultant cost savings.

When we visited Clarke, we went over the four forces for change. He thought they were all pretty good, except that we hadn't included the burst of communications. Exhibit 10 shows the increase in the use of telephone, air miles traveled and television sets. These increases are having a profound effect upon us. Everyone can communicate today; everyone is more knowledgeable; audiences are larger; and messages are instantaneous.

THE RISING TIDE OF EDUCATION

We referred earlier to the postindustrial period. This period envisages also the movement beyond industrial workers. Exhibit 11 illustrates that in 1900 the majority of the workers in the United States were engaged in agriculture. In 1940 the majority were in industry. By 1980 Drucker prophesies that the majority will be engaged in what he calls "knowledge work." The only way you can work in "knowledge work" is with education. The average American today has a much higher degree of education than ever before, and the forecasts indicate that this is going to keep increasing.

What is the world of 1985 going to look like? I think everyone will agree that the world of 1955 until today has been somewhat business dominated; the corporation being the main factor in our well-being.

Many people think that by 1985 government in the United States will be the main factor. This is based on polls conducted to find a consensus. It might be interesting to examine the consensus opinion. The question is which of three possibilities do you see occurring by 1985. Business will continue to be the significant factor in our lives. That's what we might identify as Scenario One.

Scenario Two says that government is doing more and more, and there is total agreement on this. I saw a projection not too long ago that said that by 1990, 75 percent of our GNP would be controlled by government. That

Exhibit 11.   Rising Tide of Education

Characteristics of the Majority
1900—Agricultural workers
1940—Industrial workers
1980—Knowledge workers

Educational Capacity of Colleges
1965	1975
5,000,000 students	9,000,000 students

Emerging Third Force

Traditional	Future
Business	Business⟷Knowledge
↕	↕
Government	Government⟷Institution

doesn't mean all government spent, but *controlled* by government, government contracts. So Scenario Two is that by 1985 we will live in a politicized society; a society where government is very much the strong force. Incidentally, this exists in many other countries, particularly the Communist and some of the Socialist countries. I think the average person in Sweden would say that the country is government dominated.

The third Scenario is that some new force we don't know of today will be dominant. It could be educational institutions; conceivably it could be a religious movement; it could be something different—the third force. Let's call it "think tanks" or "the educational force."

The standard response on these three Scenarios is somewhat consistent. Sixty percent usually vote for a politicized society; thirty percent think that business will still be the dominant force; and ten percent on the third force. I think business represents a way of life that made America great. In spite of the standard responses, I think that if we all study the future and do the right things about it, we can keep it there.

INCREASING CORPORATE SOCIAL CONSCIENCE

The next force for change has to do with increasing corporate social conscience (Exhibit 12). I don't think we need to say too much about this except that it is a very important part of the future. In 1925 Calvin Coolidge said, "The business of America is business." Most of our board chairmen today say, "The business of business is America." I think that has even been broadened, and people are saying, "The business of business is the community—it's all of us—it's the world." One can't be shortsighted on these things.

Exhibit 12.   Increasing Corporate Social Conscience

Calvin Coolidge (1925)
    Business of America is business
Board Chairmen Today:
    Business of business is America
Produce useful goods in a socially responsible
        way
Urban renewal
Pollution
Transportation
Black problem

I think we do have to make sure we all produce useful goods in a socially responsible way; and I think if that's done, and if business and government get together, we can solve some of these other social problems. I believe very strongly that the term "social conscience" is wrong. I'd like it to be called "market development," because that is what it is. We are not going to have markets if we have nothing but ghettos in cities people can't live in. We ought not think of it in terms of doing good or giving a contribution. Some of the social responsibility work of Westinghouse Company is done as market development, and that's the way it ought to be. If we are going to continue having markets, we have to solve these problems.

INCREASING NUMBER OF MULTINATIONALS

Exhibit 13 includes a couple of quotations about multinational corporations. I think the important thing to recognize is that the multinational corporation is one of the fastest growing activities in the world today, the average growth rate being around 15 percent. It is by far the highest growth rate. All the developed countries are getting into multinational corporations. The United States, of course, has dominated. There is an obvious reason for this. The multinational has many possibilities: you can work between countries; you can get the technology of every country; and you can take your markets in other countries. The only cause of difficulty is nationalism. It doesn't appear that nationalism can compete with the enlightened multinational. DeGaulle, toward the end of his regime, tried to do this in France and was most unsuccessful. There are just too many good things multinationals do. As long as multinationals keep doing those good things, and not exploiting the countries they're operating in, they are going to continue to grow.

Exhibit 13.   Increasing Numbers of Multinational Corporations

Output of multinational companies is $120 billion per year. Greater than GNP of any free nation outside the United States. [S. E. Rolfe]

Multinational corporation only institution . . . that creates a genuine economic community transcending national lines and yet respectful of national sovereignties and local cultures. [P. F. Drucker]

EXPLOSIVE CHANGES IN THE BIOMEDICAL FIELD

This is an interesting force with a little of the business flavor. Exhibit 14 comments on it. I must confess when we first started to study the explosive changes in the biomedical field, my reaction was that it was foolish to deal with any other forces for change, because these would make such a fantastic difference to all of us that the rest would be meaningless. What do I mean? Well just let's imagine tomorrow there is a newspaper article that says that some biologist has come up with a pill that absolutely controls the sex of children, so that every wife can take a pill and it'll be a male or a female, no question about it. Do you know what would happen with current statistics? Currently, in the United States, boy babies are about twice as popular as girls. If this circumstance were to happen tomorrow, we would suddenly have 50 percent more men than women. If this were to happen in India where boys are nine times more popular than girls, just imagine how out of balance things would get. That's a very simple example of gene control. When you go a step further and consider the possibility of not just determining sex, but determining the appearance, size, attitude, and degree of intelligence of children, we couldn't cope with it. I certainly hope it doesn't come in my lifetime. I'm somewhat encouraged, however, because in one of my trips I was with a chap by the name of James Watson, who is the head of the Cold Spring Harbor Biological Research Laboratory. He was one of the discoverers of DNA, the substance that controls genes. You recall this discovery earned a Nobel Prize. I asked Jim, "What do you think? Do you think we're going to see complete gene control in our lifetime?" He responded, "No, I don't. I don't think we'll ever see it. The more you get involved in this work, the more complex it gets." There are other aspects in this biomedical field that could be equally frightening. But I hope and pray that these fellows are right, and it's going to be a long time before we make any discoveries of this type.

Exhibit 14.   Explosive Changes in Biomedical Field

It is generally agreed that over the next couple of decades the most dramatic expansion in scientific understanding will be in biology.   [Donald Michael]

Genetics
Behavior Control
Organ Transplants

We can be affected in other ways to an equally great extent. For example, Dr. DelGado of Yale, who is a surgeon, inserts probes in the heads of monkeys and even bulls to affect their emotions. He can slow down emotionally excited animals, like a bull ready to charge at a red cape, by sending out a radio wave to control its brain. The bull will slow down and start to eat daisies or whatever a bull does that isn't emotionally charged. I asked Del-Gado, "Don't you get concerned that you may start to work on people or change them?" He answered, "No, I don't think there's a chance. I don't think any surgical work is going to affect people nearly as much as people have been affecting themselves in the last few years." I got to thinking about it and decided he may be right. I don't know what movies the reader goes to, but most of us go to the movies that are popular. I can assure you that had we gone to one of our modern movies five years ago, my wife would have walked out. I don't know how much she's enjoying them today, but we don't walk out. We've changed. We've changed in a very marked fashion. If anyone had told me five years ago that we would let my 17-year-old daughter go away unchaperoned for weekends, I'd have said, "You're crazy.!" But we're doing it, and so are many other parents. It's a different world. We're changing.

EMPHASIS ON LONG-RANGE PLANNING

The last topic that I want to mention under forces for change is the emphasis on long-range planning. There are several hundred organizations looking at the future. I'm sure the Hudson Institute, and Stanford Research Institute are familiar names to the reader. There are many smaller organizations of this type. There is a chap in Florida who has one research associate and keeps getting research grants. He is studying the future use of leisure time. Many of these studies are now directing their efforts to business. The fellow studying leisure time has worked for the Aluminum Company of America and several other corporations to assist them in their profit planning. The reader must certainly be familiar with *Future Shock,* by Alvin Tofflers, which deals with the future. There is also the very interesting book called *Limits For Growth,* written by MIT professors. It emphasizes that we have to do something about the future population and GNP before too long, or by 2020 at the very latest we will be in real trouble. This book has been a shocker, and it has had all kinds of reviews. I think most of the world agrees that population has to be slowed down. This no longer comes as a shock to anybody. But this is the first book that emphasized not only the need for population to slow down, but also the GNP in developed countries as well. This has started a great debate. I don't intend to take either side of this, but I do think people should be informed on the subject.

The Japanese and Europeans are far more involved in future studies than are Americans. They are far more interested in the longer term future, a circumstance I can't explain. The Japanese interest I can understand because they are interested in everything. But you usually think of the Europeans as being more traditional. Actually, they're not. They are really more involved, and there are more activities on future studies in Europe than there are in America. In Japan they're going all out. The Japanese did a tremendous Delphi Study in which they had 5000 leading Japanese sitting on different panels; the best study anybody has ever done. The Japanese Delphi Study on the future of Japan is available in English. It's very interesting reading, because they have gone into detail on just everything conceivable—clothing, transportation, communication, welfare, the Japanese islands, energy—everything. I think most American businesses would benefit a great deal by reading that study.

In summary, there are three methods: the method of scenario work, the method of Delphi studies, and early warning systems monitoring these changes. I've gone over a sample of some of the changes. I would like to illustrate applied future research to give you an idea of how this technique is being used. The Ford Motor Company, for instance, had recognized forces for change. They also introduced another idea, "forces for stability," and then compared these with fundamental beliefs. They say, "Now if the Ford Motor Company has had a fundamental belief that automobiles ought to be

Exhibit 15.   Emphasis on Long-Range Planning

Future-Oriented Institutions and Activities
   (several hundred now functioning)

Importance of Futures Literature
   Future Shock, by Alvin Toffler

Hudson Study, Corporation 1975–1985
   (90 corporations worldwide participating)

Delphi Studies
   (1000 in process)

made in America, and Americans have reached the point where they don't want to make automobiles," which seems true, "it's very hard to get people to do the kind of work that you can get done in underdeveloped countries." Well it's obvious what you do about it. You make them in other countries. And that's what's happened. In 1953, 75 percent of all the cars in the world were made in the United States. By 1965 this figure dropped to about 30 percent. You have to be aware of these forces if you're going to remain in business in a viable way. The way you do it is to continue to design products, as both Ford and General Motors are doing, but you manufacture them where people are still willing to work on the assembly line.

Mobil Oil has been doing great work in the field of studying the future of energy. I'm sure all the oil companies have done some of it by just becoming more familiar with what they are doing.

TREND ANALYSIS

The Institute of Life Insurance, an organization of approximately 80 percent of all insurance companies, has an interesting early warning system. As indicated in Exhibit 16, they use a matrix. Across the top there are such headings as science and technology, social science, values, attitudes and opinions, and political systems. On the political side of the matrix they have such categories as government, business, and media. Executives of the various member companies are asked to read two magazines on a particular subject. In academia, for example, they would read *The Harvard Business Review* and some other good academic paper; in business, perhaps *Fortune* and *Business Week*; in the mass media, a news magazine such as *Time*. They ask a pair (they have two people who read the publications in each of the boxes) to look for things that have to do with the future of science and technology. They ask for another pair of people to look at what might have to do with social science—what has to do with changing values. Then the "readers" submit a report quarterly to the research department at the Institute for Life Insurance. These reports are summarized, and from the information in them the analysts' reports are prepared for insurance management on *major* trends that will affect the insurance industry. An example: in one of their early trend analysis reports the idea of a government health plan was said to be just a matter of legislation now. There's no more debate; we're going to have a complete government health plan in the United States. (I think everyone is

Exhibit 16.   Trend Analysis Program "Tap"

	SCIENCE TECHNOLOGY	SOCIAL SCIENCE	VALUES ATTITUDES OPINIONS	POLITICS & GOVT.
GOVT.	Govt. Pub. on Sci. & Tech. ———	U.S. Economic Indicators ———	——— ——— ———	National Journal ———
BUSINESS	Datamation ——— ——— Wall St. Jour. →	Harvard Bus. Rev. ——— ———	Harvard Bus. Rev. ——— ———	——— ——— ——— ——— →
FORERUNNER MEDIA	The Futurist Technology Review	Journal of Social Issues	——— ———	→ ——— ——— ———
MASS MEDIA	N.Y.Times →	——— ———	——— ———	——— ——— ———

58 Publications   125 Reviewers
Quaterly Reports

INSTITUTE of LIFE INSURANCE
New York
Arnold Brown

agreed that that's going to happen.) All that one debates is the nature of the   117
program. There is also agreement that standing in the wings is complete
government supervision of retirement. Of course, this will have a tremendous
impact on insurance companies. So they are alerting all companies to watch
closely to see what is going to happen.

Every quarter a report goes out with four or five of these trends. The
General Mills Company has been developing a similar warning system, which
is used in their operation so their executives know the things that are affecting   118
them. Coca-Cola is doing quite a job. They have an interesting operation
called *The Book of Hazards* in which they ask each division to point out three
or four significant occurrences that could become hazards to Coca-Cola in
their operation and ask for information on what they are doing about it. The
importance of the early warning system, of course, is to know the forces for
change that are going to affect you, to be prepared, and then to take action at   119
the proper time.

Finally, I want to suggest that no one questions that women are going to be
in business in much larger numbers. So an early warning system ought to say,
"When do we begin to do something about this?" Let me illustrate that point.
If you move up on this too soon and get, perhaps, one third women for your
management within a year or two, I think you might find you look foolish
and it might not benefit you. On the other hand, if you wait till every other   120
business has promoted the good women, it's going to be too late. so the trick
is knowing the right time. Nobody has the answers. But I do think the exploratory profit planners do have ideas and thoughts that will help management in business make the right decisions at the right time. I want to make
sure that I leave you with that thought; it's a matter of making the decision
today. Too many people consider exploratory planners to be long-range   121
dreamers, but they're not. I know many of the leaders in this field. I know
they are interested in today. They just want to make sure that the decisions
made today are better decisions. This can be done by practicing some of the
things that I have reviewed briefly with you in this chapter.

*"The Japanese and the Europeans are far more involved in future studies   122
than we are in America. American businesses would benefit a great deal by
reading the Japanese Delphi Study."   William W. Simmons*

CHAPTER 3

SYSTEMS THEORY IN MODERN ORGANIZATIONS

RICHARD J. TERSINE

"Because of the knowledge explosion, disciplines have been breaking up into isolated subdisciplines with nonexistent or tenuous lines of communication. The less the communications among the disciplines, the greater the impediment that is created to the total growth of knowledge."

We hear constant reference to mountain systems, river systems, solar systems, body systems, transportation systems, community systems, and so forth. Generally the term "system" is used to denote a phenomenon that is complex by having numerous interrelated aspects. The term is so pervasive that it can refer to a myriad of phenomena. Anybody using the term "system" must define its content and boundaries so ambiguity can be dispelled.

The systems concept on a macro level represents an attempt to integrate the knowledge of the physical and social sciences into a unified framework.[1] Because of the knowledge explosion, disciplines have been breaking up into isolated subdisciplines with nonexistent or tenuous lines of communication. The lessened communication among the disciplines results in an impediment to the total growth of knowledge. The usefulness of a general systems theory lies in spotlighting of areas where gaps exist in knowledge. A simple analogy is the Periodic Table in chemistry and how it was instrumental in new element discovery.

For the last few centuries, the sciences have vastly expanded the frontiers of human knowledge by the process of analysis. The movement has been

[1] Kenneth E. Boulding, "General Systems Theory—The Skeleton of Science," *Management Science*, Vol. II (April, 1956), pp. 197–208.

towards specialization. Division, dissection, classification, separation, partition, and segmentation characterize the process of analysis. However, research in each of the separate fields of systematic knowledge has resulted in narrowing specialization. Walls of ignorance have tended to rise, blocking the flow of intelligence from discipline to discipline. The synthesis process is necessary to assimilate existing knowledge and avoid costly duplication of efforts. Summation, integration, unification, amalgamation, and combination characterize the process of synthesis.

The systems approach is primarily a point of view and a desirable goal rather than a particular method. It is not something new, but just a change in emphasis that considers internal and external environmental factors.

Systems can be classified as natural or man-made:

1. Natural
   a. Galaxies of which our solar system is a part.
   b. Man who is composed of skeletal, organic, nervous, and circulatory subsystems.
2. Man-made
   a. Economic systems,
   b. Social systems,
   c. All organizations in our society.

Professors Johnson, Kast, and Rosenzweig demonstrated the application of general systems theory to management practice as early as 1964.[2] We shall confine our discussion to organizational systems theory which is a subset of general systems theory.

The management processes require decision theory for the selection among alternatives. Decision theory utilizes system theory to determine the outcomes of the available alternatives. In this manner the requirements for systems analysis are precipitated by the management processes.

Organization is one form of activity that is pervasive in our society. A way of life has evolved that is characterized by the proximity and dependency of people on each other and organizations.

The systems concept is primarily a way of thinking about the job of managing. It provides a framework for relating internal and external environmental factors into an integrated whole. The organization is a part of an environment which it influences and in turn is influenced by it. System con-

[2] Richard A. Johnson, Fremont Kast, and James E. Rosenzweig, "Systems Theory and Management," *Management Science,* Vol. 10, No. 2 (January, 1964), pp. 367–384.

cepts help management reduce some of the complexity while indicating the complexity of problems.

Diversification, growth, consolidation, merger, and the closer interrelationship between organizations and their environment have all contributed to the intricacy of business operations. Organizations must adapt internally, adjusting their information flows, organizational structures, policy patterns, and operating procedures to the dynamic cultural changes in progress. Managerial adaption requires the acquisition of new knowledge for use in modifying the existing structures and procedures.

An organization is a man-made system which has a dynamic interplay with its environment. It is a system of interrelated parts working in conjunction with each other to accomplish the goals of both the organization and its participants. It has functional subsystems variously named—procurement, finance, marketing, production, and so on.

The elements of organizational systems can be categorized in the following manner:

1. Boundaries—define what is inside and outside the system. The subsystems are inside and the external environment is outside.
2. Parts—define the content of the system. They include:
    a. Individual—skills and personality belonging to organization members.
    b. Formal organization—formal structural arrangement of people and functions.
    c. Informal organization—the interaction of individuals and informal groups.
3. Interrelationships—functional relationships among variables in the system.
    a. Independent variables—explain, predict, and cause changes in dependent variables.
    b. Dependent variables—are influenced by other variables.
    c. Parameters—represent limiting constraints in descriptive equations such as the intercept and slope of a straight line.
4. Balance—refers to the equilibrium of a system.
    a. Stationary balance—the system returns to its previous position after a disturbance.
    b. Dynamic balance—the system shifts to a new equilibrium position after a disturbance.
5. Feedback/communications—control and coordinating mechanism that

permits the decision makers to influence the balance of the system in a desirable manner.
6. Decision makers—individuals or groups that determine the goals and service objectives.

Systems analysis has resulted from the growing complexity and near unmanageability of modern organizations. Its use can be related to measures of efficiency and effectiveness which are indicative of performance. In a more tangible sense, it can have a significant influence on the balance sheet as well as the income statement.

MULTIVIEW SYSTEMS CONCEPT OF THE ORGANIZATION

The model builder faces the dilemma that the more complicated and realistic his model, the more unwieldy it becomes as a tool for analysis. The model builder has had to restrict himself to simple models that can be solved by analytical techniques. However, the electronic computer with the aid of quasi-analytical and heuristic search techniques has increased significantly the probability of finding a near optimum solution to more complex models.

Concepts are only figments of the imagination, but they can help the analyst present constructive explanations of the behavior that he has observed. The question is not which version of a model is right or wrong, but whether or not any version is truly explanatory. A conceptual model becomes useful when it assists in making order out of chaotic and confusing data. The postulates of any theoretical system must be tested experimentally before they are given operational status.

In viewing an organization, no single model is appropriate in depicting the multiplicity of relationships. Numerous models can be utilized to convey conceptual and functional relationships. A model is neither true nor false; the standard for comparing models is utility, that is, adequate description or successful prediction. We shall use three models to provide different views of an organization. The three models are the Systemic Environmental Model, the Systemic Functional Model, and the Systemic Operational Model. The models represent perspectives that move from the very broad to the specific, and from the long-term to the near-term time frame. The models assume a physical product is produced, but they are easily adaptable to the production of a service. (Exhibit 1.)

Exhibit 1

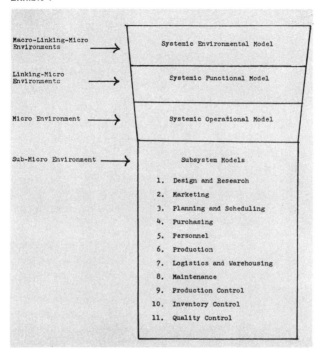

Macro-Linking-Micro Environments →	Systemic Environmental Model
Linking-Micro Environments →	Systemic Functional Model
Micro Environment →	Systemic Operational Model
Sub-Micro Environment →	Subsystem Models

1. Design and Research
2. Marketing
3. Planning and Scheduling
4. Purchasing
5. Personnel
6. Production
7. Logistics and Warehousing
8. Maintenance
9. Production Control
10. Inventory Control
11. Quality Control

It is useful to classify the environments that impinge upon the organization. A threefold segmentation includes the micro- linking, and macroenvironments. The microenvironment represents the organization itself and its internal affairs; the linking environment represents the interfaces the organization has with the external environment; and the macroenvironment represents the external environment to the organization.

The Systemic Environmental Model (SEM) includes the three environments; the Systemic Functional Model (SFM) emphasizes the linking and microenvironments; and the Systemic Operational Model (SOM) puts major emphasis on the microenvironment. (See Exhibit 1.)

SYSTEMIC ENVIRONMENTAL MODEL

This model abstracts from all three organizational theories (Classical, Neoclassical and Modern) and it contains elements of scientific management, human relations, small group theory, economics and decision making. (See Exhibit 2.) Each action has a reaction. A change in an input or rela-

Exhibit 2

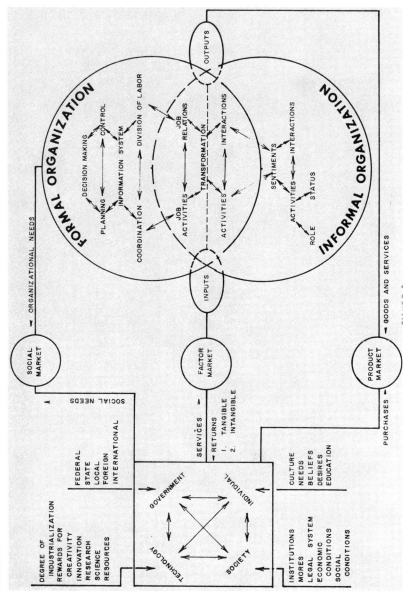

50

tionship results in a reorientation of the entire system to some degree. The model does not depict the efficiency of transfers among different sectors, but it does emphasize the path of the flow. The models attempt to unite the macro- linking, and microenvironments.

Microenvironment

It includes the firm and its internal affairs. The mutual dependency of the formal organization upon the informal organization is depicted by the area of their overlay in the transformation section. The organization imports inputs which it uses in the transformation operation to produce an output. In economic organizations, the value of the output exceeds the value of the inputs or the firm will go out of business in the long run.

The formal organization is an arrangement of tasks or duties to efficiently accomplish its goals. The formal organization is impersonal and usually defined by job descriptions and organization charts.

Under the concept of division of labor, job activities and job relations are determined by job descriptions and organization charts. Having divided complex jobs into smaller jobs it becomes imperative that all the operations be coordinated. This is the function of an information system. The information system provides the input to planning and control so the decision maker can coordinate activities to meet the organizational goals.

The informal organization is a product of the formal organization and it is derived from the needs and requirements of people. People have needs and objectives that may or may not be congruous with organizational objectives. The informal organization is made up of groups of people with shared orientations. The groups provide support and certainty to their members. The formal organization neglects these needs or does not know how to cope with them.

When people interact because of their activities on the job, they tend to develop positive sentiments (feelings of friendship) towards each other. People who share a common activity are likely to seek each other off the job for social intercourse. They presume that people who do the same thing are somewhat similar to themselves. Hence common activity leads to interaction, which in turn results in an increase in the strength of sentiments, presumably positive. People who like each other tend to interact frequently and work well together on common activities.

From their activities in the organization, people develop status and roles that may not be legitimately conferred by the formal organization. Operating within the structure of the formal organization we find this "organizational shadow" that accommodates the human needs of its members.

Linking Environment

The linking environment impinges upon the organization in three modes—when inputs are obtained from it (factor market); when output is sold to it (product market); and when the goals, objectives, and methods of the organization are sanctioned by it (social market). The factor and product markets are well defined by microeconomics, but the social market is much more vague.

The organization needs certain inputs to meet their goals and objectives. They purchase services and material inputs from the factor market. The output of the organization is sold in the product market for which the firm receives revenue.

The social market is where the public puts constraints on the organization to meet its needs or protect itself. Examples of social constraints are requirements for social security, workman's compensation, minimum wage, overtime for over 40 hours, safe working conditions, retirement programs, pollution control devices, antitrust laws, tariffs, and federal, state, and local taxes.

The linking environment represents the connecting systems between the organization and its external environment. Business areas that deal with the linking environment are finance, procurement, personnel, sales, legal, and so forth. Unfortunately, many firms have tended to ignore the social market, and they have given more emphasis to the more economically oriented factor and product markets.

Macroenvironment

The macroenvironment represents everything external to the firm. It is difficult to characterize since it can be different for two firms. An organization that provides a product to and operates in a given political unit could define the external environment by the single political unit. However, an entity that operates in and supplies an output to numerous geopolitical units may define its macroenvironment in a broader sphere. Generally, where a firm obtains its inputs and sells its outputs, defines its external environment.

The macroenvironment can be considered as a complex interacting mixture of man as an individual, society, government, and technology, all of which are not mutually exclusive. It is important to realize that not all organizations have a macroenvironment of the same consistence. As a simple example a computer hardware firm may have little governmental influence while technology could be ultraimportant, an automobile manufacturer may have little technological change, but a great deal of governmental influence.

The individual has needs, beliefs, and desires through which he influences and is influenced by society, government, and technology. Society is a structure of man-made institutions that develops values and norms for acceptable behavior for its members. The existing economic, social, and political conditions modify society's institutions as well as its mores as a function of time. Government through statute laws and its economic purchasing power has an influence that filters down to the individual level. The decisions of government can affect the lives of people for generations. Societal pressure groups try to direct government action in areas that are to their advantage.

Technology relates to the application of science to achieve human sustenance and comfort. Technology has a large influence on economic conditions. It alters and modifies the composition of the labor force, the design of organizational structure, and social relationships. John K. Galbraith, in his book *The New Industrial State,* describes technology as a major factor directing our lives in a nonsalutary fashion.

The interaction of society, government, technology, and the individual provides the structure that can define the macroenvironment of most organizations. It is important that an organization defines its macroenvironment for it has tremendous influence on intermediate and long-range planning. For example, changes in the macroenvironment of the tobacco industry via government influence has modified their long-range objectives considerably. As a consequence these firms are now diversifying. The influence of the macroenvironment through the social market can have a more pronounced effect than through the factor and product markets.

Micro-Linking-Macro Factors

The key factors of the Systemic Environmental Model are balance and reciprocity. Balance refers to the ability of the system to absorb shocks and still survive. The system can be shocked by the process of decay where products become technologically obsolete or by an overheating of the system which results in a constriction of flow to and from the markets. It is imperative that the system be able to take various shocks from both inside and outside the organization and still return to a state of balance. Some examples of shocks are undesirable merger takeover attempts, government ban on the sale of cyclamates, union strikes, acts of God, failure of a new product to be accepted, and so forth.

Reciprocity can be called a means by which different interests are satisfied. It is the "live and let live" attitude of multi-influences. Complementing, supplementing, and conflicting forces allow the organization to continue its existence because they benefit directly or indirectly from it. The relationships are symbiotic because two or more dissimilar groups receive mutual benefit. An organization must provide mutual benefit to its owners, employees, and the public or its existence will be in jeopardy.

It is clear that adaption to change over a period of time is necessary to maintain balance and reciprocity. Without the factors of balance and reciprocity the organization could not survive over an extended period of time.

SYSTEMIC FUNCTIONAL MODEL

This model emphasizes to a greater degree the linking and microenvironments. (See Exhibit 3.) The perspective of this model is much narrower than in the Systemic Environmental Model. The concern is for the functions that must be performed by the organizations in getting a successful product to market.

The Systemic Functional Model can be subdivided into five interdependent categories—policy decisions, product decisions, process decisions, plant decisions, and operations decisions. These categories give answers to questions of why make it, what to make, how to make, where to make, and when and how many to make.

Policy Decisions

This begins with the statement of the broad long-range objectives of the organization. (Typical examples are growth, market share, sales maximization, market leadership, social responsibility, customer satisfaction, product leadership, survival, return on investment, etc.) These broad objectives are modified to account for internal and external restraints. These restraints are limiting factors such as technology, financial resources, sources of capital, market conditions, size of the firm, competitors' actions, strength and weaknesses of the existing organization, and so forth. The redefinition of "broad objectives to a nearer time frame in line with the capabilities of the organization" results in strategies. From the strategies, specific plans are developed to attain the strategies. The plans are inputs to market analysis that help to determine what goods or services the public wants that are within the framework of organizational plans.

Product Decisions

Product decisions begin with general specifications from market analysis that indicate customer requirements. From the general specifications, technical specifications are written which define the product in much greater detail. Technical specifications are the structure for the functional design which includes both form and function of the product. The next step is production design or the effort to design the final product so it can be produced for low manufacturing costs. The final release of drawings and specifications of what to make terminates product design.

Process Decisions

Process decisions determine how to best produce the product. They begin with product analysis, which utilizes assembly and flow charts for analyzing each component of product in detail. The decision to subcontract or build in-house is made. Process decisions are made for all in-house work, which includes a definition of the processes as well as the steps and procedures for each process. Operations sheets are made that specify in detail how to perform each operation of a process. Finally, route sheets are developed to plan the physical flow of the product through the different operating departments.

Plant Decisions

Plant decisions begin with a decision to utilize unused capacity, expand existing plant, or build a new plant to accommodate the product. After this decision, the layout of the physical facilities is necessary including work station design and the selection of materials handling equipment.

56

Exhibit 3

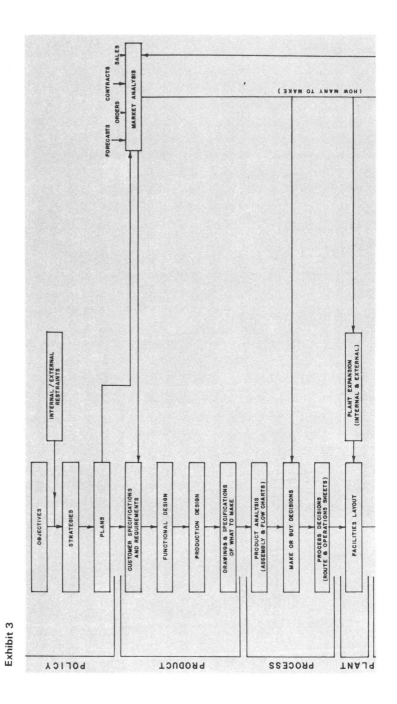

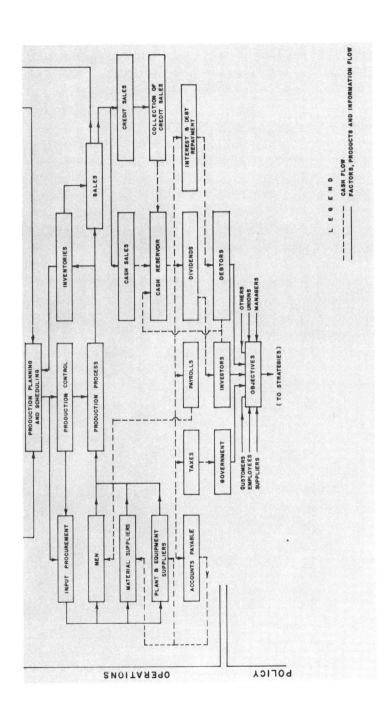

LEGEND

----- CASH FLOW
—— FACTORS, PRODUCTS AND INFORMATION FLOW

57

Exhibit 4

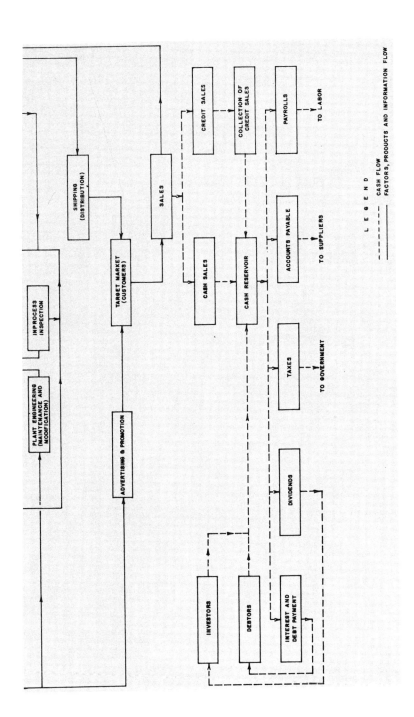

OPERATIONS DECISIONS

Operations decisions decide when and how many units to make. They begin with production planning and scheduling orders for the acquisition of men, materials, plant, and equipment. Activation and organization are achieved during this phase.

Production control concerns itself with the short-term scheduling of the resources into the production process. The production process generates inventories of products which, in turn, are depleted by sales. Sales, as well as investors and creditors, generate an inflow into the cash reservoir. Many parties have claims on this reservoir—employees, investors, creditors, government, and so forth.

Objectives are met when these claims are balanced with expectations. Any party able to modify this balance, in turn, influences the objectives of the firm. At this point, the model reflects a full circle return to the objectives in policy decisions.

SYSTEMIC OPERATIONAL MODEL

This model places its emphasis on the microenvironment (the firm itself) and it is short-term in its perspective. (See Exhibit 4.) It assumes that the plant and personnel are already in existence. The optimum operation and control of the system is the paramount consideration. The major decision areas are forecasting, planning and scheduling, procurement, production, plant engineering, sales, and control (production control, cost control, and quality control).

The system operates from forecasts and firm future orders which are transmitted to the "brain center," planning and scheduling. This central decision area determines what must be done to meet the future demand. It establishes the type and mix of inputs and schedules them for the production process. Procurement obtains the desired mix of human and nonhuman inputs. Production uses and transforms the inputs into the output product. Plant engineering maintains, modifies, and installs new plants and equipment. The sales function provides the successful interaction of the consumer with the output product. The control areas relate to quantity, quality, and cost. Inventory control maintains quantity control; quality control maintains quality; and cost control is exercised by planning and scheduling.

A close examination of the Systemic Operational Model reveals that many long-run decisions are omitted. It does not give adequate attention to the location of the system, physical facility layout, job design, work measurement, selection of equipment and processes, and so forth. The advantages of a short-term model are manifested in many short-term decisions that must be made that do not require a larger time perspective. (Should a marginal producer be allowed a line of credit in slack production periods?)

CONCLUSION

The models developed (SEM, SFM, and SOM) have been used to emphasize inadequacy of any single model for all occasions. Different conditions and situations require an adaptive view that can only be obtained from multiperspectives. The systems approach spotlights the objectives of the total system rather than a separate department. This more realistic approach reduces suboptimization. (The condition where department optimization is not optimum for the total entity.)

Particular models must be developed to represent specific systems (companies, industries, or economies). Each organization must be designed as a unique system. A focal organization is only one system in a larger order of systems. Since the subsystems and supersystems of a given system are frequently interdependent, the structure of changes in one substantially affects the others. The importance of defining system boundaries is paramount. Much organization literature focuses on intraorganizational factors with insufficient concern for interorganizational influences. Perspectives are broadened by the interorganizational and intraorganizational confluence. By examining the consequence of different organizational relationships, more effective structures can be designed to meet the specific requirement of the focal entity. A descriptive account of realtionships among the major systems provides a better understanding of the problems in its administration.

Differences between subsystem goals account for system conflict. While conflict can serve functional purposes, frequently the result is dysfunctional consequences. Some types of conflict arise from inherent structural differences which are not easily resolved. However, recognition of this type of conflict, although not sufficient to resolve it, can reduce some of the strain by permitting agents within the subsystem to anticipate it. Change should not be understood in terms of one subsystem but in terms of its possible effect on all subsystems. The systems approach is not meant to provide a historical perspective, but to provide the structure necessary for goal achievement with a mechanism for conflict resolution. It also provides a framework for explaining and predicting the outcome (behavior) of various strategies on the focal organization.

There are certain drawbacks and things systems theory cannot do. It cannot improve managerial judgment, identify objectives of the manager or his organization, nor can it aid in the prediction of future conditions and consequences of decisions. It does not indicate in what business to be, whether to diversify or consolidate, how to divisionalize, or whether to centralize or decentralize operations.

Structuring an organization to the systems concept does not eliminate the need for the management functions. There is a change in emphasis. All activities revolve around the system with its objectives, and the functions are executed only as a service to this end. In this capacity the organization is viewed as a set of flows of information, men, materials, and behavior.

Modern organizations are combinations of socioeconomic-technical systems. The systems approach attempts to integrate their complex functionings into a realistic synthesis.

"Differences among subsystem goals account for system conflict. Some types of conflict arise from inherent structural differences which are not easily resolved. However, recognition of this type of conflict can reduce some of the strain."   *Richard J. Tersine*

PARTICIPATION, THE BRICKS AND MORTAR OF PROFITABLE OPERATIONS

Specialization in labor is the outgrowth of our modern production methods, which have been instrumental in achieving the highest standard of living in the world. Although specialization is lauded as having made an important social contribution, its accomplishments have been downgraded by many because it has made "robots" of labor. The high degree of monotony that has been imposed on labor is cited as one of the disadvantages because the work becomes highly repetitive and therefore tedious.

SPECIALIZATION NOT ALL BAD

There are those who contend that specialization does not necessarily lead to unhappiness on the part of the worker. The skilled worker who is assigned skilled tasks is certainly not likely to become bored with his work. Many who are relegated to the simple routine jobs are also not likely to complain when they are temperamentally attuned to such work. The bench assembly type of operation, for example, would attract many who are interested only in working an eight-hour day and then being free to pursue other off-the-job activities.

In Ralph De Biasi's opening comments, he quotes Chris Argyris' sad commentary that 85 percent of the people would rather die than work. However, the author makes the observation that this was just as true in the agricultural period preceding the industrial period—indicating that there is a basic characteristic in people that might be blamed on one set of circumstances when, actually, it would exist irrespective of the circumstances.

PEOPLE MUST BE MOTIVATED

Mr. De Biasi points up the trend away from the sanctity of management rights. To achieve economic goals it is necessary to recognize the factors that motivate people. By motivation he refers to responsibility and sense of achievement. The author introduces the term "participation," which he uses synonymously with "motivation." He therefore recommends a partnership relationship with management—or to state it another way—teamwork.

In closing his chapter, Mr. De Biasi stresses that if people are to achieve, they must be given realistic goals. He also reminds the reader that control is not in the books of account but in the minds of men.

PARTICIPATION BY TOP MANAGEMENT

George Ingram, in outlining what his expectations are from the executives responsible for profit planning, emphasizes the importance of participation or involvement on the part of the chief executive and his principal officers. Although this sounds contradictory to what Mr. De Biasi stated, actually it is not.

Mr. De Biasi starts with the premise that top management should not dominate—that it should participate in a joint team effort with the lower levels of management. Mr. Ingram, on the other hand, is critical of the type of management that abdicates it responsibility, and urges involvement. Actually both authors are in accord—their starting assumptions are different.

George Ingram cautions against the Ivory Tower approach on the part of corporate staff people; he is strong in his admonition to get out to the scene of action—which could be the market, the factory, or the laboratory.

THE EMPLOYEE SHOULD "TALK BACK"

The author is not only a strong advocate of teamwork and management involvement—but also he is strongly opposed to the employee who tends to be a bag carrier or who is the timid, servile type. He wants to see the lower level members of management speak up not only to their peers but to their superiors as well.

CHAPTER 4

THE "PEOPLE" FACTOR IN PROFITABILITY

RALPH M. DE BIASI

"In setting goals at the top and sending down crash orders to achieve them or else, management often loses more than it can hope to gain through employee resentment at not being consulted—"

About 5 percent of the people work, 10 percent of the people think they work, and the other 85 percent would rather die than work. . . . I think there is a definite need for more pressure, people have to be needled. . . . Man is inherently lazy, and if we could only increase the pressure I think the budget system would be more effective."

"There are hundreds of workers who don't have the capacity to do things other than what they are doing. They might be able to develop some capacities, although I think there are many who couldn't even if they wanted to; because they don't have the desire."

Have I shocked you? I hope not.

Did it sound familiar? It should have.

These are all quotations from surveys Chris Argyris reported on in his classic study of *The Impact of Budgets on People,* New York Controllership Foundation, 1952, which reflect behavioral assumptions implicit in the structure of most present day accounting systems.

The view that holds that people are ordinarily lazy, inefficient, and wasteful; that if money is available it is to be spent; and that work is an unpleasant task that people will avoid whenever possible, reflects a management philosophy prevalent in the early 1900s and one that is still dominant to this day.[1]

[1] Caplan, Edwin H., *Management Accounting and Behavioral Science,* Reading, Mass., Addison-Wesley Publishing Co., 1971.

The emphasis of this philosophy is on economic gain for the enterprise, on economic incentives for the individual, and on economically oriented decision-making processes. We continue, with minor modification, to use an organization theory that is concerned with men primarily as adjuncts to machines, to be taught and economically motivated to maximize productivity through increased efficiency.[2]

To implement this philosophy, accounting techniques are established that help management to plan, coordinate, and control, so as to achieve the maximum profits. The resulting accounting system serves as the control device so that management is able to identify and correct the undesirable performance of those so-called lazy workers.

Interestingly enough, it is a pretty good description of most business accounting systems today. The behavioral assumptions inherent in these systems have endured for a long time. But today, they are—and rightfully so—being questioned, doubted, and challenged in many areas.

The world of the 1970s in which we find ourselves, is far removed from what it was 50 or 60 years ago. Technological change, economic change, changes in the structure of the family, and changes in education have all had a profound effect on attitudes, thought, and approach to life.[3]

Fundamental changes in values, particularly among our younger workers (veterans and minority workers, if you will), are having a strong influence on managerial behavior and the underlying assumptions on which traditional accounting has rested for so many years.

SHIFT TOWARD AUTONOMY

In the business setting, directional changes can be seen toward more autonomy for the individual, wider participation in planning and decision making, greater dependence upon individual judgement, and more widespread recognition of the potential power of nonmanagers to help (or thwart) business in the realization of its goals.

We are moving away from the sanctity of management rights and organizational policies and procedures. To achieve the economic goals of manage-

---

[2] Toan, Arthur B., Jr., "Does Accountancy's View of Human Behavior Meet Today's Needs," *Price Waterhouse Review,* Summer-Autumn, 1971, also "Is Accounting Geared to Today's Needs?" *Management Adviser,* November-December, 1971.

[3] Lee, James A., "Behavioral Theory vs. Reality," *Harvard Business Review,* March-April, 1971.

ment (on a long-run as well as short-run basis) it is necessary to recognize what motivates people. Failure to do so will adversely affect the long-run contributions people can make, which are so important to any company.

Now, what do I mean by this? If the system emphasizes short-term profits and cost savings, if the system does not offer motivation, then the attainment of the higher priority of long-term profit contribution is jeopardized or even impossible.

Working conditions, fringe benefits, and so on, are essential but not motivators of people. The real motivators are responsibility, achievement, the work itself, and advancement. These are the keys to improving worker performance and productivity.[4]

The management of human resources should have the same, if not greater, priority as the management of other business assets. I am afraid that in some of our companies this is not the case.

ARE TRADITIONAL THEORIES TRUE?

At this stage we can begin to see that serious doubt exists as to whether the economic and organizational theories underlying our accounting systems properly or fully describe the forces that motivate both managers and employees.

Digressing for a moment, I recall reading some figures recently that showed how poorly the United States has been doing in the international race to increase productivity. During the last decade, the United States increase in output per man-hour was the lowest among all of the developed nations of the free world—less than one third of what the Japanese accomplished.

Although it is understandable that the newly developing nations should make rapid gains in productivity, still there is a nagging doubt that our productivity is increasing as much as it could. I can't help but think there is some relationship between lagging productivity and the "people" problem. We can make rules and regulations, and set forth all kinds of plans and procedures, but it means little if we have neglected our human resources and lost their productive interest. We, as managers, must share some of the responsibility for seeing the United States go from first to tenth in productivity.

[4] Hertzberg, Frederick, Bernard Mausneo, and Barbara Snyderman, *The Motivation to Work,* New York, John Wiley & Sons, 1959.

INDUSTRY'S ATTITUDE SKEPTICAL

What we are really dealing with is human behavior. And, unfortunately, since the field of behavioral science as related to business has been exploratory at best, we are left with more questions than answers.

As an example, management accounting is not in a position to assign values to human assets and measure changes in them over periods of time.

Although we can still appreciate the plight of the manager who attempts to build high morale and motivation, to increase productivity, and who is hamstrung by the short-run orientation of accounting indexes, can we help?

Management, on occasion, has taken a dim view on the subject of human relations. I am sure at one time or other you have all heard management respond to pleas for consideration of human behavior with such terms as . . ."not useful . . . too fuzzy . . . theoretical . . . soft . . . not operational,"[5] particularly when attempts are made to incorporate the human equation into profit planning.

However, in all fairness, industry in recent years has shown a willingness to experiment—even though many such experiments fail or offer questionable results—and its attitudes are changing as far as "fuzzy, theoretical, and soft" are concerned.

You may well ask, "What part can I play in this period of change?" Very little if you accept the view that managerial behavior change is primarily a function of cultural change. To me it is evident that, as managers, it is our responsibility and that it will not happen until we properly assume the obligation to bring about the change.

If we agree these changes are desirable, are we going to say they will come about as cultural changes and sit back and wait for them to happen? Or are we going to take an active role and make it happen?

In this connection, let us examine some of the issues we will face in taking on the challenge. You will find as we deal with the issues raised that there are no clear cut paths to the correct solution.

First, let us consider the "people factor" in profitability.

While a lot has been said and written about the ideal approach to profit planning—with participation at the lowest possible level of responsibility and the need for built-in feedback to monitor and control performance—my

[5] Lee, James A., *op. cit.* Also David R. Hampton, Charles E. Summer, and Rose A. Weber, *Organizational Behavior and the Practice of Management,* Glenview, Ill., Scott Fresman and Company, p. 5. See also Conference Board, *Studies in Personnel Policy,* No. 216, 1969.

experience is that in actuality most profit plans are set by committee (this is true whether for sales, operations, administration, or even corporate profits); *not* by the line supervisors and foremen expected to carry out the plan, but by the top managers and owners of the business most desirous of the results (and who stand to gain the most), whether the goals set to achieve these results are reasonable or not. We don't admit this, but I think it's a fact of life.

Frankly, I am not convinced this is altogether bad, and not the most practical approach, and (within the context of reality), provided the profit planning is realistic and set constructively to "help" the line supervisor and his people achieve their goals—not to "police" their activities or legally bind them. It is my experience that at this level they are sincerely seeking assistance that we rarely give them.

This is where I'd like to get into what I call "humanizing" the profit-planning process to make life easier and more productive for all echelons of management. While my information is derived from experience in privately held corporations, it is equally applicable, I feel, to publicly held corporations and businesses.

We must ask, "Are the goals realistic? Or will they merely tend to create stress and pressure?"

In the dirve to force through very real and important goals it is easy to lose sight of the fact we need "people" to get the job done. And sometimes we become so committed that we are blind and deaf to these same people when they voice doubts or raise objections abount being able to meet the goals within the time scheduled.

I am not talking now of the line supervisor or foremen who will always find ways and reasons why "it can't be done" but the man who honestly questions the plan—rightly or wrongly—and has the guts, experience, and loyalty to speak out (because it takes all three). Again, I must emphasize, he is the man who honestly questions the plan.

"TRICKLE-DOWN" DIRECTIVES

Such situations are usually the result of a chain reaction that starts at the top and is bucked down through successive layers of management until it trickles down to the foreman and his assistant. The president tells the vice president who calls in the manager who passes it on to the supervisor who

⟩ the foreman—and there it terminates. Usually accompanied by
\s-out" cry that, "We don't care how you do it but it's got to be
.eople can do it. Sell them on it!"

.ne result is build up of stresses throughout the chain of command in
direct proportion to the importance of the end result. All of which lands
without recourse, on the manager, supervisor, or foreman—not the workers
who have a union to protect them from retribution or blame if the plan
fails.

This might be particularly applicable as a result of a response to an
emergency competitive situation or drastic change in market conditions
which calls for a sudden revision of budgets and goals.

What happens when such situations don't follow the textbook? A lot of
companies talk a good game about "participation at the lowest level" but
play a bad game or none at all.

How many of us work for companies in which the lowest level of management responsibility enters into every budget action—and here I'm talking
about the foreman who gets the job done—to set objectives when planning
budgets that affect his operation? Not too many, I would venture to say,
based on the stories I've heard.

What it means then is that it is up to you, or one of your people, to make
sure the channels of communication are open. And that when a seemingly
impossible task is seen as such by the people expected to get the job
done—justifiably or not—that you investigate their concerns.

Let me give an example of a situation that developed at my company. We
were up against a competitor who suddenly started selling a consumer
product at a much lower price than ours. He was beginning to make serious
inroads into a market we traditionally dominated. This was definitely having an adverse effect on our sales volume.

While our product was of a much more rugged design, and of superior
quality it was actually overdesigned for the market. So we assigned
engineering the job of coming up with a simpler low-cost unit without
reducing reliability or product life, within a parameter of a 30 percent cost
savings; concurrently advising manufacturing that it had to be in full
production by the end of the year.

Like many "crash" programs, this one collapsed. We finally ended up
with our product at the price quoted—but several months later than
scheduled. And we almost lost our engineering and manufacturing supervisors (who had been with us for years) in the process.

Why? Because the timetable we set was unrealistic and the supervisors were subject to interdepartmental pressures at an uneven level. We were not smart enough to see what was happening. In addition, we underestimated the manufacturing design problem and overestimated the urgency—because the competitor could not deliver.

The story has a happy ending because it turned out we increased our share of the market thanks to the new design, but that doesn't alter the fact that we made a management mistake in planning and we abused our human resources.

How do you conceive of your role in planning profits?

Is it one of control or support? Is your staff looked upon as the "watchdog of the company?" Are there conflicts in goal setting within your organization? Do your budget men believe they are almost solely responsible for cost reductions, that they alone are expected to seek and find opportunities for cost savings? Have line managers abdicated part of their authority to you or have you usurped part of the line authority from them?

These questions are rhetorical. For, in the final analysis, you must test your ideas against the specific nature and objectives of your company. The leadership styles, autocratic, democratic, or some combination thereof, affect attitudes throughout the organization. The type of industry you're in, and the particular jobs it requires, and the personalities of the managers are significant.

I do not expect that there are ready answers to these questions. But they do point out that the attitude and approach brought to the job has a significant impact on the people who will be attempting to realize the company's goals. Of course, your attitudes and approach all conform to a large extent to what your management expects from you.

In conclusion, it would appear to me that profit planning has an impact on the behavior of people, and that people's behavior affects the effectiveness of such plans. The effects of these relations are not always clear. Changing attitudes toward the concept of man and his relation to work brought about by changes in technology, affluence, family structure, and education are influencing the way an organization functions.

The simplistic views of the past, upon which much of accounting theory rests, are giving way to the recognition that in a modern complex society there is no single universal goal, such as profit maximization, that a company can claim for its own. We cannot be oblivious to this change. We must accept the challenge of the present and search for the answers that have meaning for us even if it means discarding ideas that have served us well in the past.

It has been said that control is not in the books of account but in the minds of men. If we can solve the people problem, the other problems will be easy.

"A chain reaction starts when a goal originates at the top and is then bucked down through successive layers of management without adequate time for discussions or reactions on the way."   *Ralph M. De Biasi*

CHAPTER 5

WHAT I EXPECT FROM MY PROFIT PLANNING EXECUTIVES

GEORGE INGRAM, JR.

"I expect my profit planning executive to exercise mature business judgment. I want him to speak out forcefully when he has something to say. He must also operate in a manner that will elicit teamwork rather than grandstanding."

I cannot really get into the topic of expectations from my planning group without talking quite a bit about what I think planning is; the organization of it and what we are trying to accomplish. In this chapter I would like to give some basic ideas, about profit planning, and the basic philosophy of planning, a number of comments about organization for sound profit planning, and then comments about the characteristics of executives who are good profit planners. I cover the matter of setting corporate objectives and then the inevitable thoughts on acquisitions and mergers. These topics play an important part in this whole picture. Then there is the matter of implementation of the profit plan, the objectives and the measuring of results. After discussing these matters I can give a more meaningful comment of what I expect from my profit planning group.

BASIC PHILOSOPHY OF PROFIT PLANNING

Before I get into this I want the reader to know that I am presenting my own feelings and ideas but that most of the ideas are not original with me. I may be packaging them differently, and I hope you will find this particular way of presenting the material useful. With that let's get into some specifics—let's talk a bit about the basic philosophy of profit planning. I believe very strongly that profit planning, if it is to be effective, must be the primary job of the chief executive officer and the principal officers who support him in managing the company. What I'm really saying is that we are never going to get anywhere, if we simply say: "Okay, we'll hire a half dozen fellows to work on profit plans and we will let them go in that room and talk to them twice a year." It can't be done that way. I'm sure you will agree with this. The real planning that means something to the company, that determines the objectives of the company and results in some significance in the company's results and image, will only come about when there is prime involvement on the part of the chief executives—usually five to ten in number—depending on the particular organization. I don't mean that it should be limited to these, but they are the ones who must become involved.

So we start off with the very basic thought that we must have top management involvement, and I believe that profit planning is the most important single thing that any of those top people can and should do. The second point is that there really isn't any one way to do planning. I've been in several organizations where I have been involved in this activity. The way that it works effectively in a particular situation is the right way to do it. There are different arrangements, different people, different organizational possibilities, and different techniques. This is so because you have different businesses and different conditions. It takes a great deal of imagination to recognize the inner relationships of these elements and to come up with the right organization and approach to planning in a particular case. Just to reemphasize, I think it is very important not to try to do it in your company the way it is done in another company just because it was successful there. Your situation could be quite different.

Technical Analysis and Problem Identification

The next thought on this general subject of profit planning and philosophy is that technical analysis and a very careful approach to identifying problems are extremely important for success. We ought to recognize from the beginning that success is also dependent on the proper proportions of opportunism. That may surprise you, but I believe it to be the case. There is a place for business instinct in this matter. So it's not just a question of knowing scientific techniques for planning and knowing about the financial characteristics of a particular product line, the process, or the market. We must go beyond that and make sure there is a place in our organization, thinking, and philosophy for opportunism to a reasonable extent. Let us recognize that business instinct is still one of the strongest forces for success in the business world. This is very difficult to depict in an organization chart or a job description. But somehow or other top management and the planning management must understand that those elements are important to any successful program.

Assignment of Priorities

Now something else that is obvious to everybody, but that needs to be repeated from time to time, is that every business detail does't deserve the same amount of attention or skill, as far as profit planning is concerned. Each product line doesn't have the same problems, or the same opportunities, or the same impact on the company. Each division doesn't have the same impact, and each technology or whatever it is we are dealing with can also have different importance. Let's realize that what we are really interested in doing is maximizing the overall profits of our company on a short term basis *and* a long term basis. But we don't want to say that every division, regardless of size, should spend exactly the same amount of money, or time, or degree of skill on profit planning because some divisions don't need anywhere near the sophisticated planning that others do. I think this is obvious, but we have a tendency when we set up our plans and put out general memoranda and procedures to treat everybody the same. To a certain extent this is necessary; we shouldn't overdo that uniformity of procedure.

Avoid the Ivory Tower Approach

Another point on profit planning philosophy, which I think is very important, is that most of the work should not be done in the ivory tower, the Corporate Headquarters. Although there are certain things that can't be done anywhere but at Headquarters, most of the real planning and analysis has to be done where the action is; in the market or the factory or the laboratory. This is where the opportunities are. An effective planning organization will have to be out wherever the problems are if it's going to be successful in identifying these problems and helping in the solutions.

ORGANIZATION FOR PLANNING

The second general area of comment has to do with organization for planning. In most companies I think it is fair to say that planning jobs can be broken down into four functions, or four subfunctions. The terms that I use for these may be different from the reader's, but I think you will recognize in each case what I'm talking about.

Planning for Existing Operations

First of all, we have the planning for current existing operations, the budgets, and the profit plans we deal with each year as they come along, sometimes for two, or three, or four, or five years depending on the particular situation. This is where the energy of most people in planning goes, and this is what most companies call planning.

Expansion or Contraction of Operations

The second area, which I think is quite separate from the first, is the possibility for expansion or contraction of current operations. Maybe we should be closing down a plant, maybe we should be redirecting from large ones to small ones, and maybe we should be going into new markets with existing products. These kinds of questions require a little different approach from the planning for established operations, although they have to be coordinated.

Should We Diversify?

The third area raises the basic question of whether the company should diversify. This is a much broader question involving the development of corporate strategy—what you are trying to do with the company. Then the fourth area is the corporate strategy itself. This has to do with the priority of the things I just mentioned and the question of allocation of resources among the units and where you want to expand; whether you should diversify and how you sort out these resources. Timing, I believe, is a very important consideration in planning. This is particularly so when you are moving into new product areas, new markets or planning acquisitions.

Corporate Objectives

The other important part of corporate strategy concerns corporate objectives themselves. So current operations, expansion, or contraction of the current operations, diversification, and the corporate strategy are the four areas I see in this whole picture. Each of these can be looked at from different points of view. You can view them from short range, and in many cases it is proper to do that. You can also look at them long range. Some might look at these same things from a mechanical point of view. What forms are we going to design, or what period of time do we want to have reported. All too many profit planners overfocus on the mechanical aspects.

THE BIG STRATEGY

There is another area that many profit planners don't get into at all—the big strategy. Every company, no matter how large or how small, has questions relating to strategy. There can be five, six, seven, or even ten questions that have to be faced up to but are sometimes completely ignored. I think it is the planning function's job to see to it that these big questions, as I call them, are identified and that they are faced up to. There is very frequently no one to organize the strategy approach.

Differences in organizations will come about as a result of differences in individual personalities and the motivations of the people involved. Even factors like ages can have a significant effect on approach. In addition you have particular combinations of people with specific business skills. Some are strong in some areas and weak in others. Frequently you can organize around that problem.

Of course, the magnitude and the diversity of the business will have a lot to do with the way you organize. In addition the degree to which the corporate objectives dictate change can affect the approach. When the indicated change is small you don't have the complications in organization that you would have in a big change. If you are trying to make your company ten times as large, and if instead of being in one business you are trying to get into ten, you have a different kind of organization problem. Obviously just sticking with what you have been doing for the last ten years stifles the flexibility that a healthy business requires.

We must bear in mind that businesses vary widely. There are insurance, women's apparel, wholesale, retail, mining, transportation, and service organizations just to mention a few. These differences naturally affect the way you organize for planning. Profit planning responsibility is usually shared. The comptroller or other financial people have important inputs into this, and they usually relate to the budgeting and short-term profit planning aspects. In a larger and more aggressive company there is probably someone who concentrates on acquisition and mergers. He may even have a department. Usually there is a separate planning function, the assignments to this office varying from company to company. This office in one company may be responsible for the entire profit planning program or it may merely consolidate the profit plans prepared by divisional profit planning executives.

PULLING IT ALL TOGETHER

Also to be considered is the very important matter of basic responsibility of the line officers of the various operations of the company. So far, we have been talking mostly about staff responsibilities. In the final analysis, though, if your company is going to accomplish what you are after, the line people are going to have to carry the major part of the responsibility. They are going to have to play a major part in any planning effort that you organize for. The top executive pulls this all together in whatever configuration he may select. He is responsible for coordination and leadership. He and his key group make it all go or make it fail.

"Pulling it all together" can also take many different forms. In some companies there is much detailed involvement and detailed planning. In some cases objectives are set as to what is to be accomplished by the profit plan. In other cases the principal mechanism is one of reviewing the plans after they have been revised and setting up an approval procedure. The reader is familiar with all of this. I think the main concern is to make certain that the chief executive sets the objectives of the planning effort and stays involved so he is satisfied that he is getting what he wants.

PROFIT PLANNING GROUP SHOULD BE SMALL

The number of people involved in profit planning departments should be small, and I have several reasons for suggesting this. Since planning is the job of everyone in the executive category, let's not set up a parallel function to duplicate their efforts or their skills. A planning staff should do analysis, prodding, coordination, and seeing to it that the job gets done. But in seeing to it that the job gets done it ought to use the skills in the legal department, the financial department, the comptroller's shop, wherever those skills may lie, to accomplish the objective. When you do this, you accomplish several things. In the first place you tend to coordinate the efforts of everybody in the company so that people are working as a team. This helps to minimize the internal political tendencies that frequently create jealousies among the various functions.

I'm for small planning departments but with a big responsibility. It is a mistake to give all profit planning responsibility to one executive because it's just too much to do. My experience is that if you give all this responsibility to one man he will concentrate on the short-term matters because "the house is on fire and he has got to put the fire out." The long term aspects of planning get little attention; this can be a very serious deficiency. It is important to analyze the different levels and types of planning that you need in your business and to make sure you do not end up by giving the assignment to one fellow who isn't going to be able to handle it satisfactorily.

FOUR BASIC QUALITIES OF A GOOD PROFIT PLANNER

There are four primary requirements for good profit planning.

1. Sound Business Judgment. The most important one, and very often this is lost sight of, is that the planning executive must be a sound businessman. After all, he is planning a business; he is motivating and coordinating people who have business responsibilities and he ought to have enough background to have the basic "feel of the goods" as it were.

2. Maturity. As a second requirement the planner should be mature enough to be able to deal with top executives in the company on a very close basis, and particularly the chief executive and those other top level people who advise him. This means that he must have personal qualities so that he can identify with these people as well as have a satisfactory breadth of experience to get his message across and have a good give-and-take rapport.

3. Poise. The planner also must be able to deal appropriately with outsiders. He is going to be involved in acquisitions; maybe he is going to be talking to bankers, not necessarily on financial matters, but on contacts. You certainly want a man who will be respected in these circles.

4. Wide Ranging Points of View.   Finally, but very important, he has to be able to understand and anticipate a wide range of points of view. You may think I'm talking about understanding everyone in the organization. Well that is a must; he has to understand what the product managers think, what the advertising department thinks, and what the financial people think. But I'm really going beyond that; he has to be able to anticipate the way the board is going to think, because sometimes they have an entirely different point of view. They may be of different experiences; they may come from different economic situations themselves so their points of view may be surprisingly different from what you think to be logical. And you have to be able to anticipate this. It is important to understand the reaction of stock-holders and the investing public to some of the major things you are working on. A lot of very important plans have been stymied by failing to anticipate the reactions of some very important people who are not sitting in the organization on a day to day basis.

BACKGROUND OF PROFIT PLANNING GROUP

There are three other matters I would like to mention in this general area. One is that I don't think a planner is likely to be as effective if he has been only a member of the planning staff all his life.

Varied Business Experience.   He must have had some range of business experience besides planning. There is nothing wrong with planning, but I'm getting back to the basic point, that he should be a rounded out business man.

Bright Young Man Syndrome.   In addition, we have to avoid what I call the perpetual bright young man syndrome. We are all familiar with the bright young man who graduates from one of the fashionable business schools and goes into the planning department in his middle twenties. He stays there for two years and he still is regarded as a bright young man; 12 years later he is still there and still a bright young man. Pretty soon he is 45 and he isn't a bright young man anymore; he goes stale and you haven't got the life and vitality in your planning function over that big span of years that I think you need. On the other hand, I don't mean for that to be negative at all. I think the planning department should be the place where people get exposure to a breadth of business problems that they can't get any place else in business. I think we should look at the planning department as a place to develop people whether you are talking about the very top people in the department or whether you are talking about the analysts and the younger people.

Additions to the Staff.   My last point is that I don't think the techniques of planning and procedures of planning are the be-all and end-all. We must have them, and we must have them in the proper prospective. But if I were selecting an addition to the planning staff to come in on the top level today, I would go back to those four qualities I stressed earlier. Then, if I found out he knew something about planning technique and planning procedures, I would consider this to be a plus, but I wouldn't look for this first.

CORPORATE OBJECTIVES

Setting corporate objectives, in my opinion, is the most important job that top management has. It's important to remember that objectives are established by executive action. The planner does not set the objective. It is usually done by the executive action of a board of directors, chief executive, or some kind of committee of top executives in the company. If a company is so structured, the objective could be greatly influenced by the division making it up. It is a line responsibility to run the company. It is a line responsibility to set the objectives, so the planner must put himself in a position where he sees to it that the job of setting the objectives is getting done, and he feeds the ideas to help in this process but doesn't set the objectives himself.

While good management requires that each person, each department, and each division should have its own specific detailed objective, the primary focus is to set overall corporate objectives, rather than the detailed objective of the individual segments of the company. There are several other considerations.

The first is that objectives should be few in number. Obviously if you have 500 corporate objectives you are not going to achieve the required impact on any one of them. You are not going to get the focus or the attention. But if you have ten and you can articulate them in a clear meaningful way you are more likely to get your point across. These should obviously be top priority items. As an example, maybe one of the objectives is to get your return up to 20 percent on equity. You shouldn't then throw in as the next objective: "Let's get the productivity of file clerks up 3 percent next year." This only gets things out of perspective, and you won't get the respect for your program from your management group that you want.

It is very important to establish clear-cut and meaningful objectives and then communicate them throughout the company. These communications should be established throughout the entire company. There may be some reason why you don't want certain people involved. But you certainly should communicate your objectives to the entire management group, including foremen, because all have a very important role to play.

Objectives can vary at a particular time in a particular company. In some situations, if you are in a desperate situation, where a company is losing money, the only objective may be to get out of the red. That seems rather obvious, but let's go further. If our products are losing acceptance and our market penetration is declining today we may not have opportunities ten years away unless we focus on that problem first. So the objectives could be justifiably short range in one period of time. In another time period when things are in better shape in the same company, a long-range objective should get the focus. Objectives can have financial, marketing, or technical orientation. But it is important to stay "loose." This year it may be one thing, and two years from now it may be something else. The tune should change as the company's needs change.

One more point on objectives. We are all aware of the trend in the emerging area of social issues, as far as corporate citizenship is concerned. All kinds of things are embraced in this; matters of employment practices, pollution problems and the like. It is very important that a proper perspective on these matters be worked into the overall objective. I bring it up here to make sure you don't overlook it. It will have a growing impact on your company, and I think without giving proper consideration to those things and getting them in the right perspective here you may miss something important further down the road.

MERGERS AND ACQUISITIONS

Acquisitions and mergers are very glamorous subjects. Everyone likes to participate in "deal making." But acquisition is only one way to help achieve a broad corporate objective. It is not a never-never land separate and distinct from planning; it is part and parcel of the profit planning function. "Closing a deal" in itself seldom accomplishes the corporate objective. Before we can say we have done that, we have to go through the process of assimilation and realignment. There may be product shifts and there may be plant consolidations. Before we can say we have achieved our corporate objective, we not only have to close the contract and get the new company aboard, but also have to have a management in place that we are satisfied with. Acquisition is the most expensive way to achieve certain corporate objectives, so we want to be very realistic. We must be very careful in our evaluations of make or buy decisions on the matter of going into new product lines. Let's recognize that there is a significant failure rate on acquisitions in American industry. Acquisitions can be quite expensive; on the other hand, acquisition can save a lot of time in getting to a particular market place. They do have the advantage of not creating another competitor, which in some cases, can be advantageous. Timing of acquisitions is a very much more important factor than has been recognized in the past. Usually when you talk about timing on acquisitions everyone thinks in terms of the stock market, as it relates to your stock, the other company's stock, and the psychology of the market place. I am talking beyond that however; I am talking about the business cycle. Let's consider where we are in the business cycle, where the company we are acquiring is, what is going to happen to the business cycle, and how it is going to affect our products and his products. It's amazing how many purchases of companies are made at the wrong time.

FOLLOW-UP

When the objectives and plans have finally been delineated we must not think we have finished, because we haven't really done our job until the results we are after have been achieved. In some ways the hardest part still lies ahead. I don't think that good plans and good objectives get accomplished very often unless we have a proper follow-up procedure. Most companies issue routine short-term reports put out by the controller. These are extremely helpful. Whatever method you use it is important to have a follow-up system; one that tells what the results are.

I want to emphasize the results don't always come in terms of dollars spent, number of units produced, or whatever usual statistics you may be thinking of. It is just as important to know where you stand in ordering the new tools. If you are coming out with a product 18 months from now, it is important that your advertising program is properly organized and that it is going to start at the right time. Is it on schedule? These things are just as important as the financial details. When I say follow-up on the plans, I mean for all of those other things to be followed up as well. The follow-up should be very clear as to who is responsible. There must be reports wherever possible on the things that can be measured by reports. The further you get toward the long-range situation, what I called earlier the big questions, the more difficult it is to do this follow-up on an organized routine basis. Usually the long-term factors and the big questions, as I call them, involve the very top people in the company. It isn't a question of getting a lot of details together and merely listing them in numerous reports; that is the least demanding kind of follow-up. The planning officer certainly has a major responsibility to see to it that follow-up of the unique features as well as the more routine types are implemented.

Implementation of short-range operational plans and budgets is usually fairly easily handled, but you can get bogged down in detail. It is unfortunate if this should happen. Every six months, the planner should look at the reports that are being issued and see if they really answer the key questions. Do the reports contain a lot of trivia? Are they too bulky or too difficult to read? I think this is very important. I am sure that some of this seems old hat to the reader but I thought it necessary to review all the factors.

WHAT I EXPECT FROM MY PLANNING EXECUTIVES

I expect mature business judgment from the planning officer in the company and the people in his department. If I don't get it, I feel we are missing a major contribution to the overall management of the company. We don't want a bunch of bag carriers or servile employees; we want people who will speak up and will have something to say when they do speak up. The second point is that they should have a method of operation that encourages all executives to pull together on their planning jobs—not a group of politicians who are more interested in grandstanding than in teamwork. Third, I am looking for business judgment and perspective applied not only to individual problems but also to determining the priorities we have been talking about. It is important to be able to focus on what is important. Too many planning executives get bogged down in detail. Let's stay on the things that are really important to the company. Someone has got to keep administrative control over the detail, but not to the point of overwhelming our top people. We must have in our planning function sufficient mechanical techniques to get the job done. But let's not be overwhelmed by these techniques. It's getting the job done that really counts.

We must have adequate follow-up. I would say that a good planning officer probably spends more time on follow-up than on anything else. The most important consideration in many companies is to make sure that he does the needling in the prodding sense; it is a high-class executive action needling. It all boils down to this: if we accomplish all our objectives and meet our plans, the plan has been successful.

In any organization, whether it is profit planning or anything else you should have a balance of relatively new people and established people—mature people if you want to say it that way. While we need continuity and maturity in the department, we ought not to have people coming to the planning department very early in their careers with any objective on their part or ours of keeping them there for a long period of time. When we do that, I don't think we are doing the most for the company, or for them. The other side of the coin is that I have never had a planning officer at the executive level who hadn't been in planning for five or ten years anyway; he has also had other business experience—he has done other things. He has been in marketing, or he has been in manufacturing, or perhaps both, and even been in a different kind of business somewhere along the line. We need to have balance. The biggest thing we can do for ourselves—and it applies to finance, and to some of the other departments or functional areas—is to move people around. I really intend planning to be the prime area for future management development and strong company growth.

"Follow-up, an important ingredient to effective profit planning, is not just dollars spent or units produced. It's just as important to know where you stand in ordering those new tools, whether your advertising program is on schedule, and whether your new product will be ready for the market on time."   George Ingram, Jr.

THE PRACTICAL APPROACH TO PROFITABILITY

Responses to the question, "What is practical profit planning?" which was asked of top level executives, yielded varied answers. This suggested that there could be as many different answers as there were respondents.

The differences of opinion are not in the basics of profit planning but in where the emphasis is placed. Undoubtedly, when the question is asked, respondents react by expressing opinions and caveats that are the result of personal experience. It suggests further that the section on practical profit planning should include discussions on strategic profit planning as it relates to use of stockholder assets, marketing, budgeting, and cost effectiveness.

STRATEGIC PROFIT PLANNING

Richard Osgood, in Chapter 7, raises the question as to the value of many numbers and the resulting "5-foot shelf of schedules." The reader should challenge his own company's profit planning activities by raising such questions as: "Do we put too much effort into 'grinding out' numbers?" "Would we obtain better results if we devoted more of our time to obtaining a sound overview of the various facets of the business?" Too often, the profit plan boils down to a formula rather than common sense logic.

Another important consideration is the attitude of the key executives toward the profit plan. If pragmatic department heads scorn the formality of setting down a well thought-out plan, perhaps this is an indication that the top executive does not get sufficiently involved himself.

CHALLENGING TODAY'S FINANCIAL EXECUTIVE

The financial executive, by the nature of his training and background, is a creature of routine. When a task arises for which he has responsibility, he frequently attempts to slot it into the routine so it can be handled automatically. While this is necessary in order to cope with the thousands upon thousands of documents that must be processed in billing customers, making payments to vendors, costing production, and maintaining all the other transactions related to the business, some financial endeavors require "customized" treatment.

An example pointed out by Dr. Goodman is distribution costs. Products that require heavy marketing effort, such as cosmetics, require more than routine treatment. Dr. Goodman, in Chapter 8, recommends a departure from the conventional treatment of "below-the-line" expenses. Some of this cost is identifiable by product lines; therefore it should be recast to reflect product line profitability. He also emphasizes the need for a return-on-investment by product line.

This author makes a further point when he reminds the reader that the product life is relatively short. He quotes a Nielsen survey made in 1968, which establishes that the average life is 2.9 years; yet, he continues: "profit plans assume that products will last forever."

ZERO-BASE BUDGETING

The typical budget prepared each year assumes that the prior year's expenses were fairly representative of each department's needs. These costs are then used as a base to add additional costs needed in the coming year.

Peter Phyrr, the author of Chapter 9, feels that this procedure "freezes in" the past inefficiencies and does not result in a true budget. He feels that each year's budgeting should start with a clean slate and that all budgeted expenses must be completely justified rather than "adjusted."

COST REDUCTION BEGINS WHERE COST CONTROL LEAVES OFF

"Cost Control" often becomes a magic phrase that connotes the ultimate in cost effectiveness. "Not so" says the author of Chapter 10. He contends that cost control merely monitors progress toward achieving a level of cost established as the current year's budget. Since the budget is based on the current method of operating, cost control is limited. Cost reduction, on the other hand, looks critically at the present method of operating and looks aggressively for possibilities for more cost effectiveness.

SUMMARY

Each author in this section has cited his own area of interest in improving profits. In each instance some facet of existing procedures was challenged by the authors. Does this not suggest the answer to the question, "What is practical profit planning?" The unanimous response seems to be "Look critically at all the steps while making up the plan—don't let anything go unchallenged."

CHAPTER 6

WHAT IS PRACTICAL PROFIT PLANNING?

PLANNERS DO NOT PLAN

ROBERT M. SCHAEBERLE

"A good profit planner does not plan. He coordinates, guides, presents, questions, challenges, communicates, systematizes, and most important, he innovates."

While probably an old saw, I believe the initial responsibility in a job description for the person charged with *planning*, be it business, government or an institution, should be, "Planners do not plan." The job description must contain such action verbs as:

coordinate
guide
present
question
challenge
communicate
systematize and, most important, he must
innovate

But I do not find the quiet verb "plan." The practical approach for planners is to get others—starting right at the top—to *understand* the *difference between* financial budgeting and its subsequent measurement techniques, *and* long-range planning (LRP).

Once this is understood—and this does not come from reading articles or attending a few meetings, the *challenge* to the planner is to persuade top management to:

1. buy the *concept* of planning.
2. actively promote LRP to key managers.
3. and finally take the *time* to participate with management groups in planning meetings and reviews.

In some instances this is a very time consuming and traumatic experience "the first time around." Of course, this is one of the first hurdles to clear safely. I truly believe that, in the end, unless the efforts put into LRP do not save time in managing an operation *more* efficiently, there should be no LRP.

I realize that many companies are well advanced—ahead of our company—in installing an *effective* planning system. We are an infant in absorbing these techniques.

Nevertheless, for what it is worth, let me give you a very brief case history of how we got started a few years back.

First, one piece of history. We have had a formal corporate *budgeting* system, both one year operating budget and five year forecasts, since the late 1940s. In fact, the gentleman who introduced, sold and implemented this system, Mr. Frank Gurgone, was one of the charter members of the Budget Executives Institute. I can state without reservation, that every management member in our company would affirm the statement:

"We could not operate—i.e. we could not stay in business today without our budgeting and forecasting system."

Yes, it does require black and white projections; yes, it does highlight variances—controllable and uncontrollable; yes, it does create a fish bowl world. But, we accept it and could not compete without it.

Now to L.R.P. . . . A few years back we took our senior management team, only six in number including the CEO, an absolute prerequisite, to a retreat. The word *retreat* to some may connote peace, quiet solitude, deep inner contemplation. This type of "meeting in the woods" was far from that. In fact, starting each day at 8:00 AM and carrying far into the night, for two weeks, locked in a room, was a unique experience. We had a pro as the only outsider. He merely guided our discussions and kept us on the track. He noted what was said, challenged obvious contradictions, kept us together, and separated us when necessary. This in-depth discussion was our introduction to the *concepts* of planning.

In our first week we discussed the building blocks of planning; that is, statements in black and white for our:

corporate mission
basic corporate policies
assumptions
our strengths
weaknesses
long-range goals—probably the most important decision to be reached and agreed upon.
Once agreeing on this—then on to our:
overall objectives
trend analysis
plans and discussions of establishing the planning gap
Which in turn lead to:
priorities
strategies
programs
assignments
time schedules
review

and now you are ready to start all over again.

We do not look at LRP as a bound book; it is a loose-leaf system, but to be successful not loose in the sense of pages and sections omitted or incomplete.

If our management, including the CEO, had not gone through the exercise of asking, "Where do we want to be 10 to 15 years from now?", LRP would have very little sense of being. After you answer and have agreement to that complex question, the other questions flow fast and hard.

We use the philosophy of overall corporate planning goals established at the very senior corporate level. These total corporate goals are freely communicated to operating division and supporting department levels.

But, then the latter are charged with the responsibility to develop their *own* planning programs. While told to live within corporate *policies*, their mission, their goals *are not* established for them. In fact we do not even give them guidelines. This part of the planning process is theirs.

When all the pieces are brought together, it would be surprising if they spelled "Mother." Here of course is the realization of the "planning gap." To *fill* this gap, takes consideration of:

reviewed plans by the existing divisions.
acquisitions
new products
possible divestitures
or even a rude awakening that you cannot get there from here. Thus you, they, may have to change or shall we say modify division, or in the end, corporate goals.

While the goals must provide "reach," stretch, and *personal* commitment, they must be attainable through *coordinated* long range plans of our:

manpower planning
facility planning
technological planning and results reduced to a common language in our
    financial planning

A natural question would be: "How do budgets and LRP integrate?" We carefully analyzed this problem and our answer is: "One planning system." This is accomplished by:

1. our assignment of responsibility to line and supporting staff.
2. a formal step-by-step approval process.
3. and such tied together with a specific timetable.

A 14-month year would help, but the moon and the stars limit us to 12.
Our process timetable starts out with LRP meetings in the spring. Each spring the task becomes a little easier since basic goals and missions do not change to any great degree from one year to the next.
Next, we sit down with all operating divisions to review their annual marketing strategies. If you are in the business of satisfying consumers, this is paramount.
This in turn is then welded into what we call operational planning—known to some as the annual budget—presented to our board of directors each December so that *all* measurements the following year are against the budget, *not last year*. In all the foregoing we have specific roles

set out for: corporate management, supporting staff management, and line management. LRP and operational plans in our thinking must be welded together in a single planning system.

Back to where we started. The profit planners have to be a fantastic management group. Their challenge as practical business planners is to get the job done without becoming too involved with the passive connotations of the verb "planning."

CREATIVE PROFIT PLANNING

JAMES W. MCKEE, JR.

"We have to be careful that we do not have everyone caught up in the fascination of looking ahead and working for things to come at the expense of today's business, which is our vehicle for getting to tomorrow."

One of the keys to practical profit planning may involve being somewhat impractical. Profit planning is an art. This is not to be interpreted as advocating that we discard all of the values we have established in our business life. It does mean that we should look at new approaches to the problem which may not be susceptible to the analyses and short-term returns to which we are accustomed.

BALANCING INNOVATION AND PRAGMATISM

Within the total effort there has to be the proper balance of innovative thinking with the pragmatic necessities of our economic life. As with artists, there are certain basic tools that are common to all planners, but the methods for using these tools will be unique for each individual situation. The personality and the character of the corporation will largely determine how it organizes itself to accomplish its planning task.

It would be gratifying to be able to report that we at CPC have all the solutions to corporate planning and by proper organization we have developed the master programs that will guarantee our economic well-being for years to come. This would be, to say the least, somewhat of an exaggeration. But rather than try to discuss short-range planning, long-range planning, or budget planning as separate types of planning, I will attempt to give you a brief outline of how we are organizing for practical planning with some of the reasons for doing it this way.

Just about every individual, whether philosopher, economist, or businessman, who is concerned with the total world in which we live, has repeated time and again that the only constant we can expect is change. Recognizing that looking into the future is a precarious occupation even in the best of circumstances, the planning function that will guide our future must maintain a flexibility that will permit adapting to the lack of certainty that exists with changing conditions. It must also be concerned with the interrelationship of all the various pieces and functions of a diverse operation that will be involved directly or indirectly, because they either change or react to change elsewhere in the corporation.

Since it is virtually impossible to plan for one area without affecting other operations, the planning process needs adequate participation at the various corporate and operating levels. We have to be careful, however, that we do not have everyone caught up in the fascination of looking ahead and working for things to come at the expense of today's business, which is our vehicle for getting to tomorrow.

PLANNING MUST BE FLEXIBLE

As a result, our planning work is organized differently in the different parts of the organization to meet individual requirements. There is not necessarily one person in any group, regardless of size or importance, whose sole responsibility is planning. Our aim is to consider our operational budgeting programs as the reflection of our planning process. Planning is not left just to the financial departments, although they have to perform the indispensible task of putting the programs into numbers and bringing these together to set out our total corporate projections.

Each of our divisions understands that it has its own planning responsibility. Each division head understands better than anyone else that which is happening either to benefit or harm his area of operations. Future operations cannot really be divorced from today's. So, without reducing the individual's responsibility or authority, we encourage the managers of key operations or functions to make use of teams to assist in looking at alternatives and evaluating these for their impact on their particular area. These teams are sometimes formalized as boards of directors of major operating divisions or more informal groups set up as councils or steering committees. But they all have a common organizational concept. The participants are managers with diverse functional backgrounds. Each group contains not only individuals from within the manager's area of responsibility, but also from other departments or operations. The division managers, in turn, are advisors and councilors at progressively higher echelons in the corporate structure.

This organizational concept cuts across the rigid lines of the formal organization chart. The various groups are part of practical planning and contribute to the decision-making process at a point different from their own function. Management at all levels is involved in developing and incorporating creative solutions into, first, the ongoing programs, and second, the corporate planning for the future. The recommendations that are developed may go forward either with the manager as he participates with other groups or in formal investment programs which have to meet and compete with other similar programs throughout the corporation. As these managers themselves progress, they will bring these experiences with them. Possibly, more important, they will bring a greater ability to recognize the limitations of planning or, if you will, what it is not.

These arrangements do more than encourage the involvement of a broad spectrum of managers. They also reflect the dynamic process—the continuous changes in business conditions—and the environment—not the least of which, is the movement of personnel within any corporation. A continuing reappraisal of business goals and objectives, therefore, becomes a necessity. While it is realistic to accept the premise that the future is crouching in the present, each organization has to determine its particular position and interpret its own special requirements. It has to understand better than any other, its own strengths on which it can build. The amount and total concentration of the resources that can be brought to bear on developing that part of the future which crouches in "our" present will depend to a large degree on how successfully we have managed the programs that came to us from our past "presents."

But this then brings me back to where I started. We believe that planning has to be a continuing process. It is the responsibility of all our managers and cannot really be separated from current operations. Our organization is designed to encourage participation at appropriate levels in the three critical phases of planning: first—the formulation of corporate-wide objectives and strategies; second—agreement on strategic programs; and third—the monitoring or control of performance following the implementation of the programs.

We expect to obtain the proper combination of creativity (too often associated with the unreal) and the practicality of formal business systems that will permit achieving our total corporate purpose with the necessary blend of originality and economic justification. The continuity of our progress as evidenced by our year to year results, will be the determination of how successfully we have organized for planning profits.

TO PLAN IS TO MANAGE

RALPH P. MOORE

"A misconception that should be dispelled is that profit planning is an attempt to avoid taking risks. On the contrary, a good profit plan seeks to identify risks and to recognize problems so they may be profitably and prudently exploited."

What is corporate profit planning? In looking for an answer to that question, I am reminded of what it is not.

So let's look for a moment at what corporate business planning is not.

It is not next year's budget, the five-year plan, forecasting, or other management exercises for which it sometimes passes.

These are, however, the tools, the effectors, the manifestations, if you will, of corporate planning. Another misconception that should be dispelled is that planning is an attempt to avoid taking risks. In fact, it is quite the opposite. It seeks to identify risks and to recognize problems so they may be profitably and prudently exploited.

The best definition of corporate planning I have encountered is by Mr. David Ewing in his book, *The Practice of Planning.* He says, "Corporate planning is a method of guiding managers so that their *decisions* and *actions* affect the future of the organization in a consistent and *rational* manner, and *in a way desired by top management.*"

When one reflects on Mr. Ewing's quotation and remembers that management is the art of getting things done through people, it follows that *to plan is to manage.* Through its planning, or lack thereof, management expresses in its deeds its commitment to manage, and no other activity so clearly reflects a given management's style.

Documented, quantified, and detailed plans do not necessarily represent the fruits of good planning, for it is the planning process that is important, not the prose, graphs, charts, and reports that it produces.

In an article published in the *Harvard Business Review,* Mr. Robert Mockler succinctly dissects the corporate planning process into two segments: *strategic planning* and *implementation planning.* He further defines implementation planning as "the term generally applied to day-to-day efforts to carry out the overall corporate task defined in strategic planning."

This leads us, in order to understand more fully the corporate planning process, to seek answers to six vital questions:

What is this strategic planning?
Who are the strategic planners?
What are the pitfalls that can derail this strategic planning process?
Why does implementation planning differ from strategic planning?
Who are the implementation planners?
What are the obstacles to practical implementation planning?

Strategic planning presumes a desire for introspective knowledge, an intellectual "gut feel" that there is a better way to do things, an awareness of the hostile environment external to your company, and a healthy respect for the uncertainties of the future. But most of all, strategic planning presumes a strong desire to shape the character of your company in that uncertain future, and it requires the emotional and intellectual capacity to make those hard decisions and to commit resources today and tomorrow that will bring about the success you desire for your enterprise in the form in which you want it.

We'll get back to the strategic plan in a moment, but first let's discuss who these strategic planners are. Since good strategic planning is incumbent upon those with the power to make decisions and to commit the resources to see those decisions through to a conclusion, the only strategic planners in any firm are the senior management of that organization, including, and sometimes solely, the chief executive.

If senior management is the strategic planner, what is the role of the corporate planning staff? One of a planning staff's inherent values lies in its ability to devote its full energies to *identifying* and *analyzing* corporate opportunities and problems and *recommending a course* of action to senior management.

We must keep in mind that the strategic planner, in dealing with the future, must be constantly alert to a changing environment and business opportunities that are external to his company. He must weigh his organization relative to these factors. A full-time planning staff can better advise senior management in these areas than can operational management. Operational management, involved with the day-to-day management of its line responsibilities, may not be able to give the time, vision, and objectivity that should be brought to broad strategic planning.

Take the strategic plan a step further. Obviously, it starts with establishing, reaffirming, or changing corporate objectives. It is a continuing process. Strategic objectives continually need monitoring for validity. These objectives must meet the *needs of the owners* of an enterprise and *must reflect the desires* and wishes of *senior management*. Owners, management, and the external business environment change; thus, strategic objectives will change. Also, strategic objectives should be broad, but no matter how broad, they should never be static.

To effect strategic objectives, strategic goals must be set. The essence of these is in recognizing opportunities and problems. Strategic goals quantify the strategic plan, add to it the dimensions of time, and enable the establishment of benchmarks to measure progress. They should be ambitious and should inspire superior, rather than adequate, performance. Unattainable strategic goals are self-defeating, and goals narrowly constructed would never have resulted in a 4-minute mile or a man on the moon.

Like objectives, goals are subject to continuing review for validity. To conduct such a review it is necessary that the major assumptions upon which they are predicated be spelled out. This includes *identification of those assets,* tangible, intangible, and human that form the cornerstone for building the enterprise, and the identification of those *weaknesses and liabilities* that must be overcome to achieve successfully the desired objectives.

A good strategic plan should *establish the priorities* for committing resources to accomplish company objectives, must *fix the management responsibilities* for achieving the goals of the plan, and *must be communicated* to those to be held accountable for execution.

What are the serious pitfalls to strategic planning? First and foremost, *the strategic planning* process *involves people*. Without the unwavering commitment of the chief executive, the process cannot be effective. Without a consensus of senior management, the strategic plan will be hollow. The plan must reflect the company, the time, and the people who develop it. We must remember that it is the continuing planning process which provides the stimulating desire to manage, and that is the essence of corporate planning.

A *poorly conceived, unrealistic* plan will undermine the planning process; a *narrowly conceived, unambitious* plan, while attainable, will result in mediocre performance; an *uncommunicated* strategic plan will leave the future to happenstance.

Now let's turn our attention to implementation planning. What makes it different from strategic planning? Previously we quoted Mr. Robert Mockler who defines it as "the term generally applied to day-to-day efforts to carry out the overall corporate task defined in strategic planning."

This is a planning area with which we are more comfortable. It is more specific, its guidelines are more generally accepted, it is more tangible, it is less perilous. It also is a continuing process, and the process is more beneficial than a finished, bound product but, unlike strategic planning, implementation planning is illustrated better by its component parts.

It most certainly is the five-year plan or any other appropriate period for which business planning falls under the long-term category.

It is budgeting.

It is the specific programming of resources.

It is the evaluation and ranking of investment opportunities with hardnose capital budgeting techniques; discounted cash flow, rate of return, the present value resource apportioning tools.

It does bring into plan forecasting techniques, model building, and the other management science tools.

It demands monitoring systems by its nature and time frame.

Implementation planning is made for rolling up your sleeves and plunging in. But if senior management represent the strategic planners, who are the implementation planners?

Unlike good strategic planning, which is so sensitive to the external environment and which requires a degree of detachment, implementation planning is the stuff of today and literally, rather than figuratively, of tomorrow. It is best accomplished by the line people: operating management.

To succeed, implementation plans must employ the expertise of each of the functional areas within an operating organization; marketing, production, research, administration, finance, and control.

We know that the most effective way to gain and maintain adherence to any plan or planning system is to involve, at the formative stage, those directly affected by it. It then becomes their plan and, having been involved in the setting of specific objectives and goals, operating management is more likely to work towards and gain the achievements outlined by the plan.

A corporate planning staff can play a very important part in the implementation planning process but, again, as in strategic planning, their appropriate role is a staff function. Their purpose should be to educate and advise operating management in form and technique. Planning administration, not planning, is the appropriate role for planning staffs.

What are the obstacles to successful implementation planning?

First, *if* we reflect back to Mr. Ewing's definition of corporate planning, he speaks of leading or guiding managers. If we accept this definition, which I do, it follows that implementation planning cannot be classifed as successful *unless* senior management has provided a *good strategic plan* with which to *guide its operational managers.*

A second serious obstacle to implementation planning would be and is *handing down plans from the top.* Communications must be direct and open with the charge clearly spelled out.

And we must remember that plans and planning systems are not ends in themselves. They should give outlines for direction and must be appropriate to the company.

As an example: five-year plans are most important. But even more important, if the five-year plan stands on its own, and if annual budgets, short-range profit plans, and capital budgets are not constructed and reviewed in relation to the contribution they make to that five-year plan, the efforts expended on the five-year plan will have been largely wasted.

Another must of successful implementation planning is timely monitoring and control. I would put heavy emphasis on the word "timely." Most phases of implementation planning are relatively short; if deviations from plans cannot be spotted quickly, the game will be over before corrective action can be initiated.

And that, with a little hard common sense thrown in, is the textbook approach to practical business planning.

Now let me tell you how we approach this difficult and important area at Liggett & Myers.

A decade ago this planning function was the prerogative of the Executive Committee. In the spring of 1964, a new president and chief executive officer, Milton E. Harrington, was elected. Under his strong leadership the strategic planning group was galvanized into a viable, thought-provoking, and action-oriented group. The groundwork for Liggett's future was laid; lines of business we wanted to be in; management to carry on and execute the probable thrust of our business, economic, and political forecasts were researched. All of this was done with very little paperwork and a minimum of formalized reports.

Then a department was created to implement the program. Staffed with competent people and consulting with the Executive Committee and the operational heads of the subsidiaries, industry studies were prepared in great detail, economic and political considerations were cranked in, and follow-up procedures for the operating heads were instituted.

So we believe that today, operating in a broad framework of strategic planning and a more formalized framework of implementation planning, Liggett is equipped to meet the challenges of today and the future.

CHAPTER 7

STRATEGIC PROFIT PLANNING

RICHARD M. OSGOOD

"Creation of the strategic plan provides the manager an opportunity to show his superiors that he is putting stockholder assets to prudent use and that he is alert to the opportunities and pitfalls within his sphere of activity."

GTE Sylvania has been doing long-range planning throughout our corporation on a formalized basis since the early 1960s—but until the late 1960s, this process was so structured as to have limited constructive value to corporate management and direction. Several years ago, we overhauled the whole process and created a strategic planning program.

BACKGROUND

By way of background, GTE Sylvania is a manufacturing company doing about $850 million in sales annually. Its products and services are primarily related to the electrical and electronics industries. These products and services are sold in many different domestic markets, including consumer, industrial, commercial and government. It sells these products through multiple channels of distribution, ranging from wholesalers, retail chains, jobbers, as well as direct to various end-customer classes in a variety of industries and government units. We are also vertically integrated to a fair degree with several business centers making products consumed by other business centers, as well as outside customers. Well, all of this is only to convey that we are a fairly complex diversified company. We are organized into five operating groups, each of which has several operating divisions or subsidiary corporations within the group. Because of this diversity of products and of markets, the corporate officers have a challenging task to stay reasonably current on the opportunities and problems of its many businesses and, thereby, to make the necessary central decisions on capital and other resource allocations or, perhaps, more fundamentally to guide and direct the development of all these businesses.

ADOPTION OF STRATEGIC PLANNING

The formal long-range planning process was devised with the intent of both improving and facilitating this process of corporate direction of its businesses. It fell considerably short of its aim for a variety of reasons, among which was a tremendous volume of paper and details of future plans that virtually inundated the corporate staff.

We abandoned this annual exercise of creating 5-foot book shelves and went to a Strategic Planning. This program is not terribly unique; it is fairly straightforward. Our intent, in adopting this approach, was to enable senior management throughout the corporation to face and make current decisions faster and more intelligently. It is conceived now as a part of an integral annual process of setting corporate long-range objectives—reviewing and revising the strategic plans of present businesses—and then, towards the latter part of the year, creating short-term, two-year profit plans in the context of these strategic plans. The operating groups and divisions develop these strategic plans, covering five future years, early in the year. They develop them in the framework of the corporate purpose and objectives, and the corporate staff is directly involved in the process of selecting the objectives and strategies of the group. We stress an absolute minimum of number work and a maximum of thought—not words—on the key objectives and strategies of the business.

The structure of the formal document is shown below. It outlines six steps in the plan, which are:

1. Corporate Purpose—A brief statement of the business mission or scope, or horizon of the enterprise.
2. Situation and Environment Analysis—An identification of the major factors and facts in that particular business that are determinants of its objectives and strategies covering such topics as strengths and weaknesses, competitor status, technological forecasts, market trends, legislative/legal trends, and so on.

3. Objectives—What measurable key achievements does management want to record in the time period?
4. Strategies—Broadly, how are we to achieve these objectives? What rational alternates exist and why were certain ones selected?
5. Financial Performance—How is the business expected to perform under these strategies, both in a gross profit and loss and balance sheet sense?
6. Resources Required—What principal capital and people needs are required to support these strategies?

After two years of operation on this program, we have made real progress in our basic objective to better inform corporate officers of the critical opportunities and problems of the corporation's various businesses and to facilitate their impact on the future direction of these businesses. This is not to say that we are satisfied, that we feel we have a fully effective system for evolving and implementing business strategies; we have a long way to go indeed to get to that point. But, we have taken the tremendous number of manhours of creating documents with a myriad of business details and converted this into a constructive effort to think about a business and make some fundamental decisions now affecting its future course. Now, with this background I want to tell you a few of the practical challenges we struggle with in trying to make this strategic planning process effective. I bring these out because I suspect they are endemic with all large corporate entities having diversified businesses—and, despite the plethora of literature on corporate planning, good answers do not yet exist.

CHALLENGES TO STRATEGIC PLANNING

There are three basic challenges to strategic planning.

The Intuitive Business Manager

The first is the matter of the intuitive business manager—the man who manages his particular business domain by his wits—by the "seat-of-his-pants." When confronted with a need to formalize his thoughts on what he is in business for, what critical factors dominate his long-range thinking, what is he trying to realistically achieve, what alternate rational courses of action exist for achieving it? What does he do? How does he react? Well, instinctively he rebels at the thought. He thinks: "What 'knucklehead' thinks he can reduce such a complex process of understanding a living, breathing enterprise, diagnosing its condition, and prescribing a grand course of action to make it a bigger, better enterprise and set it down on a few sheets of paper?" I am no industrial psychologist, but inherently I think he feels that it can't be done and, if it can be done, then they don't need him. So he compromises by putting forth a dissertation in his own fashion, which provides some fodder for the grist mill, but is anything but a penetrating analysis, a carefully thought-out fundamental approach to improving the business. What do you do with this sort of reaction?

We just don't have the answers. One obvious method, of course, is to get the whole program actively led by the president or chief operating officer. If he doesn't lead it, it isn't worth anything anyway. After that or along with that, take pains to make it clear that this is not a detailed blueprint of the future actions in the business; it is simply an assessment today—just like a balance sheet—that it will surely change as time goes on; it is no immutable set of laws we are trying to establish.

This creation of a strategic plan is, in fact, rather an opportunity—an opportunity to assemble at one point in time facts that he needs as an intuitive manager—an opportunity to show his superiors that he is prudently using the stockholders' assets under his charge and consciously aware of the possibilities and pitfalls in his sphere of activity. Despite the superiority of this logic, and all the other preparatory steps we have taken, this reluctance to formalize a strategic plan is still a very real challenge to us and, I think to all large corporations.

Projected Financial Performance

Let me go on to another difficult nut to crack—projected financial performance. You saw earlier that we ask for such a projection as an essential ingredient of the plan. Based on the appraisal of the current situation and the objectives and strategies that have been identified, how will the business perform over the next five years? That is the question. You all know, as well as I, there is no rigorous way today where you can proceed from a set of broad strategies and develop, unequivocally, the financial results that will eventuate.

The problem that you seem inevitably to get into is untrammeled optimism—who tempers his forecast with intransigent competitors, with an unresponsive factory, with inharmonious cost-price relationships, with clogged channels of distribution? Yet, that is what happens in the real world—and aren't we trying to predict the most likely sales, profit, and investment situation for the business in the real world?

How does one prudently inject practicality in these future estimates? We have tried "minimum," "maximum," and "most likely" to get some ranges. We are experimenting with economic models as a means of closing in on this. And, while I am mentioning models, I would like to mention the very interesting work being carried out by the Marketing Science Institute in Cambridge, Massachusetts. Their activity is capitalizing on some earlier pioneering work by General Electric and aimed at validating the applicability of business models to a wide variety of industries and levels of business. This is called "Project PIMS" for "Profit Impact Of Market Strategy." This work, and other econometric modeling work going on in the country, promises to give us an important tool to combat the unrealism that inevitably creeps into the financial projection process.

What Is Strategy?

A third difficulty that we have continually encountered in strategic planning is trying to get a fix or a good working understanding on precisely what is a strategy—as distinguished from a tactic or a policy or operating technique? Now, this is fairly fundamental. If we can't define what a strategy is, what are we doing developing strategic plans? Fundamental as this sounds, and the tomes on planning are full of descriptions and definitions on this point, it is nonetheless an illusive and evasive concept. To establish a proper grasp of this concept—and to put it in practice consistently across a large corporation, with continuing turnover in people and responsibilities—is an art we at least have not yet managed.

It could be argued, indeed it is argued, that this is a "tempest in a teapot," a semantic exercise. What difference does it make if, in conceiving how you are going to succeed in a business, you evolve a better policy, a better procedure, some better tactics, or a better strategy? After all, if they are better, they will indeed improve the business, and that is what we really are after, isn't it? Well, there is a lot of logic to the point, you have to concede. But, our point on strategy is that any normal business in our economy, should get a better yield over the long pull on its committed resources, both capital and people. As the manager of that business, you have certain discretionary power over the amount and employment of these resources—so you must decide the magnitude, the direction, and application of these. That is all that strategies are.

To only delineate a comprehensive set of tactics, a clever set of procedures, an astute collection of policies, is to avoid the central issue in the competitive struggle. So we continue to stress the distinction and ask that the critical issue of strategy not be confused with these other matters, important though they may be. The best test then, that we have found, is one of whether the strategy is a *broad* course of action and directly involves, in carrying out this action, a *significant* use of resources—financial resources or effort of people resources. Again, the point here is that developing a widespread appreciation of a strategy is a very difficult task. Yet it is central to the whole issue of corporate strategic planning.

These are a few of the challenges/impediments that plague the full development of corporate strategic planning. There are, of course, many others involved to perfect this process of stimulating strategic thinking in the many businesses that make up the diversified corporation.

And, speaking of stimulating strategic thinking, I would like, before closing, to show you a few examples of the kind of data collection and data presentation that we have tried in order to foster strategic thinking about a business. These are not very sophisticated, but they do help to draw attention to the conditions of the business—the situation analysis section of a plan—that have proven effective in stimulating strategic thinking and planning.

THREE ANALYSES

There are three different analyses that we have carried out, aimed solely at getting a better grasp of the business situation—analyses that tend to bring out, rather simply, conditions of the business that should be recognized when developing the objectives and strategies.

Mainstream Product Analysis

The first of these is called a mainstream product analysis—identifying the basic momentum of the business. It merely calls for a listing of the major present product lines of the business, relating them, using the forecasted market growth rate of the product classes and their present sales volume in order to get a composite growth rate for the collection of product lines over a finite period of time. This calculation assumes no change in market share over the period examined. Exhibit 1 shows a simple listing of this sort with the composite growth rate. It simply says to management that the

Exhibit 1.   Mainstream Product Analysis. Five Year Projected Market Growth

Line	Sales	Growth
A	75	5.2%
B	85	5.8
C	40	6.0
D	100	6.5
E	90	8.1
F	45	8.3
G	50	10.1
H	120	+1.0
I	70	−1.0
J	30	−20.0
90% of total sales	705	+4.2%
GNP		+5.1%

mainstream products account for 90 percent of the sales of the business—and with the variety of growths of the various markets they serve, if no further penetration or loss of market share takes place, the momentum of this corporation's main businesses are leading it along a path of 4.2 percent/year sales volume growth over the five-year time period.

If the mainstream products account for, say 85 percent of the enterprise, then this indicates a basic rate of growth for the business unit or corporate entity. As you can see, this is not very sophisticated, but it is an important factor to keep in mind if you are aiming at a specified overall growth rate in your business planning. Obviously, increasing rather than static market shares will enhance this calculated composite growth rate; by the same token, decreasing market shares have the opposite effect.

Comparative Commitment Analysis

Another technique we have used is called a comparative commitment analysis. In looking at a given collection of businesses, you can usually group them into a few categories, whether these categories are based on organizational structure, markets served, technology of manufacture, or what have you. Then having grouped them, you should be able to assemble the investments involved, the sales performance, and the profit yield either on the basis of past performance or future predictions. By ratio or proportioning these three factors, you can readily portray the relative performance and spot the strong from the weak, as illustrated in Exhibit 2. You can't look at this very long before you spot the weak sister and the star performer and recognize what needs attention in your profit generating mechanism.

Product Life Cycle

The final technique first came to our attention from the Boston Consulting Group, but, in one form or another, has been advanced by other consulting organizations as well. It goes like this:

To evaluate a collection of product lines or businesses and to try to assess whether you have a fair balance of investments between growth and mature businesses, you group them according to two yardsticks: market growth rates and your competitive position in those markets. The low-growth and low-market-share businesses are familiarly known as "dogs"—the market is going nowhere and you are a weak participant in the field.

The "cash cows" are in the euphoric state of a very strong competitive position, even though the market is very low or no growth. The "problem children" are in the high-growth market side, but you have a challenge to get to a substantial competitive position. The "stars" are in the happy present state of being high-growth markets and you have a strong market position. These four "bins" or segments have dramatic differences in characteristics. For example the cash-flow characteristics are markedly different: the problem child unquestionably sucks up cash as you strive to get a stronger position in a rapidly growing market. On the contrary, the cash cow is generating a great deal of cash throw-off as the market growth has slowed down. In the other two quadrants, there should be a small or zero net-flow condition. Another characteristic is the style of management. The problem child category calls for your most entrepreneurial-style manager,

Exhibit 2.   Comparative Commitment Analysis

	Sales	Profit	Investment
Industry Group A	58%	19%	51%
Industry Group B	16%	31%	17%
Industry Group C	26%	50%	32%
	100%	100%	100%

the creative risk-taker. The cash cow calls for the cautious administrator who makes the most of your strong position, who faces few large gambles in the direction of the business.

These are dynamic situations. Markets change and competitive positions shift. It is one thing to talk in general groupings such as this and another thing to get down to cases with your product lines and your markets. The Boston Consulting Group suggests a practical chart for categorizing your business units. The ordinates are in a linear form, using annual growth rates with the horizontal divider at the predicted GNP level. The abscissa are in logarithmic form and plot the ratio of your size (sales volume) to the average size or sales volume of your three largest competitors. In this case, the vertical separator is drawn where this ratio is 1—where you are equal in size to the average of your three biggest competitors. What happens as a function of time on a successful product life cycle? As a new product business opens up, it is generally in a high-growth state. If you are not the introducer, then you start out in the low-share category—the problem child state. As you succeed, you move over to the star condition. As the market subsides or matures, it drops down sometime into the low-growth condition, hopefully, to become a cash cow.

The Success Path

So the success path goes counter clockwise as the successful life cycle unfolds. The unsuccessful entrant goes inevitably to the "dogs." We have used this format for appraising our inventory of businesses to the extent that we have reasonable estimates of market growth rates and competitive sales.

I have related to you our efforts in this promising field; some of the practical impediments we have encountered; and a few of the ways we attempted to stimulate fundamental thinking about our businesses. I hope you find our experience helpful.

"A major deficiency of many financial projections is overoptimism. How many forecasts are tempered to allow for intransigent competitors, unresponsive factories, and illogical cost selling price relationships."

R. M. Osgood

CHAPTER 8

CHALLENGING TODAY'S FINANCIAL EXECUTIVE

SAM R. GOODMAN

"The average financial executive is oriented toward what has happened yesterday rather than what will happen tomorrow. There is a general reluctance to get involved in marketing, an area that has a great potential for improvement of profits."

The profession of finance is in danger of being drowned by its own rigidities. The profession has made a point of concentrating its efforts on the reporting function. However, in interpreting the problems of reporting, the profession seems to give the heaviest weight to those problems that deal with how best to report yesterday's results. The most prestigious accounting firms are now engaged in a searching effort to look at themselves inwardly and to discern those accounting practices that have given rise to the tremor of discontent on the part of the investing public and professional securities advisors. Inevitably then, the efforts are directed towards the proper element of corporate reporting to stockholders. Questions such as the proper reporting of investment tax credits, long-term leases, goodwill, mergers, and acquisitions have occupied the minds of the professional financial people. What has been lost in the shuffle and continues to be lost, is the completely overlooked area of *internal* corporate reporting, which is designed to assist the management of companies to make interim, impact decisions. These decisions are those vital to the daily conduct of business and reflect deeply on the ability of the decision maker to influence the daily course of operations through his understanding of the variables contained within the framework of the problem. Regretably, finance has almost always ignored this aspect of reporting.

THE RELUCTANT FINANCIAL MAN

It is the rare marketing decision that does not result somehow in a financial equation. In turn, that decision will ultimately lead to a dollar sign. Marketing is the area to focus upon for decision making because in reality, it is the reason for existence of any company. No company can truly claim to be in business for the purpose of making products; rather they are in business for the purpose of selling products. Marketing is the total purpose of a business enterprise. As such, it transcends its usual status as a functional discipline and in the larger picture becomes the totality of all efforts of a company.

Whenever I see an accountant coming into a room, my mind pictures him as walking into that room backwards. The reason is that, for the most part, he is much more concerned with where he has been. In reality the professional discipline of accounting has been weaned on that type of perspective. From birth all of us are instilled with different types of disciplines and moralities. In our lifetimes our parents try to teach us many things. The discipline and morality in the lifetime of a professional accountant, however, mean that the individual must be geared to having an end fulfillment of creating an income statement and a balance sheet. In the interim, the financial executive must, of course, regularly report to the stockholders of a company, internally, and to other externally interested parties.

Essentially this means that the financial man is oriented towards reporting what happened yesterday. To the contrary, the marketing executive, the decision maker, must pursue a policy that is much more concerned with the probability of what is going to happen tomorrow. Compounding the above by what I consider to be a reluctance on the part of the financial function to enter into this sphere of marketing, I think that the magnitude of the gulf existing between the two functions will be obvious. An example of the orientation of the financial executive towards reporting what happened yesterday can be seen in the formally defined controllership duties issued by the Financial Executives Institute. These duties are:

Planning for Control: To establish, coordinate, and administer as an integral part of management an adequate plan for the control of operations.

Reporting and Interpreting: To compare performance with operating plans and standards, and to report and interpret the results of operations to all levels of management and to the owners of the business.

Evaluating and Consulting: To consult with all segments of management responsible for policy or action, concerning any phase of the operation of the business as it relates to the attainment of objectives and the effectiveness of policies, organizational structure, and procedures.

Tax Administration: To establish and administer tax policies and procedures.

Government Reporting: To supervise or coordinate the preparation of reports to government agencies.

Protection of Assets: To assure protection of the assets of a business through internal control and internal auditing.

Economic Appraisal: To continuously appraise economic and social forces and government influences, and to interpret their effect upon the business.

Recently a revision to the above list by the Financial Executives Institute has given recognition to the shortcomings of the definitions by including in the list the responsible assignments in the area of management information systems. What perhaps should be added to the delineation of duties by the Financial Executives Institute would be the following:

Utilization of Creativity: To establish alternative reporting and analytical methods designed to measure the effectiveness of performance responsibility under the marketing concept by measuring the fiscal implications of media, promotion policy, and profit responsibility under the product manager system.

I alluded above to what I perceive as a reluctance on the part of the financial man to enter into the sphere of marketing. Frankly, the variables of consumer behavior and marketing techniques are simply too complex for the average financial man to comprehend. In addition to that, the disciplined financial man runs up against the undisciplined marketing man who always claims he cannot be measured because he is creative.

THE NEED FOR FINANCIAL EVOLUTION

The profession has not had very much to boast about lately. Inevitably when asked for its recent innovative developments, the professional group answers that it has developed direct costing and that it has perfected the return on investment concept. In reality, each of these techniques is quite dated. Direct costing and the return on investment concept can be traced back as far back as the late 1800s. This type of innovation hardly bespeaks a progressive type of professional group.

As a consequence, I think a new evolution is required of the profession. I am also not at all convinced that the evolution will come about through self-motivation. I think it may be forced upon the group by decision makers who will pull and urge and demand. Essentially, financial people have been reluctant to change because everything they have done has been in the "comfortable" vein. Most practice in financial reporting has been oriented toward manufacturing. The chances are probable that you have within your own company some variant of standard costing, absorption costing, or direct costing. All of these analytical techniques measure the performance of a company in the environment of a factory. The greater problem, however, is what happens to the merchandise once it leaves the factory door.

When the factory door is closed and the finished goods are moved out, the world of marketing opens up with a vengeance. It was only 20 years ago that the Twentieth Century Fund commissioned a study attempting to estimate the cost of distribution. At that time, 20 years ago, approximately 60 cents out of every revenue dollar was consumed in distribution. Of course, in defining distribution for that study, advertising, sales promotion, freight, warehousing, and so on, were included. Nevertheless, the major impact of expenditures lay beyond the factory door. If we were to bring that study forward in time in an attempt to update it, I would intuitively suspect that such an amount would easily be increased by 10 cents. In those terms then, it is logical that over two thirds of all expenses are consumed in some type of distribution effort.

This is the precise area where the financial people have been reluctant to intrude. In order to appreciate this, one must understand the financial mentality. There is a comfort in being able to walk into a manufacturing plant and see a machine turn over 100 times a minute. With each turnover, the accountant can observe that a widget is produced. It is easy for him then to stand up and say, "I can create a system—look what I've done. I have been able to calculate the cost of a widget." That same man, however, placed into the area of sales promotion would be extremely uncomfortable because, once questioned and asked to evaluate the profitability of a given sales promotion, he would probably be at a loss as to how to proceed. This would occur because he is now entering a different world where there are a multiplicity of variables.

First, there is the subject of measurement, which is implicit in evaluating the profitability of something. Against what base is the effectiveness of a sales promotion measured? What motivates the consumer to react to the sales promotion? What were the objectives of the sales program? Were the qualitative objectives met as well as the quantitative?

As individuals, we are all imponderable variables. As consumers, we don't know what we are going to do tomorrow with any degree of certainty. We may have an idea of probable plans. However, is that idea a sufficient base for someone else's plan? We do not know tomorrow how much money we will have in our pockets at a precise moment. If we use this logic and project it into the reasoning process of the financial man, we can understand his fright. He doesn't want to be a part of this type of world because everything he touches becomes like a grain of sand. I think, then, that this is one of the large reasons why marketing has not been served very well by the financial area. Nevertheless, I think there are concrete things that the financial area can do to assist the marketing area.

WHERE DOES THE FAULT LIE?

Part of the fault leading to the present schism between marketing and finance lies within the function of marketing itself. Marketing men have always had a great deal of trouble trying to define their own profession. Even though it is an academic approach to a pragmatic problem, a definition of marketing is required if we are to help solve the problem. One such definition was proposed about seven years ago by th American Marketing Association. It says that marketing is the "performance of business activities which directs the flow of goods and services from consumer to user." As a definition of marketing, I think it is a superb explanation of physical distribution. Sometime after that, in 1967, Remus Harris wrote an article in *Advertising Age* and said that "Marketing is the total process of creating consumers efficiently." I think this latter definition is a giant step forward because included in the definition are three essential elements. He has recognized that marketing is a total process. He has further recognized that a consumer must be created, and lastly, he gives homage to the fact that it must be an efficient process. Even with the improvements in this latter definition, it is still not complete enough for use by the new breed of financial man.

Easily the finest definition of marketing that I have ever heard was written by Clarence Eldridge in the year following that of Mr. Harris. In 1968 Eldridge wrote a series of purely pragmatic essays for the Association of National Advertisers. In one of these statements he said that, "Marketing is ascertaining, creating, and satisfying the wants of a consumer; *and doing it at a profit.*" This is the first time that anyone has ever defined marketing in terms of making a profit. Suddenly we are taken out of the sphere of being magnanimous; away from being the type of individuals who say "I am creative, you cannot measure me." Suddenly all, encompassed by the marketing concept, are going to be concerned with profit responsibility, profit awareness, profit consciousness. It will no longer be possible for the marketing man to go to the sales manager and simply give him a goal of volume attainment for salesmen's quotas. What can be done now is to make the sales manager responsible for the profitability of the product mix being sold. The definition encourages selling on the basis of the mix of profitability. We need no longer listen to the sales manager tell the salesman "Sell, sell, and get rewards for selling." In fact, he may be encouraging the salesman to sell what is easiest for him to sell; and what is easiest for him to sell may be the least profitable item for the company.

What I am suggesting is only one example of what might stem from a redefined marketing function. Another example is the concept of how to create a realistic incentive plan for salesmen. Why must it be like a medieval castle with a moat around it? Why must the only people who can raise and lower the drawbridge be the sales managers? Why not have the sales managers sit down with the financially oriented marketing man (or conversely, a marketing oriented financial man) and together create an incentive plan based upon a product mix and further, calculate the product mix that will optimize the profitability of the line, the division, or the company. It is no longer practical to have an incentive plan based simply upon volume attainment.

Another fact of the redefined marketing function is involved with the product manager concept. Ostensibly product managers are held responsible for the profits of their products. Although this is not true in every company, by and large the vast majority of companies in the United States hold managers responsible for profits. Yet, if we realistically look at the product manager, we must ask ourselves how he can exercise his responsibility. He cannot, in fact, purchase the raw materials for his products, he cannot go into the factory and tell the plant manager to increase his output by 10 percent (the union shop steward would be highly unnerved by this type of affront). He cannot unilaterally accomplish a price change for a major product, and sometimes he cannot even create his own media program, especially in cases where companies now have staff directors for media. Nevertheless, we attempt to continue the charade that the product manager is responsible for profit. There is a tremendous anomaly here.

EFFECTING THE EVOLUTION

When we attempt to measure the performance of people under profit responsibility, we are measuring them on the wrong base. We are first concerned with the word profit—a misleading word. In all honesty, profit is what is left over. What we should be concerned about is the semantic distinction of *profitability*. Profitability is far different from profit in that it is a *new rate* of profit. It is an incremental rate of profit that is derived from every transaction. That, then, is the key to the precise measure that we can apply to individual performance.

The remaining point then is, how can we establish these concepts? The first step to accomplish this is to be willing to look the controller in the eye and ask, "Are you willing to take a different look at your system? For all these years, you have been telling me that the magic things to look at are gross profit and net profit, and you have been so accomplished in your craft that you have even broken this down to a product level. Well, standing up here as a heretic, I can say that there isn't any such thing as a net profit for a product. Products don't pay taxes; companies pay taxes."

In addition, wearing my financial hat, I can realistically state that I, as a financial executive, can influence the magnitude and the direction of corporate profit. Within legally and morally accepted accounting principles, I can accomplish this type of change. Sooner or later, if I do choose to exercise this power, I can distribute that effect over the products. I would reasonably have to ask whether any marketing man should be willing to be judged by the controller's changes to the profit measure. Should careers be judged by a financial man's ability to change numbers? It is hardly a fair type of measure. There is another way of accomplishing fair measurement and it is contained within the elements of relevant costing, of product life cycle analysis, and of the return on investment technique. All of these, of course, are exciting innovative financial tools and can best be implemented through creating the position of marketing controller.

RELEVANT COSTING

Relevant costing is neither standard costing, direct costing, nor absorption costing. It is a completely different type of costing analysis. It is an analytical tool that recognizes the concept of value. Value is what is inherent in every decision that must be made about factors that will affect tomorrow. The financial profession is disturbed about the concept value because there is nothing in the entire theory of accounting that recognizes value. Looking at an income statement is the same as looking at cost. Looking at the balance sheet is the same as looking at cost. For example, the value of assets on the balance sheet is based on the cost at which the items were purchased, less the depreciation accumulated against the assets. Nothing in those statements has to do with the value of an asset.

I am suggesting that the following be considered: scrap the traditional income statement; it is oriented towards custodial reporting. In fact, custodial responsibility for control and reporting is nowadays becoming less and less important, not more. Besides, there is really not too much of a challenge left for solving reporting problems. Even if your controller cannot do it correctly, there is always the independent outside auditor to correct him. So, therefore, this is not the nub of the relationship problem that exists within the corporate organization. The challenge is to create the system that is going to orient itself towards decision making.

The essence then of relevant costing is to begin by separating *all* types of costs. In saying this, I am referring not only to manufacturing costs, but marketing costs, functional distribution costs, administrative costs, and so on. Under relevant costing they are first separated into a classification of a *direct* or *indirect* cost. For the sake of simplicity, let's assume that the definition of direct or indirect refers to whether the costs are directly attributable to the existence of the item being measured. This type of procedure is necessary. It is the classification procedure I am referring to. Accounting is preoccupied with the classification of costs and has rarely been concerned with the behavior of costs. The distinction in practice between the term classification and behavior is immense. Classification does not consider variable or marginal elements of profitability. In essence, relevant costing is concerned much more with the behavior of costs than it is wih the classification of costs.

Once the split between direct and indirect has been accomplished, costs are further separated into two other classifications, variable and nonvariable. The essence of this distinction is "does the cost vary with volume or not?" Examples of different types of costs that might vary directly with volume are commissions, manufacturing costs, spoilage, obsolescence. Freight, in addition, may vary directly with volume. Adertising, on the other hand, is a direct cost but it is nonvariable. It exists because the product exists but does not vary directly with volume. The nature of this type of cost is that it is akin to a period cost. Advertising, over the period of the planning horizon, is generally a fixed, planned amount. If a successful campaign is launched, the unit rate of advertising based upon the number of units sold will decrease compared to the planned unit rate. If the campaign is not successful, the per unit rate will be far more expensive because fewer units will be sold. This is essentially the type of distinction that we are looking for when we separate variable from nonvariable costs. In a purely variable cost, the unit rate remains the same, while aggregate dollars change following volume. In a nonvariable cost, the aggregate dollars remain the same but the unit rates change in response to volume changes.

Out of all of this come *two new decision making levels of profit*. We will be scrapping the traditional gross profit and net profit measurements because they are not realistic for making a decision. The levels of profit created through relevant costing are *variable profit* and *direct profit*.

Variable profit *answers all questions of change*. "What happens if I drop my selling price by 10 cents a ton?" "What happens if I increase my volume by 500 thousand pounds?" "What happens if I increase the output of my plan from 80 to 90 percent of utilized capacity?" The foregoing are questions of change that are asked every day. This type of system will give an almost instantaneous reply to the question that deals with the effect of such changes on coporate profits. In addition to that, it will provide *instantaneous break-even analysis*. No longer will the decision maker have to suffer with the old statistical break-even charts showing horizontal lines and 45-degree lines representing fixed costs and sales revenues. That type of construction took hours because, before the chart could be drawn, fixed and variable costs first had to be separated. Under relevant costing, this has already become a built-in part of the system.

Direct profit, which is the second decision making level of profit, answers another type of question. It responds to a question regarding the economic impact of operations. Direct profit is a profit that exists because a product exists. Correspondingly, if a product is done away with, that amount of direct profit will also be eliminated. In this vein, it answers such questions as "Should I close plant A and leave plant B open? What would the effect be?" "What would the effect on profits be if I discontinued the operations of division C?" "Should I keep product D in the line or should I discontinue the product?" "Should I go ahead with the marketing of new product E or not?"

Relevant costing is only one of the techniques that can be used to help the financial area assist the marketing area. Another vehicle incorporates the decision making applications of return on investment.

The Return On Investment Problem

Return on investment is an old war-horse that has been trotted out quite a bit lately. It is most commonly used for purposes of stockholder reporting in annual reports. Usually the numbers used will be for purposes of divisional return on investment or aggregate return on investment measures. The sad truth is, there are so many other uses for the concept that can be applied to decision making but that are almost totally ignored by the financial profession.

Why not use the return on investment concept for obtaining the return on investment for a geographic selling area. Compare the profitability of district 1 versus district 2. Certainly there is no technical problem involved. All of the data input is there in any available system. The hang-up encountered by most financial people is that of the base that should properly be used for the denominator of the equation, investment. The financial people question how they can apportion the stockholder's equity to achieve geographic district profitability. The obvious answer is that you don't distribute the stockholder's equity to achieve measurements of geographic profitability. In effect, one should render unto Caesar what is Caesar's; the investment in the geographic area may only be in accounts receivable or in inventory. That, therefore, will become the common investment base for all of the geographic areas. The return on investment equation on a geographic basis would measure the profitability of the product sold in the geographic area aganist the incremental investment base of accounts receivable and inventories.

The return on investment concept can also be applied to measuring the efficiency of the sales force. An individual salesman can be evaluated in terms of his return on investment. In effect, the equation can evaluate the profitability of adding salesmen to the sales force.

The concept can be used for product pricing. There is a fine formula, developed by Wayne Keller some years ago, that is not highly complex and is valid, especially for the pricing of unique products. It helps to relate the selling price of a product to the return on investment objective of a company. It will not give the marketing man the exact price that he should charge; rather, it will tell him how low he can price his product and still maintain his target return on investment. In the above sense, the marketing man may have his cake and eat it too. He knows how low he can price the product but he does not know how high he can go. Obviously the answer to that question is that he should price the product as high as he economically can and still maintain his basic demand for the product. It is, of course, an excellent vehicle for determining a ball park pricing structure for unique products that do not have the conventional parameters of an established market or a built-in customer demand for the product.

The concept is also highly applicable for the evaluation of new products and capital expenditures relative to the new products. If we assume that we have a fine new product but do not have the factory to make it, the options that arise from that type of situation are manifold. One can build a factory to make the new product in order to sell it, or one can build a new plant, then in turn sell the plant to a third party and lease it back from him. This type of situation is a perfect example for an application of return on investment techniques.

These pitifully few examples, among many, should demonstrate that one must demand, or at least convince, the financial people to expand their horizon to include other applications of financial techniques so that marketing will be in a position to make the best decision for the company. There is another problem that has been largely ignored by the financial area and, in fact, by the marketing area: product life cycles.

Product Life Cycles

In 1968 the A. C. Nielsen Company published the first definitively realistic study of product life cycles. They studied 250 major household products for Lever Brothers covering the period 1960 to 1965. The startling conclusion of that study was that the average life span of a new product is *2.9 years*. The 2.9-year measure covers the product from conception to prototype; from test market to national distribution; from maturity to obsolescence to death—and in addition, the marketer has to make a profit.

The marketing world has been inundated by the demise of what once were highly touted new product introductions. The consumer's mind has been ingrained with the names of prominent new products which, in fact, are on the downturn of their own quick, untimely down spiral. Has anyone heard of

Reef Mouth Wash lately? or Hidden Magic Hair Spray? or the FIII? Or Three Layered Jell-O? When was the last time you had breakfast cereal with freeze-dried fruit in it? Right now there are products in development on the drawing board that are going to replace many existing products today. For example, current information is that Xerox is working on a copier innovation that could obsolete everthing that is currently on the market. Their development will not come to fruition until four or five years from now. However, even then, it will have a profound effect upon its market.

When was the last time you segregated your products into the stages of their life cycles and then looked at the *quality* of profit? If the attribute of quality to profit strikes you as being odd, consider that it is an entirely normal reaction. I would assume that we are all American capitalists. We open up the stock pages of the *Wall Street Journal* each day and say, "The stock is going up or the stock is going down." Usually, the correlation for stocks going up or down is with the earnings per share. What I am submitting to you is that a company whose earnings per share is increasing may be a very sick company. No one questions *how long* the sources of those earnings are going to continue.

For example, the coffee market in the United States is declining about 1 percent a year. The leading companies that make coffee, though, have managed to increase earnings. Somewhere, at some future time, a curve will intercept those earnings; it will occur because the per capita consumption of coffee has been going down from about 3 cups a day in 1963 to 2.6 cups a day at present. At that point, the companies will be in for a rude awakening. It is prudent at this point to ask youself, "What is the quality of the dollar of profit attributable to coffee, compared to the quality of profit of a good, new product that is expanding its market?" Further ask, whether there is a difference in the quality of profit?

Why not then take this innovation in profit planning and view your situation in the light of the life cycle stages in which your products are located. The point of all of this is, that when doing profit planning for marketing, the conventional method encourages *planning in a vacuum*. Profit planning always assumes that the product is going to last forever.

IMPLEMENTING THE MARKETING CONTROLLER CONCEPT

It is reasonable, of course, to ask how all of this can be accomplished, especially if one has a conventional controller. I think that the accomplishment of this concept leads us to a discussion in detail of the marketing controller concept. The only excuse for not having a marketing controller is if you happen to have a conventional controller who appears to have a single head but in reality has two heads.

A marketing controller really is a man with two heads. Ostensibly, one can make a search and in a job specification specify that this man must be more powerful than a speeding locomotive, be able to leap tall buildings in a single bound, and be faster than a speeding bullet. Obviously, there aren't too many of these fellows around. In a pragmatic sense, I think one must create him. Further, I think that he can be created by taking a financial analyst and simply immersing him thoroughly and completely in the marketing sphere—even to the extent of having him participate in sales force and product management activities for a period of time, concurrent with the financial training. It has been my experience that after about two years, one *might* develop a marketing controller. The key to the position is that the man has to report to two people; I think that it is the only way that it will work. I am speaking about a marketing controller who will be a staff member of the marketing function and who will primarily report to the marketing head. He will secondarily report to the financial controller. It will obviously take an extremely mature individual to undertake this type of relationship. I think to do otherwise, having him report to the financial controller first and then the marketing head, would tend to brand the man as a misfit from out-of-town, or as a controller's spy. It would defeat the very essence of the program.

THE FAULTS OF "ORGANOGRAMS"

Many of the problems about which I am writing stem from the common conception of corporate organization charts. There are two basic faults with an organization chart. The first fault is that there are a lot of little boxes in it, and one box has a tendency to say to the other box, "This is my job; keep your hands off." There is an additional problem. Most often the big boxes have little boxes that hang down and that denote assistants. One assistant will quite often look at the other assistant and say, "Why is his box higher than my box?" When hard put for an answer, one can obviously see that the other box is making more money or his boss is more important. In essence then, conventional organizational charts breed insularism.

A better concept of an organization is in the shape of a good old fashioned wagon wheel. The wagon wheel I envision has an axle, a hub, and spokes. The hub of the wheel is marketing because that is what the company is in business for. As indicated earlier, the company is in business to sell products, not just to make them. If you, the reader, can accept the logic stated above, then perhaps this logic can be stretched and you will accept that the rim of the wheel is composed of service areas that augment the hub's function. One of the service areas may be finance, one may be purchasing, one may be manufacturing, and so forth. The spokes, in turn, are simply lines of communication among these elements of the corporate organization. This then produce's a modern functional, pragmatic organization chart. If this is acceptable to the reader, then I ask that you further accept the concept of the marketing controller. He is there as a service function to marketing, and he is there only to help someone make a decision. He is not there to make debits or credits; he is not there to perform routine assignments. He is there to be a quantitative financial advisor and a financial conscience. There is no proper name to call this type of individual. For better or for worse, he has been called a marketing controller. Further, such individuals really do exist.

In 1965 The Nestlé Company innovated the concept of a marketing controller. Marketing controllers are stationed in each of the major marketing divisions, and figuratively they sleep in the same bed with the people of the division. It has been an eminently successful program. In fact, it has been so successful that an offshoot of that program was created, the position of a manufacturing controller. More recently a further step in the evolution of the marketing controller was created, the position of physical distribution controller. In the future this concept might be expanded further to include the functional decision making areas of purchasing and administration.

IMPLICATIONS OF THE MARKETING CONTROLLER CONCEPT

The evolution of medicine has brought about profound changes in our perception of doctors. When we have problems with our throat we no longer go to a general practitioner; we would rather see an ear-nose-and-throat doctor because he has the special skills required in that area. If we have problems with our eyes, we go to an ophthalmologist. In this sense finance is no different. The kinds of decisions that have to be made in each of the functions are simply too complex to permit the corporate staff man to assist a functional area. In addition, the corporate staff financial man is usually isolated in his ivory tower. Besides that, there is always the spectre behind his shoulder of generally accepted accounting principles and the obligation to report what happened yesterday. Therefore, one must recognize that finance has not one responsibility, but many. Obviously and essentially one of these responsibilities is a reporting function for yesterday. More importantly, though, the mission in life of the financial executive should be to help someone make a sound decision.

A marketing controller would control media expenses, advise on the optimum timing for different strategies, measure the efficiency of promotional spending, analyze media production cost; evaluate the profitability of an individual customer, evaluate geographic profitability, and monitor the production efficiency of scheduling manufacturing. The role of the marketing controller is, and will be, different depending upon the type of company.

Quite often they present sales-oriented financial reports, and by that I do not mean to imply sales by district, by territory, or other such types of reports. I am referring to sales by customer, compared to how much of an inducement was paid to a customer to perform certain services. In that manner the marketing-oriented financial man will be able to determine the profitability of our selling efforts to an individual customer. The customer is frequently paid performance payments, especially in the consumer products industry, or he gets some other type of sales promotion incentive. These can be measured against the *performance* of the customer, not just the number of items he has purchased. In addition, one can measure the purchase performance of the customer against his own neighboring competition for a company's products. In a sense the marketing controller can custom tailor a market measure that competes with a particular customer to whom the company sells. When that is concluded one can give the salesman a tool to say to the customer, "You increased your purchases almost 10 percent a year for product A; in addition to that, we gave you $60 thousand of incentives for purchasing our product. But you know, your own bedfellows, your competition, who also buy from us in this area, increased their purchases by 15 percent we only paid them $50 thousand." This is the type of warning flag that a marketing-oriented sales report can raise so the salesman covering a customer can have a viable sales tool with which to confront him.

Marketing controllers in other companies quite often design incentive plans based upon profitability attainment. Further, they assist direct accounts to optimize their purchasing and inventory policies. If necessary, some marketing controllers have gone on loan to various major customers. In that respect, what better goodwill device can be employed than attempting to assist one of your major customers by sending him a qualified man to help?

Companies are now beginning to recognize the worth of the marketing controller concept and are fondly embracing it. In fact, Johnson & Johnson has really reorganized their financial area to employ this concept. In addition, it is currently being actively explored by Bristol-Myers and Crown Zellerbach.

Change is not going to come if one does not display a curiosity sufficient to cause the change. In order to accomplish the transition to a marketing controller concept, you, the reader, are going to have to ask for it; you will have to demand it, because I don't think the change will come from within. Moreover, when the change comes I think it will be through evolution, certainly not revolution. Revolution makes people defensive, and there is no place for that type of atmosphere within any company. Thus far, the experience of major corporations with the marketing controller concept has proved that it is an eminently successful tool to achieve better decision making. What more could a company ask for.

"A better concept of an organization is in the shape of an old-fashioned wagon wheel. The hub of the wheel is marketing—because that is what the company is in business for. The rim represents the service functions—which, instead of being self-serving entities unto themselves—provide support to the marketing function."   Sam R. Goodman

CHAPTER 9

THE ZERO-BASE BUDGETING PROCESS

PETER A. PYHRR

"In practice, department managers need justify only increases over the prior year's budget. This implies that what is already being spent is automatically sanctioned. Under the zero-base budgeting concept each department's functions must be reviewed completely and all costs, rather than only the increases, must be approved."

ORIGIN OF THE ZERO-BASE BUDGET CONCEPT

On December 2, 1969, at the Plaza Hotel in New York City, Dr. Arthur F. Burns, then counselor to the President of the United States, addressed the annual dinner meeting of the Tax Foundation on the "Control of Government Expenditures." In this speech Dr. Burns identified the basic need for zero-base budgeting, but he also expressed his concern that such a process would be difficult if not impossible to implement:

Customarily, the officials in charge of an established program have to justify only the increase which they seek above last year's appropriation. In other words, what they are already spending is usually accepted as necessary, without examination. Substantial savings could undoubtedly be realized if [it were required that] every agency . . . make a case for its entire appropriation request each year, just as if its program or programs were entirely new. Such budgeting procedure may be difficult to achieve, partly because it will add heavily to the burdens of budget-making, and partly also because it will be resisted by those who fear that their pet programs would be jeopardized by a system that subjects every . . . activity to annual scrutiny of its costs and results.

However, as experience in Texas Instruments, Inc. and the State of Georgia has indicated, this kind of budgeting need not "add heavily to the burdens

131

of budget-making." In fact, effectively planned and properly managed, zero-base budgeting can actually reduce the burdens of budget making while significantly improving management decision making and the allocation of resources.

The zero-base budgeting process, as used by both Texas Instruments and the State of Georgia, is identical in philosophy and general procedures, although the specific mechanics of implementation differ slightly to fit the particular needs of each organization. Zero-base budgeting is readily adaptable to organizations that have significantly different operations, needs, and problems, and the following sections discuss the available adaptations that make this budgeting process an effective management tool in both industry and government.

THE PLANNING AND BUDGETING PROCESSES IN PERSPECTIVE

Many managers have suggested that zero-base budgeting be renamed "zero-base planning" or "zero-base planning and budgeting" because the process requires effective planning and immediately shows up any lack of planning. The planning and budgeting process can be contrasted as follows:

> Planning identifies the *output* desired.
> Budgeting identifies the *input* required.

Planning is more general than budgeting. Planning establishes programs, sets goals and objectives, and makes basic policy decisions for the organization as a whole. Budgeting analyzes in detail the many functions or activities that the organization must perform to implement each program, analyzes the alternatives within each activity to achieve the end product desired, and identifies the trade-offs between partial or complete achievement of the established goals and the associated costs. Exhibit 1 shows the relationship required between planning and budgeting. This relationship is dynamic because the resources required to achieve the desired goals are not unlimited. Therefore, we must determine whether achieving the last 10 percent of each goal requires 25 percent of the cost, or vice versa; whether we *can* achieve each goal; and whether we must eliminate and/or reduce some goals. If we fixed our goals, the zero-base budgeting process would be a suboptimization tool, telling us how best to achieve the given results. However, the realistic requirement to modify goals based on a cost/benefit analysis makes the zero-base budgeting process both a suboptimization and total-optimization tool.

Exhibit 1

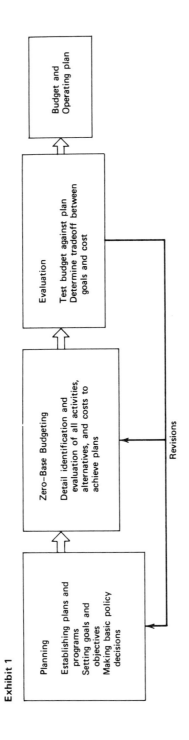

Planning	Zero–Base Budgeting	Evaluation	Budget and Operating plan
Establishing plans and programs Setting goals and objectives Making basic policy decisions	Detail identification and evaluation of all activities, alternatives, and costs to achieve plans	Test budget against plan Determine tradeoff between goals and cost	

Revisions

If we take a look at this same budgeting and planning relationship from the point of view of those managers who will design and implement programs and activities to achieve the desired goals, we have the relationship shown in Exhibit 2. These managers need to have an understanding of the current organization and operations before they can design each program. This need is created by several factors:

- Goals may be achieved through extensions of current programs.
- New Programs must still operate within the total organizational framework and may require support from existing activities.
- Costs may depend heavily on the effectiveness and efficiency of current activities or may reflect the capability of the organization to develop effective and efficient activities for new programs.
- Cost constraints may require the funding of new high priority programs and goals at the expense of current programs and lower priority goals.

From this basis (or starting point) managers can build programs, either modifying them to fit the capabilities of the current operations or designing them to change the current operations and modifying the goals to meet the capabilities of the programs, and then modifying both goals and programs to meet cost limitations. This determination is an interactive process that can be achieved by effective preliminary planning and the zero-base budgeting process.

Regardless of the budgeting technique used, there is no substitute for good planning. If we should not have been producing the product or providing the service in the first place, even the best operating plan and detailed budget will not buy us anything. At the very least, any budgeting system should point out such a mistake, but a lot of time and money can be saved if this conclusion is reached in the preliminary planning stage.

THE TWO BASIC STEPS OF ZERO-BASE BUDGETING

There are two basic steps of zero-base budgeting:

1. *Developing "decision packages."* This step involves analyzing and describing each discrete activity—current as well as new, in one or more decision packages. (These packages are discussed below.)

Exhibit 2

	Basis (Starting Point)	Direction (How To Get There)	Goals (Ending Point)
A.	Ideal planning situation		
	Detailed knowledge of current activities and operations, including costs and efficiency	Detailed evaluation of directions, activities, and programs, with specific expenditures and set of established priorities with each program	Realistic, measurable, and attainable goals; with established expenditure ranges, and a set of priorities among goals
		← Modification →	← Modification →
B.	Poor planning situation		
	Lack of detailed understanding of activities, costs, and efficiency	Programs and directions very broad and general; no cost guidelines; operating managers have few or no specific directions	"Motherhood" statements (increase profits; provide the best education possible; reduce air pollution; etc.)
C.	Impact of zero-base budgeting		
	Current activities, alternatives, costs, benefits, and effectiveness evaluated in detail	Identifies and evaluates both current and new activities and programs in detail: alternatives, costs, benefits, and effectiveness; establishes priorities within each program, identifying level of goal achievement at varying expenditure levels	Identifies trade-offs among programs and goals so that top management can make the decision as to what funding level they can afford versus the programs and goals they must afford to do without

2. *Ranking "decision packages."* This step involves evaluating and ranking these packages in order of importance through cost/benefit analysis or subjective evaluation.

Once decision packages are developed and ranked, management can allocate resources accordingly—funding the most important activities (or decision packages), whether they are current or new. The final budget is produced by taking packages that are approved for funding, sorting them into their appropriate budget units, and adding up the costs identified on each package to produce the budget for each unit.

Step 1: Developing Decision Packages

Concept of Decision Packages. A decision package is a document that identifies and describes a specific activity in such a manner that management can (1) evaluate it and rank it against other activities competing for limited resources, and (2) decide whether to approve or disapprove it. Therefore, the information displayed on each package must provide management with all needed information for such evaluation. We can generally define the decision package as follows. A decision package identifies a discrete activity, function, or operation in a definitive manner for management evaluation and comparison with other activities. This identification includes:

- Purpose (or goals and objectives)
- Consequences of not performing the activity
- Measures of performance
- Alternative courses of action
- Costs and benefits

The activities for which decision packages should be prepared—including all information required for management evaluation—will vary slightly among different organizations.

The key to zero-base budgeting lies in the identification and evaluation of alternatives for each activity. Two types of alternatives should be considered when developing decision packages as follows.

1. *Different ways of performing the same function.* This analysis

identifies alternative ways of performing a function. The best alternative is chosen and the others are discarded.

- If an alternative to the current way of doing business is chosen, the recommended way should be shown in the decision package, and the current way should be shown as an alternative.
- Only one decision package is prepared. It shows the recommended way of performing the function and identifies the alternative ways considered, giving a brief explanation of why they were not chosen.

2. *Different levels of effort of performing the function.* This analysis identifies alternative levels of effort and spending to perform a specific function. A minimum level of effort should be established, and additional levels of effort identified as separate decision packages.

- This minimum level of effort package may not completely achieve the purpose of the function (even the additional levels of effort proposed may not completely achieve it, because of realistic budget and achievement levels), but it should identify and attack the most important elements.
- In many cases, the minimum level of effort will be between 50 to 70 percent of the current level of operation. (One exception to this rule of thumb would be start-up functions or operations that were not up to full speed during the preceding budget year.)
- The minimum level of effort package would be ranked higher than the additional level(s) of effort so that the elimination of these lower ranked packages does not preclude the performance of higher ranked packages.

Managers should consider both types of alternatives in identifying and evaluating each function. Managers will usually identify different ways of performing the same function first, and then evaluate different levels of effort for performing the function for whatever way or method chosen. The most common questions asked at this point are:

- Why should different levels of effort be identified?
- Why should a manager not choose the level of effort he thinks necessary, and then recommend that level?

Perhaps the most significant result of zero-base budgeting comes from identifying and evaluating different levels of effort. There are two reasons for this:

1. Limited expenditure levels (owing to dollar constraints and the desired funding of new or expanding programs) would cause the complete elimination of some functions if only one decision package at some desired level of effort were identified. Such elimination *might not* be desirable and practical, and higher management usually prefers to have the option of reducing current levels of effort in addition to eliminating entire functions.

2. The functional level managers who develop these decision packages are the ones who are best equipped (because of their detailed knowledge of their particular function) to identify and evaluate different levels of effort, and it should be the responsibility of these managers to advise higher management of all possibilities. It then becomes higher management's responsibility to evaluate the relative importance of functions and the different levels of effort within each function.

Example of Production Planning.   The following example of production planning illustrates the type of analysis that each manager needs to make to prepare his decision packages.

The production planning manager analyzed his department's purpose and efforts and decided that decision packages should be developed around production planning as a whole, rather than around separate work units within the department (such as working with marketing to determine delivery schedules, estimating production time and material needs, preparing schedules, etc.), since he had a small department and each work unit took only a fraction of the daily effort. He then proceeded to make the following analysis.

1. *Different ways of performing the same function.*
    (a) *Recommended decision package.*   Production planning department for product X, with five production planners (cost—$60,000). Maintain current organization and method of operation. This level of effort is required to maintain shipping and production schedules and inventory reports updated at the level desired by the manufacturing superintendent.
    (b) *Alternatives not recommended.*   Eliminate production planners and let line foremen do their own planning (zero incremental cost for foreman). This would result in excessive inventories, inefficient production runs, and delayed shipments. Combine production planning for products X, Y, and Z. This would save two planners at $15,000 each (total of 12 planners for combined departments), but foremen of each product line fear lack of specialized service; peak work loads on all product

lines coincide, creating excessive burden for one supervisor; product departments are in separate buildings and physical proximity of planning is desired.

Once he had defined the basic alternatives and chosen the one he considered best, this manager completed his analyses by identifying and analyzing the different levels of effort for his chosen alternative. In this particular case he believed he could eliminate one planner from the group and still satisfy minimum requirements. Hence, he developed the following decision packages:

> Product X planning (1 of 3): cost—$45,000
>> Four planners required for minimum planning support and coordination between marketing and manufacturing, and for establishing production schedules and making reports. Would reduce longer-range planning, inventory control, and marketing support for special product modifications.
>
> Product X planning (2 of 3): cost—$15,000
>> One long-range planner required to increase forward planning of production and shipping schedules from 2 to 4 weeks, to update in-process inventory reports daily rather than every other day (to aid inventory control), and to assist marketing manager with customers who need special product modifications. (Current level of staffing.)
>
> Product X planning (3 of 3): cost—$15,000
>> One operations research analyst required to evaluate optimal length of production run versus optimal inventory levels by color and size of product. (Savings of 1% in production cost or a reduction cost of 5% in inventory level would offset this added cost.)

In this example, the minimum level identified (in package 1 of 3) required one man less than the current operating level; package 3 of 3 brought the production planning staff to one man more than the current level. If the alternative to combine the production planning for products X, Y, Z had been chosen, packages for several levels of effort could have been developed for this centralized production planning activity.

For most functions, different levels of effort should be possible. By developing these levels as separate packages, the production planning manager is stating that he thinks all levels deserve serious consideration within realistic funding expectations, but he is identifying these possible levels of effort and leaving it to higher management to make trade-offs among functions and levels of effort within each function. Management can now eliminate the production planning department by disapproving all decision packages (leaving it to the line foremen to do their own planning); or approve package 1 (cost—$45,000), packages 1 and 2 (cost—$60,000), or all packages (cost—$75,000).

In a few instances, different levels of effort are not realistic because of the specific circumstances involved. In these cases, there should be only one decision package at the recommended level of effort, with an explanation of why that one level was the only realistic possibility. In the preceding example, a specific level of production planning effort might have been established by the manufacturing manager for product X if he thought that any possible cost reductions or changes from the specified production planning effort were of minor consideration compared to the resulting production problems or increased manufacturing costs. (However, most managers cannot make such an assessment until the consequences of different levels of effort have been explored, which is done formally in the decision packages. If a manager then realizes that the consequences of a lower level of effort far outweigh the cost savings, he can merely give a high priority to several or all packages for that activity.)

Separate decision packages would not be prepared for each different way of performing the same activity as well as for each different level of effort for performing the activity, since we do not want to double-count each activity and its associated costs. If it is determined that several levels of effort are possible, a separate package will be prepared for the minimum level as well as separate packages for each increment—that is, separate packages for product X planning (1 of 3), product X planning (2 of 3), and product X planning (3 of 3). The recommended way for performing each package will be displayed on that package, with the recommended way usually being the same for all levels of effort for a specific activity.

Needless to say, decision packages cannot be prepared in a vacuum. Planning assumptions and guidelines concerning direction and purpose must be provided by the higher-level managers to the lower-level managers before they can develop their packages. Managers preparing packages should also discuss their alternatives and recommendations with those affected by their function before developing the packages. In the preceding example, the production planning decision packages should have been prepared after discussions with the manufacturing and marketing managers whose work is affected by the type and quality of production planning.

The minimum level decision package for production planning is shown in Exhibit 3, which illustrates the one-page decision package format used by Texas Instruments. This basic format was established to force each manager to perform a detailed analysis of his function(s)—including al-

Exhibit 3

DECISION PACKAGE [$000] TY-14270-A   STRICTLY PRIVATE

PACKAGE NAME	MANAGER	RANKING
Product X Planning (1 of 3)	John Doe	2

STATEMENT OF PROGRAM AND GOALS

Provide minimum level of planning effort for 5 million units of product X.
Maintain updated production and shipping schedules for two weeks in advance
(currently maintaining schedules four weeks in advance).
Provide finished goods inventory level reports daily and in process inventory
reports every other day (currently being done daily).
Maintain perpetual inventory system (computerized) on raw material to
maintain a two week s supply on hand and a two weeks supply on order.

IMPROVEMENTS   Reduce overtime and clerical effort due to perpetual inventory system.
INCLUDED   Replace professional with clerk.

BENEFITS

Activity required for minimum maintenance of planning
function to deliver products on schedule.

OPERATING RATIOS	1969	1970	1971
$ M NSB/planner	3.75	3.60	5.25
Avg inventory/M NSB	10%	12%	12%
Package cost/NSB	.30%	.33%	.21%
Package cost/GPM	.90%	1.1%	.75%

ALTERNATIVES AND CONSEQUENCES

-Elimination of planners would force line foremen to do their own planning (zero incremental cost for foremen); but excessive inventories, inefficient production runs, and
  delayed shipments would result in excessive sales loss.

-Combine production planning for departments X, Y, and Z.

-Package 2 of 3 ($15,000): add back long range planner.

-Package 3 of 3 ($15,000): add operations research analyst.

RESOURCES EXPENSE/PEOPLE	1969	1970					1971					Δ70-71
	TOTAL	1 Q	2 Q	3 Q	4 Q	TOTAL	1 Q	2 Q	3 Q	4 Q	TOTAL	TOTAL
GROSS	45	13	16	16	15	60	11	11	12	11	45	15
NET	45	13	16	16	15	60	11	11	12	11	45	15
NON-EXEMPT	1	1	1	1	1	1	2	2	2	2	2	(1)
EXEMPT	3	3	4	4	4	4	2	2	2	2	2	2

CC	ORGANIZATION	DIVISION	PREPARED BY	DATE
205	DTL Planning	Circuits		

ternatives, cost trends, and operating ratios—to show work loads and effectiveness, and then to display his analysis and recommendations on these
forms.

Formulating Decision Packages. A decision package is defined as an identification of "a discrete activity, function, or operation. . . ." Generally a
discrete activity is the lowest organizational level, cost center, or budgeted
unit, and often several such activities are contained within an individual organizational unit. Determining the activities around which decision
packages should be prepared is the most important step in implementing
zero-base budgeting. At this stage, let us proceed with the understanding
that decision packages are prepared down in the "gut" level of each organization, and hope that the remainder of this chapter will provide enough
examples and insights to allow each reader to determine where the packages
should be developed in his own organization.

Decision packages are formulated at this gut level to promote detailed identification of activities and alternatives, and to generate interest in and participation by the managers who are most familiar with each activity and who will be operationally responsible for the approved budget. Exhibit 4 shows the basic formulation process.

To begin developing his packages, each manager might logically start by identifying the current year's activities and operations. The manager can then take his forecast or budgeted expense level for the current year, identify the activities creating this expense (activities around which he will subsequently develop his decision packages), and calculate or estimate the cost for each activity. At this stage, the manager should simply identify each activity at its current level and method of operation and not try to identify different ways of performing the function or different levels of effort.

After he has broken his current operations into activities around which he will develop his decision packages, the manager can start looking at his requirements for the coming year. It is extremely helpful if upper management issues a formal set of planning assumptions to aid each manager in determining next year's requirements. Such formalized assumptions might include:

- Billing levels.
- Number and types of units to be manufactured or processed.
- Wage and salary increases.
- Number of people served, such as hospital patients.
- Addition to or reduction in facilities to be cleaned and maintained.
- Planned changes from the current method of operation, such as centralization or decentralization of activities, additional scope of operations, and so forth.
- General guidelines as to realistic expenditure levels for the coming budget year.

This formalized set of planning assumptions is needed for several reasons:

1. It forces top level managers to do some detailed planning and goal setting for the coming budget period early in the budget cycle.
2. It provides all managers with a uniform basis for viewing the coming year and estimating requirements.
3. It provides a focal point for reviewing and revising planning assumptions, which in turn requires the revision of decision packages affected by

Exhibit 4

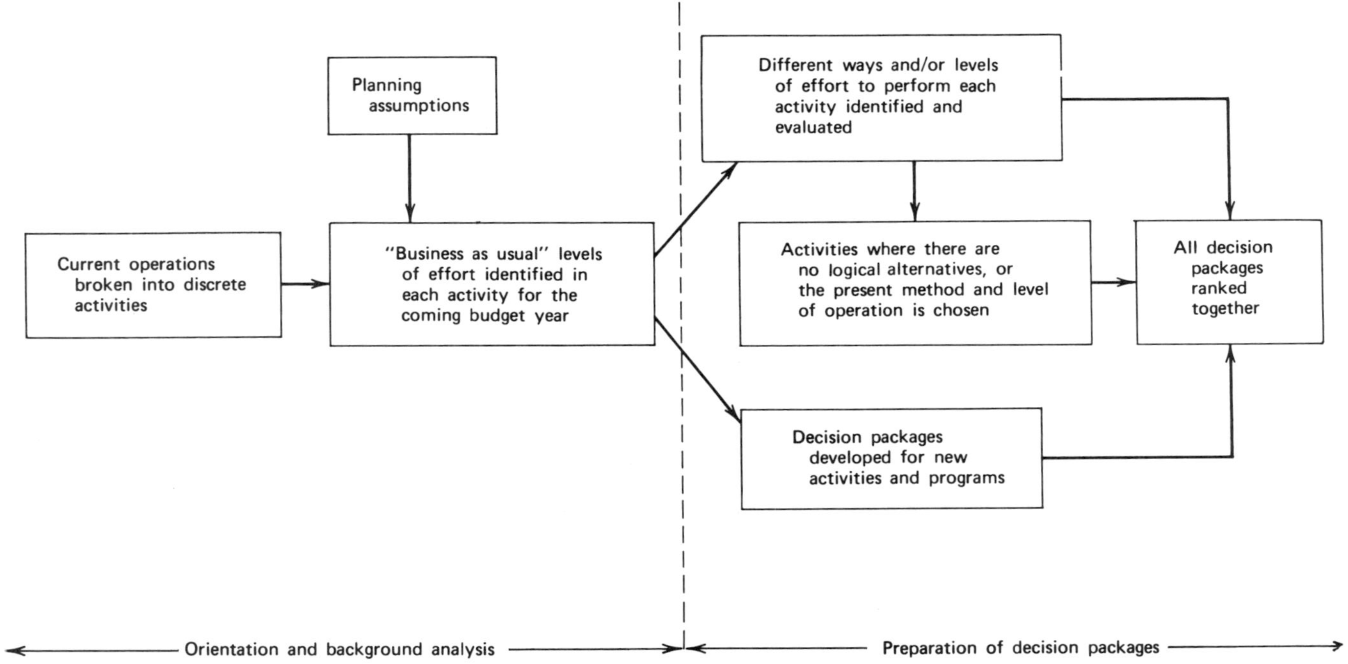

Current operations broken into discrete activities

Planning assumptions

"Business as usual" levels of effort identified in each activity for the coming budget year

Different ways and/or levels of effort to perform each activity identified and evaluated

Activities where there are no logical alternatives, or the present method and level of operation is chosen

Decision packages developed for new activities and programs

All decision packages ranked together

←———— Orientation and background analysis ————→   ←———— Preparation of decision packages ————→

143

those assumptions. The number of revisions in assumptions can be controlled to reduce both confusion and the cycling of budget inputs in rapidly changing environments.

4. It allows managers to readily identify the actual expenditure variances during the operating year that are created by inaccurate assumptions provided during the budgeting process.

Once each manager has determined the discrete activities around which he will develop his decision packages and has received his formalized set of assumptions, he can identify his "business as usual" levels of effort for each activity—which merely extends this year's operations in terms of next year's costs and requirements, with no change in the method of operations. To determine next year's costs, the manager simply adjusts the costs for changes in activity levels for dependent service functions, for wage and salary increases, and for annualizing expenses of new employees and activities not incurred throughout the current budget year.

Until this point no decision packages have been prepared, but the manager has been going through a necessary orientation and background analysis. The real starting point in the preparation of the packages comes when alternatives to the "business as usual" levels of effort are developed by evaluating different ways of and/or levels of effort for performing each activity. If an alternative to the "business as usual" method is chosen, then, as explained earlier, the so-called alternative is incorporated into the package *first* with the "business as usual" method given as an alternative not recommended.

At the same time that the manager is looking at his current and ongoing activities, he should identify all new activities and programs and develop decision packages that handle them—analyzing alternatives for different ways and different levels of effort to implement these new programs. At the conclusion of the formulation stage, the manager will have identified all his proposed activities for the coming year in decision packages that fall into one of three categories:

1. Different ways of and/or different levels of effort for performing the activity.

2. "Business as usual," where there are no logical alternatives, or the present method and level of effort is required.

3. New activities and programs.

The manager is now ready to rank his packages.

Step 2: Ranking Decision Packages

The ranking process provides management with a technique for allocating its limited resources by making it concentrate on these questions: "How much should we spend?" "Where should we spend it?"

Management answers these questions by listing all packages identified in order of decreasing benefit or importance. Managers can then identify the benefits to be gained at each level of expenditure and can study the consequences of not approving additional packages ranked below that expenditure level. The initial ranking should of course occur at the organization level where the packages are developed, so that each manager can evaluate the importance of his own activities and rank his packages accordingly. Then the manager at the next level up the ladder reviews these rankings and uses them as guides to produce a single, consolidated ranking for all the packages presented to him from below.

This ranking process is shown in Exhibit 5. The decision packages would be ranked first by the managers preparing the packages at the organizational level of D_1, D_2, and D_3. These managers would then submit their rankings to their boss, the manager of unit C_2, who would consolidate the 28 packages (5 from D_1, 8 from D_2, and 15 from D_3) into one overall ranking. This process is then repeated, with the manager of unit B_2 producing a consolidated ranking of 55 packages submitted from units C_1, C_2, and C_3. Consolidation can continue until one final ranking is achieved at some desired organizational level. This consolidation hierarchy usually corresponds to the ordinary hierarchical organization of the company, but logical groupings of similar functions may be useful even where these cut across normal organizational boundaries.

Theoretically, one ranking of decision packages can be obtained for an entire company and judged by its top management. But while this single ranking would identify the best allocation of resources, ranking and judging the large volume of packages created by describing all the discrete activities of a large organization would impose a ponderous, if not impossible, task on top management. At the other extreme, ranking at only the cost center level is obviously unsatisfactory, since it does not identify to top management the trade-offs among cost centers or larger organizational units, and these lower level organizational units are usually too numerous for top management to make these trade-offs themselves.

One can begin to resolve this dilemma by stopping the consolidated ranking process at some level between the cost center and the entire company. Such a level might be, for example, a division, department, agency, product

Exhibit 5

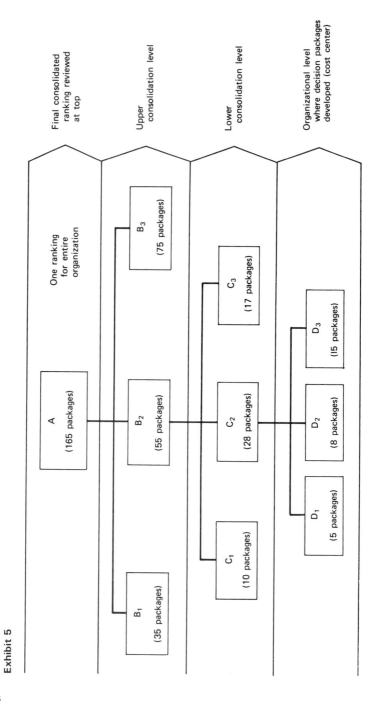

Final consolidated ranking reviewed at top

Upper consolidation level

Lower consolidation level

Organizational level where decision packages developed (cost center)

One ranking for entire organization

A (165 packages)

B₁ (35 packages)

B₂ (55 packages)

B₃ (75 packages)

C₁ (10 packages)

C₂ (28 packages)

C₃ (17 packages)

D₁ (5 packages)

D₂ (8 packages)

D₃ (15 packages)

line, or profit center. The organizational width and depth of such groupings may be determined by four factors:

1.   The number of packages involved, and the time and effort required to review and rank them.
2.   Management's ability and willingness to rank unfamiliar activities.
3.   Natural groupings that provide a logical scope of analysis, such as a product profit center in industry, where the number of packages approved for funding is directly related to profit goals and expectations.
4.   The need for extensive review across organizational boundaries to determine trade-offs in expense levels. (This factor is particularly important when deep cuts in expenditure levels are required and managers are forced to make trade-offs across larger organizational units than normal.)

The volume problem can be the most serious obstacle to effectively implementing the zero-base budgeting process in a large organization. However, the basic solution to the volume problem lies in limiting the number of packages ranked at any consolidation level and properly focusing top management's attention on areas requiring decision making, thus leaving it to lower management levels to perform the detailed evaluation and ranking.

The ranking process itself should be relatively simple, but it seems to be a stumbling block for many managers. In addition to forcing them to make decisions, which seems foreign to some managers, they may have conceptual difficulty in ranking packages they consider "requirements" and may express concern over their ability to judge the relative importance of dissimilar activities, since many packages require subjective judgment. The difficulty and the time consumed in overcoming these problems can be significantly reduced if managers:

1.   Do not concentrate on ranking high priority or "requirement" packages that are well within the expenditure guidelines (other than to ensure that all alternatives, cost reduction opportunities, and operating improvements have been explored and incorporated as appropriate) but concentrate instead on discretionary functions and levels of effort.
2.   Do not spend too much time worrying over whether package 4, for example, is more important than package 5, but instead only assure themselves that packages 4 and 5 are more important than package 15, and package 15 is more important than package 25, and so on.

The Ranking Form.   Exhibit 6 illustrates the ranking form used by Texas

Exhibit 6. Ranking Form

R A N K	PACKAGE NAME	4 QTR 19XX ANNUALIZED EXPENSE		YEAR 1 EXPENSE		PEOPLE	YEAR 2 EXPENSE		PEOPLE	CUMULATIVE LEVEL ($000)	
		GROSS	NET	GROSS	NET	NX/X	GROSS	NET	NX/X	GROSS	NET
1	Quality Control (1 of 3)	167	167	175	175	11/3	90	90	6/1	90	90
2*	Product X Planning (1 of 3)	60	60	60	60	1/4	45	45	2/2	135	135
3	Routine/prevent maint (1 of 2)	140	140	150	150	10/2	105	105	7/1	240	240
4	Industrial Engineering (1 of 4)	93	93	90	90	2/6	41	41	1/2	281	281
5	Administration	24	24	23	23	1/1	25	25	1/1	306	306
6*	Product X Planning (2 of 3)						15	15	/1	321	321
7	Relocate test and assembly						45	45	/	366	366
8	Industrial Engineering (2 of 4)						35	35	/3	401	401
9	Routine/prevent maint (2 of 2)						50	50	3/1	451	451
10	Maintenance scheduler	9	9	9	9	1/	10	10	1/	461	461
11	Quality Control (2 of 3)						83	83	5/1	544	544

12	Industrial Engineering (3 of 4)						/		20	20	1/1	564	564
13	Quality Control (3 of 3)						/		30	30	2/1	594	594
* 14	Product X Planning (3 of 3)						/		15	15	/1	609	609
15	Records and file clerk	6	6	6	6		1/		6	6	1/	615	615
16	Industrial Engineering (4 of 4)						/		15	15	/1	630	630
17	Computerized Scheduling Model						/		10	10	/	640	640
							/				/		
							/				/		
							/				/		
							/				/		
							/				/		
							/				/		
							/				/		

CC	ORGANIZATION	DIVISION	PREPARED BY	DATE
	Manufacturing Support–Product X	Circuits	J. Doe, Manager	10/5/XX

Instruments. This form serves only as a summary sheet to identify the priority placed on each decision package. The package with rank number 1 has the highest priority; the package with rank number 17 has the lowest priority. The package name, expense, and people information is taken directly from the package itself.

It is extremely useful to show cumulative levels (the sum of the expense for each decision package plus all packages ranked above it) so that if, for example, packages 1 through 12 were approved, management could readily see that the budget for the Manufacturing Support Department would be $564,000. The ranking form used by the State of Georgia is very similar to that for Texas Instruments, but it also has a space at each cumulative level to show the percent of this expense level as compared to the current year's expense level for the department.

The ranking form can be easily modified to include any information desired, but it should be remembered that it is merely a summary form to display package priority and the packages themselves must be reviewed to effectively determine which ones should be funded.

WHERE ZERO-BASE BUDGETING CAN BE USED: INDUSTRY AND GOVERNMENT

The zero-base budgeting process consists of identifying decision packages and then ranking them in order of importance through a cost/benefit analysis. Therefore, zero-base budgeting can be used on any activities, functions, or operations where a cost/benefit relationship can be identified—even if this evaluation is highly subjective.

Industry

Exhibit 7 illustrates the typical scope of management activities in industry, which run the gamut from corporate overhead to direct labor and material costs. Zero-base budgeting is applicable to administrative, technical, and most commercial portions of the budget (some transportation and distribution costs may be part of the standard cost system), but it is not directly adaptable to the direct labor, direct material, and some direct overhead associated with production operations. Zero-base budgeting is not applicable to direct production and manufacturing costs because there is usually no benefit from increasing these expenditures—that is, there is no

Exhibit 7

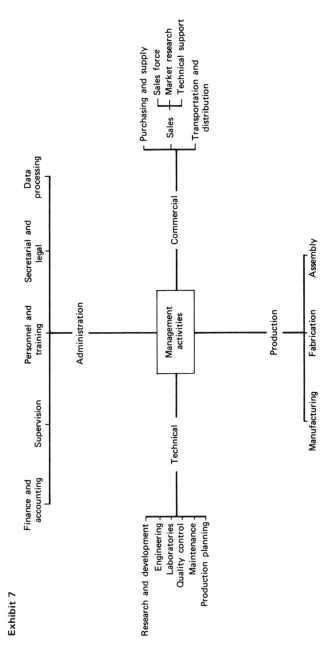

Administration	Finance and accounting / Supervision / Personnel and training / Secretarial and legal / Data processing
Management activities	
Technical	Research and development / Engineering / Laboratories / Quality control / Maintenance / Production planning
Commercial	Purchasing and supply / Sales (Sales force, Market research, Technical support) / Transportation and distribution
Production	Manufacturing / Fabrication / Assembly

151

cost/benefit relationship. The budgeting effort for these direct costs is usually an engineering study with emphasis on minimizing unit costs, with the budget developed by multiplying units of output by standard unit costs. Elements of direct manufacturing overhead fall into a gray area between standard cost budgeting and zero-base budgeting. Some direct overhead costs, such as depreciation expense on existing equipment and facilities, or utilities and power—if this expense is directly associated with machine hours or number of units produced—fall into the standard cost category because, again, there is no cost/benefit relationship. (For these direct manufacturing costs, decision packages can be developed and ranked extremely high if management merely wants to use the mechanics of the zero-base budgeting process to display all costs.)

However, zero-base budgeting is adaptable to all other expenses incurred in industry, even those that are closely related to the direct manufacturing operations and costs. Manufacturing support services (maintenance, supervision, production planning, industrial engineering, quality control, etc.) require an assumed level of manufacturing or production by type and volume but are still variables with specific benefits identifiable with increased expenditures. For example:

- Increased expenditures in preventive maintenance, such as replacing parts before failure, may reduce downtime of equipment.
- Variable levels of supervision can affect personnel turnover and employee productivity.
- Industrial engineering and production planning efforts can have substantial impacts on manufacturing costs.

Other service and support activities usually accounted for as overhead items at department, division, and corporate levels are justified directly on cost/benefit evaluations. These functions may include marketing, advertising, accounting and control, data processing, training, personnel, tax and legal activities, industrial relations, safety and security, research, and so forth.

Capital expenditures for facilities and equipment are also easily identified in decision package format, with the ranking process facilitated by rate of return or payback period calculations required on most sizable capital investments. Managers also have readily identifiable alternatives as to the type of equipment or facilities available, such as rental of equipment or facilities in place of capital outlay, and can vary the level of expenditures by such actions as delaying plant expansion, going to multiple shifts, rearranging current layouts to make more effective use of current facilities, slipping expenditure and completion schedules, or varying the capacity of the equipment or facility. These decision packages will usually show cash flow (purchase price) as well as the depreciation expense associated with each capital project. Capital projects can be ranked separately, or, in periods of extreme profit or cash flow problems, decision packages for capital can be merged into the rankings for all packages.

Although zero-base budgeting may apply to only a fraction of the total budget in a heavy manufacturing organization, the activities subject to zero-base budgeting techniques are usually the most difficult to plan and control and yet offer management the greatest lever to affect profits. For example:

- Service and overhead functions can be varied significantly over short periods of time.
- Expenses for research and development, capital, industrial engineering, production planning, and so on, can directly impact manufacturing technology and processes and can heavily influence direct manufacturing costs.
- Arbitrary cost reductions in the service and support functions without full understanding of the consequences involved can create severe problems, with cost savings proving minor compared to the resulting production problems and increased direct manufacturing costs.
- Marketing and research and development programs determine the future course and growth of the organization.

Management typically has a difficult time getting a handle on the service and support activities, which are usually made up of many relatively small—compared to direct manufacturing operations—and dissimilar functions that are not subject to the type of engineering analysis used on the direct production costs. Zero-base budgeting gives management an effective operating tool to use in these problem areas, which impact profits far in excess of their relative proportion of total dollars budgeted.

Government

Zero-base budgeting can be readily adapted to all government activities and agencies since government is a service organization that supposedly provides some benefit for the tax dollars spent. Zero-base budgeting was applied to all 65 budgeted agencies in the State of Georgia [health, highway, education, corrections, agriculture, public safety, game and fish, family and children's services (welfare), etc.], for a budget in excess of 1 billion dollars in state funds and approaching 2 billion dollars in total funds (state funds, federal funds, and other revenues).

IMPLEMENTATION PROBLEMS AND BENEFITS OF ZERO-BASE BUDGETING

The type of problems experienced with and benefits gained from zero-base budgeting by both industry and government are almost identical. However, there were wide ranges in magnitude of the common implementation problems, depending primarily on the capabilities of the managers involved, but with some specific problems stemming from the size and nature of each operation. Most of these problems can be eliminated or minimized by effective management of the process so that the benefits gained from zero-base budgeting far outweigh the problems experienced in implementing the process.

IMPLEMENTATION PROBLEMS

There are three general requirements for the successful implementation of zero-base budgeting or any other system: (1) support from top management, (2) effective design of the system to meet the needs of the user organizations, and (3) effective management of the system. Zero-base budgeting is a general system that can be successfully adapted to fit the needs of dissimilar activities and organizations. The one factor that can effectively kill the implementation of zero-base budgeting is lack of support from top management—because managers experience all the fears and problems of implementation before the benefits are realized. A member of the Texas Instruments Board of Directors (C. J. "Tommy" Thomsen) and the vice-presidents for the Staff and Research divisions (Cecil Dotson, Grant Dove, Jim Fischer, and Bryan Smith) provided this strong leadership when zero-base budgeting was first initiated in that organization, and Governor Jimmy Carter provided this same strong leadership in Georgia.

The implementation problems that should be expected when zero-base budgeting is introduced can be divided into three categories:

1. Fears and administrative problems.
2. Decision package formulation problems.
3. Ranking process problems.

Fears and Administrative Problems

There are four common problems that can be anticipated when the zero-base budgeting process is first implemented:

1. Managers are often apprehensive of any process that forces decision making and requires detailed scrutiny of their functions for all to see.
2. Administration and communication of the zero-base budgeting process may become critical problems because more managers become involved in this process than in most budgeting and planning procedures, and these problems are further compounded in large organizations.
3. Formalized policy and planning assumptions are often nonexistent, inadequate, or not communicated properly to lower level managers who will be preparing the decision packages.
4. First-year time requirements may exceed the time spent in the prior year's planning and budgeting that used other procedures. (Note the restriction to the first year.)

Zero-base budgeting is a decision making process. Top level managers must make decision concerning billing levels and other planning assumptions to be used by their organizations throughout the zero-base budgeting cycle; managers must (1) decide which activities and functions to develop their decision packages around; (2) identify and evaluate alternatives and decide on the best method as well as several alternative levels of effort; (3) decide on meaningful work load indicators and measures of effectiveness, and then evaluate their performance against those measures; (4) decide on the relative importance of each package; and (5) establish the budget by deciding which packages they can afford to fund or cannot afford to do without.

The zero-base budgeting requirement for decision making and establishing priorities is viewed as an extremely dangerous and upsetting process by those managers who place high priority on survival, and who have learned to survive by keeping low profiles or "keeping their noses clean." Zero-base budgeting takes away the blanket or security from these managers, identifies exactly what and how well each activity is doing, and forces some very difficult decisions. This fear of decision making and close scrutiny of all activities seems more common and pronounced in managers in government than in industry, and seems to be more common in poorly managed organizations than in well-managed ones.

Initial administrative and communications problems are experienced in large organizations because more managers usually become involved in this process than were involved in previous planning and budgeting procedures. Some of these new people involved are technicians and specialists, such as engineers, doctors, quality control managers, who not only have never been involved in budget procedures, but who have concerned themselves only with the technicalities of each activity with little or no regard for their cost and cost effectiveness. In addition, there are the normal problems of large organizations in effective communication, in auditing and controlling the process during implementation, as well as in the subsequent changes and revisions required owing to changes in assumptions or upgrading of poor quality and results. These are problems to be anticipated and evaluated before implementing zero-base budgeting, and their outcome will directly influence the extent to which zero-base budgeting will be installed in each organization the first year, and will influence the administrative procedures used to control the process and review the results.

Regardless of these problems, there are tremendous benefits to be derived from involving these additional managers in the budgeting and planning process, and the need in large organizations for a tool to effectively plan, budget, and control the individual activities is greater than in small organizations where top managers can more readily keep abreast of and judge the effectiveness of each activity.

One of the benefits of zero-base budgeting is the identification of the lack of coordination among activities and the lack of planning assumptions. However, this need should be anticipated by top management before the development of decision packages by lower level managers in order to avoid the revision of packages affected by these assumptions. Managers responsible for implementing the zero-base budgeting process within each organization need to identify both the assumptions required and any specific studies or alternatives they wish various activity managers to consider. If this is not done, three basic problems will arise:

1. Managers will make their own—differing—assumptions. To correct this problem, we must first find out what assumptions were made and then compare these to the appropriate assumptions before we know which decision packages need to be revised.

2. Coordination among related or service activities will usually be inadequate without a formal mechanism to provide and revise assumptions. In a service organization providing maintenance, materials, utilities, and so on, to manufacturing activities, the service activity needs specific information to determine the amount and cost of service it will provide. A formal mechanism for providing and revising assumptions is extremely helpful to assure this coordination, especially if the service and manufacturing activities are not in the same organization or division.

3. Many managers will not consider radically different alternatives to their current way of doing business, either because they have "tunnel vision" and will not identify these alternatives, or because they fear a personal loss of stature or responsibility if such a radical change is adopted. For example, a manager of a data processing activity in one organization might not consider the centralization or consolidation of his operation with other data processing units, either because he does not know of the existence of these units, or because he fears that his unit will be absorbed by a larger unit, which might cause him to lose his managerial status. Alternatives such as this may be identified to top management when they see decision packages from the several data processing units in which centralization has not been considered. Top management may then require the units to study the possibility of centralization or consolidation, but if such an alternative can be identified before the preparation of decision packages, the data processing managers can be instructed at that time to consider this alternative and save the revision cycle.

The first year's planning and budgeting time requirements may exceed those of the previous year because of the general problems mentioned above, as well as the fact that managers spend a good deal of time evaluating and setting priorities on current activities as well as on new activities, whereas in prior years they had only concentrated on new activities. In small organizations where the span of control and communication is reasonably short, as was the case within each division of Texas Instruments, the zero-base budgeting process need not take more calendar time than the normal budgeting cycle, although more managers will spend more time participating than in earlier years. In large organizations where the span of control and communication is long, such as in the State of Georgia, the calendar time spent in budgeting will probably be lengthened to allow for both additional communication and control time and the turnaround time required to revise decision packages because managers either did not understand the process or did a poor job of identifying and evaluating their packages.

The mention of the additional time and effort spent by managers during the first year of the process often leads to the comment that zero-base budgeting must be very costly, assuming we were to keep track of the hours spent and allocate costs accordingly. However, this would be an erroneous conclusion because the salaried managers can still do their normal jobs, as they did during the budget period in both Texas Instruments and the State of Georgia, although the additional effort did require some "midnight oil" and weekends—but this is not an out of pocket expense. Also, if we added the time spent in goal setting, operational decision making, and control to the time spent in budgeting, which is an integral part of zero-base budgeting but is often done outside the normal budget cycle, we would further reduce or eliminate any first year time difference between zero-base budgeting and earlier budget procedures.

Following the first-year implementation problems of zero-base budgeting, there is is a steep learning curve that flattens out during the second and subsequent years because:

- The administration and communications problems are gently reduced through experience.
- Managers become accustomed to analyzing their operations and tend to do so on a continuing basis rather than only during the budgeting cycle.
- Directions and assumptions provided by top management become much improved through the continuing analysis of all activities, and the number of revisions required in decision packages and rankings are therefore greatly reduced.

The second-year budgeting cycle at Texas Instruments was reduced to half the first-year calendar time, which was less than the time spent under the previous budgeting procedures. The most drastic time savings between the first and second years accrue to the managers preparing the decision packages. Less time is saved by top level managers, who must still review packages and/or summary analyses, establish priorities, and determine final funding levels among several organizational rankings competing for funds.

Decision Package Formulation Problems

Several problems are commonly experienced in the formulation stage of developing decision packages and administering the zero-base budgeting process. Six of these problems are discussed briefly below.

1.   Determining which activities, functions, or operations to develop decision packages for. This determination is truly a variable, as it depends on what is "meaningful" to the management involved in each particular organization.

2.   Establishing the minimum level of effort. This demands a judgment on the part of each activity manager, and is therefore subject to question. Establishing this minimum well below the current operating level is unthinkable to many managers, who prefer to identify the minimum level at either the current operating level or, sometimes above that level. Unless there are significant increases in work loads, or a given activity has had its budget cut substantially in previous years without corresponding work load reductions, it is hard to believe managers who claim that their minimum levels of effort could not be below their current operating level.

3.   Reducing the dollar cost in the minimum decision package while keeping people at the current level. Managers are naturally protective of their people, yet normal attrition and the shifting of people among activities will usually eliminate the need for layoffs except when major reductions are required. Although such a reduction in dollars without corresponding people reductions is occasionally justified, minimum levels should usually include people reductions. This is because there is often an optimal mix of people and associated operating expenses within an activity, and reducing the operating expense per person often reduces the effectiveness of the people. This problem is common in activities such as maintenance, where a large portion of the cost is related to material and supplies or other nonpersonnel costs; if a maintenance man is not provided with adequate materials and supplies he will lose some of his effectiveness. (When these operating expenses are added back in future budgets, a few more people are often added. Such a cycling of events can lead to an inefficient operation and points out the need for some standard for the mix of people and associated operat-

ing expenses, so that people and operating expenses are reduced or increased in proportion.)

4.   Identifying work measures and evaluation data for each activity. In many activities it is difficult or impossible to identify meaningful work measures for evaluation, and once measures are identified the historical data are often missing. At least the identification of meaningful measures usually initiates the development of statistical records for future evaluation, and the lack of work measures on any package should automatically be a red flag to raise the question of whether or not there *are* any meaningful measures.

5.   Costing and auditing packages to ensure the proper expenditure level for the proposed activity. There is a definite tendency for a manager to overestimate his costs to allow himself some leeway. However, any over-costing that is not corrected promotes loose budgets and allows the funding of other activities or pet projects not identified in the decision package. It also reduces the number of packages that can be approved for given funding levels.

6.   Emphasizing cost reductions within each activity. The ranking procedure identifies cost reductions by eliminating packages or ranking them low in relation to other activities so that they may end up below the approved budget cutoff line. However, activities and packages with high priority also have many opportunities for cost reductions, and the search for these reductions needs to be emphasized.

Ranking Process Problems

There are four common problems encountered during the decision package ranking process:

1.   Determining who will do the ranking, to what level within each organization packages will be ranked, and what method or procedure will be used to review and rank the packages.

2.   Evaluating dissimilar functions. Higher levels of management find this a problem when they are not familiar with the functions, especially when subjective judgment is required. This problem can be solved by each manager jumping in feet first and getting started. Once familiar with the decision packages and resigned to the ranking task, most managers are happily surprised to find how easy the process becomes.

3. Ranking packages considered high priorities or "requirements." Managers can easily avoid this problem by:

(a) not concentrating on ranking high priority packages that are well within expected expenditure levels, but concentrating instead on discretionary functions and levels of effort.

(b) not spending too much time worrying over whether package 4, for example, is more important than package 5, but instead only assuring themselves that packages 4 *and* 5 are more important than package 15 and package 15 is more important than package 25, and so on.

4. Handling large volumes of decision packages.

The first three problems are easily overcome with a little experience, but the handling of large volumes of decision packages in large organizations is definitely a problem and can become a tremendous burden on top management if it is not managed properly.

BENEFITS

In many organizations, the planning and budgeting process is conducted by financial or fiscal people, with only the top level operating managers participating in decision making and formulation of the budget. Zero-base budgeting requires the participation of managers at all levels of each organization. The process was designed that way because these lower level operating managers are the ones who actually spend the money to provide the services, they are the experts in their activities, and we want them to become familiar with planning and budgeting procedures and to be responsible for evaluating their own cost effectiveness. Also, top management should have the benefit of their recommendations and analyses. Therefore, the major benefits of zero-base budgeting result from the harnessing of the thoughts and talents of managers throughout each organization.

The benefits that each organization can realize from zero-base budgeting can be divided into three general categories:

1. Improved plans and budgets.
2. Follow-on benefits (realized during the operating year).
3. Developing the management team.

Improved Plans and Budgets

The most immediate benefits gained from zero-base budgeting, and the prime purpose of instituting this process, are improved plans and budgets. These result because:

1.   Identification, evaluation, and justification of all activities proposed—rather than just the increases or decreases from the current operating level—promote a more effective allocation of resources because managers have evaluated the need for each function and have considered different ways of—and levels of effort for—performing each activity.

2.   Top management has great flexibility in reallocating resources and allowing greater budget shifts among organizations because of consolidated rankings of activities and organizations. Further, the identification of different levels of effort for each activity offers the alternatives of eliminating an activity or choosing from several levels of effort for that activity.

3.   High priority new programs can be funded totally or in part by eliminating or reducing current activities.

4.   Combining planning and goal setting, budgeting, and operational decision making into one process requiring detailed scrutiny of every activity results in an integrated approach for the total organization in its quest for the most effective allocation of resources.

5.   Duplication of effort among organizational units will be identified, which can result in elimination or centralization of these functions.

6.   Lack of effective planning, and poor coordination among interrelated activities in different organizations, is readily identified, which can result in correction of these conditions.

7.   Changes in allowable expenditure levels during the budgeting cycle for major organizational units do not require the recycling of budget inputs, but once decision packages are identified and given a priority ranking, this ranking identifies which packages would be added or deleted to achieve the desired expenditure level.

8.   Revisions in assumptions during the budget cycle (billings, services required, etc.) do not require complete revision of all budgeting efforts. Instead, managers can identify which packages are affected by these changes and can then selectively revise these specific packages.

9.   Planning models or initial expenditure goals are subject to modification because managers can see exactly what will and will not be done (which packages will and which will not be approved) at those expenditure levels.

These models and goals can then be increased or decreased accordingly, with managers avoiding the problem of getting "locked-in" by models or initial goals.

10.   Managers at all organizational levels have the same basic information and analyses provided by the decision packages and rankings. Having assured themselves that the proper analyses have been made by the various activities (or having had the packages revised), top level managers should be able to concentrate more on reviewing the priorities proposed by each organization and establishing priorities among organizations and less on their own independent fact finding and analysis.

11.   Approved decision packages provide the basis for detail budgeting, control, variable budgeting in the manufacturing overhead activities, and the preparation of other documents. Zero-base budgeting does not require any change to the normal accounting or control procedures, it strengthens the data base and evaluation process from which these detailed documents are prepared, and it may result in the elimination of some procedures without any loss of control. (In the Staff and Research divisions of Texas Instruments, one such elimination was the requirement that all cost centers prepare a detail budget by chart of accounts. This elimination was possible because of the additional analysis and control provided by zero-base budgeting.)

12.   Identification to top management of the workloads and costs imposed by general policies, procedures, information requirements, legal requirements (in government), and so forth, helps top management take action to remove or alleviate the constraints imposed upon the operating managers. Managers are sometimes constrained by general policies and procedures that affect several organizations, and over which they have no direct control. Instead, they should be encouraged to develop their decision packages and rankings on merit alone, highlighting any recommended changes—such as in policy—to top management. Top management is often unaware of problems and costs associated with specific policies and procedures, or of information requirements imposed on the operating managers, and is usually eager to make any justified changes.

Follow-on Benefits

After the budgeting cycle is completed, and each organization enters into the operating year for which it has just completed its zero base budgeting, there are several follow-on benefits that managers can realize:

1. Managers have a tendency to continue to evaluate in detail their operations, efficiency, and cost effectiveness—not only during the budget cycle, but during the operating year as well. Although zero-base budgeting does not require this continuous evaluation, it is common for managers to initiate studies and improvements during the operating year because they know the process will be repeated the next year, and hopefully zero-base budgeting trains managers to continually think along the lines of the analyses that the process requires.

2. Managers can be measured against the goals, performance, and benefits to which they committed themselves, as identified in the decision packages and in their budgets. At Texas Instruments, about midway through the operating year a formal set of reviews was usually used to follow up on the progress, problems, and modifications or additions to the approved set of decision packages. These reviews also served as a good preview to the planning and budgeting cycle that began again two to three months later.

3. The ranked list of approved decision packages can be used during the operating year as a starting point to pinpoint activities to be reduced or expanded if allowable expenditure levels change. To reduce costs, managers can continue up the ranked list of packages (from the point where the budget cutoff was established) until they have identified enough packages to delete to provide the savings required.

4. Activities that are poorly operated and managed are readily identified throughout the zero-base budgeting process and any follow-up reviews, and top management can take whatever action is necessary to eliminate these problems.

Developing the Management Team

Zero-base budgeting is also an educational process that can promote the development of the management team. The identification and evaluation of each activity in the manner required by the decision package ranking processes can become an ingrained thought process, where managers evaluate their planning, operations, efficiency, and cost effectiveness on a continuous basis. Managers may also serve on committees that rank multiorganization decision packages, which produces an understanding of other activities and problems. This type of participation in the Staff and Research divisions of Texas Instruments produced a willingness in managers to reduce their own budget levels in order to fund priority activities in other organizations, thereby achieving the common goal of increasing profits by reducing costs, and also producing a better working relationship among organizations during the operating year.

Managers preparing decision packages were also encouraged to have their people participate in identifying and evaluating alternatives, workload measures, and the effectiveness of their operations. In the decision package example of Georgia's Highway Patrol, 45 sergeants from the 45 Highway Patrol posts throughout the state participated—with their Headquarters Staff—in a detailed study and evaluation of how the State Troopers spent their time, and developed recommendations to greatly improve the effectiveness of the State Highway Patrol at a substantial savings to the state. This type of active participation by managers and their subordinates at low levels in each organization, along with review and analysis by upper management levels, can achieve a high level of commitment and understanding for the approved activities, can develop a feeling of working together for the betterment of the entire organization rather than of each manager and his subordinates being interested only in their immediate spheres of responsibility.

CONCLUSION

In most organizations the benefits identified can be readily achieved and the problems can be effectively minimized so that even in the first year the sometimes painful process of decision making proves well worth the effort. However, this sometimes painful first year is followed by a zero-base budgeting process that produces much improved identification and analysis of activities and alternatives, with less time and effort expended because managers know the process and have started to orient their thinking to where the analysis of alternatives, costs, and priorities is standard practice.

Zero-base budgeting is a tool. It cannot be expected to solve all management's problems—which only management itself can do. What zero-base budgeting can do, however, is provide a tool to efficiently identify and evaluate activities and their related problems so that management can make decisions, take action to solve those problems, and effectively allocate and utilize the organization's resources.

ZERO-BASE BUDGETING AND THE MANAGEMENT PROCESS

Zero-base budgeting is more than the traditional process that produces a set of resource allocations in the form of dollar and people numbers for specified organizational units. Zero-base budgeting goes beyond these limited boundaries to provide management with an operating tool to adjust the organization to meet the need and demands of its environment. The previous sections have focused on the impact that this budgeting has on the planning and budgeting aspects of the management process. This section describes how it affects the entire management process, concentrating on the impact that it has on implementation and control, and identifies the impact that zero-base budgeting has on management's continuous effort to improve operations and profitability.

THE MANAGEMENT PROCESS

Zero-base budgeting affects all aspects of the management process, providing managers with an additional operating tool to more effectively manage their business. The four basic components of this process (planning, budgeting, implementation, and control) are an integrated series of events as illustrated in Exhibit 8. Management may be fortunate enough to operate in a relatively static environment, where the basic assumptions and planning guidelines remain constant during the planning and budgeting process and prove to be reasonably accurate as compared to the actual situation experienced during the operating year. With reasonable fluctuations in the external and internal operating environment, managers can readily adjust their operations for these fluctuations and can control any programmed modifications through allowable budget variances. However, changes in the external environment beyond some acceptable or manageable limits, or substantial internal operating problems or changes in personnel, force management to react in a dynamic environment that may continually change. In such a case management may be forced to completely revise its plans and budgets, implement major changes to current activities or establish new programs and operations, and revise its controls to meet the new operating situation and criteria.

Exhibit 8. The Management Process

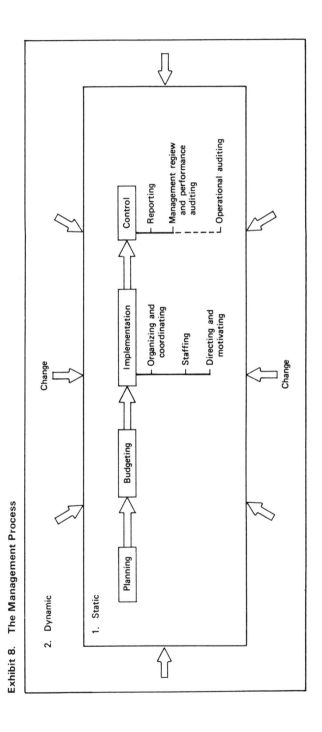

Static Environment

Zero-base budgeting provides a detailed operating plan and budget for a specified set of circumstances and a desired output. If the environment adheres to the predictions or assumptions made during the planning and budgeting process, the detailed analysis of all activities provides a roadmap for management to follow in implementing the specified plan and budget. Zero-base budgeting impacts all the elements of implementation. The process requires management to evaluate its organizational structure and to identify the interrelationships among activities and organizational units, and readily identifies the overhead costs and operating problems associated with excessively broad or deep organizational structures. The evaluation of the costs and benefits of this administrative overhead as opposed to other activities often leads to a paring or streamlining of the organizational structure to reduce costs and/or improve effectiveness. The definition of relationships between manufacturing operations and its service and support activities is essential to ensure smooth manufacturing operations, especially if volume fluctuates or the same facilities produce a variation of products (whether these fluctuations are planned or unplanned).

The organization's staffing requirements and people budgets for those activities using zero-base budgeting are determined by the summation of people numbers from the approved decision packages. In addition to establishing the number of people in each activity, the packages usually identify the types of people and general duties or activities involved. This information can aid personnel departments in determining hiring needs, establishing a "manpower inventory" of the types of people within the organization, and establishing job descriptions. Management can determine many of its staffing problems during the decision making process as it ranks the packages. Packages for current operations (and people) ranked below the anticipated funding level indicate that these people need to be transferred or laid off. Packages for new activities given a high priority indicate hiring needs or openings that can be filled internally. At the end of the planning and budgeting, top management can get a complete reading of manpower shortages and overages from across the organization and can establish its policies to bring staffing needs and availability into balance.

Zero-base budgeting also aids managers in directing and motivating employees since most managers and their subordinates will have worked together in developing and evaluating the decision packages and operating plans. In many cases, with typical planning and budgeting techniques, managers do not have the opportunity to identify operating problems and needs nor to make their recommendations to top management. Zero-base budgeting provides such a mechanism and also commits managers to a set of defined goals and objectives, performance standards, and accomplishments that they will be held accountable for. The identification and evaluation of each activity is especially helpful for managers assuming new responsibilities, since the packages and rankings provide a ready access library describing and analyzing the duties and commitments of each activity.

Zero-base budgeting allows management to hold all activities and operations to a budget as well as to the performance that each one commits to in its decision packages. The summation of approved packages for each cost center or budget unit provides the budget framework for the reporting of actual costs and budget variances. The analysis provided by each decision package is usually a much deeper analysis of a cost center (which may contain several activities or programs) than previously existed, and aids management in evaluating the reason for cost or performance variances. Typical reporting systems that indicate only cost and people variances from budget or the previous forecast can be augmented by the standard reporting of work load and performance measures for those service and support activities having readily definable measures.

Unfortunately, many of the overhead, service, and support activities using zero-base budgeting do not have readily measurable work load and performance measures that lend themselves to a standard reporting format. The evaluation and control of these activities is not determined by budget variances (which can usually be readily controlled by varying the staffing levels) but by the performance and effectiveness of these activities. Management can determine the performance and effectiveness of these activities through special reviews or performance auditing. At Texas Instruments, for example, the support organizations in the Staff and Research divisions had at least one special review with top management in addition to the normal review of budget and forecast variances to review activities in detail. With the advent of zero-base budgeting, these reviews often started with a review of the approved packages for each organization, and then proceeded with a status report on actual accomplishments versus commitment, problems, corrective action proposed or being undertaken, new programs, and changes in the environment or organizational requirements that were not anticipated in the operating plan and budget. In addition to such a review, performance auditing can be conducted by individual managers or teams of managers, or by an internal audit staff as part of their normal audit procedures.

Operational auditing is rapidly becoming a standard function in management control and is often a formal function of the Internal Auditing Department. Operational auditing aims primarily at improving operations and profits rather than merely verifying costs or evaluating performance against some standard or commitment.

Dynamic Environment

Zero-base budgeting provides a powerful operating tool for management to adjust operations and resources to keep abreast of a rapidly changing environment. Zero-base budgeting provides three assets that enable management to makes these adjustments:

1.   A well analyzed and documented base (or budget) with an existing set of priorities from which management can determine the actions required.

2.   An efficient procedure for management to follow to identify the specific actions required, including changes in the assumptions and guidelines during the planning and budgeting process, budget reductions, variable budgeting, and organizational changes.

3.   A detailed identification of the consequences of the actions taken, with the procedure assuring management that the least important activities were eliminated or reduced.

If the required changes result from cost overruns or developing new activities and programs, zero-base budgeting allows management to review the previously budgeted activities to determine if they should be reduced to provide the funding required.

Major changes implemented using zero-base budgeting techniques have the same foundation for implementation and control of the revised plans and budgets as the original process provided for the original plans and budgets. Reductions based on eliminating or revising decision packages merely revise the road map for management to follow in implementing the revised plan, and allow holding of all activities and operations to a revised budget and a revised set of work load and performance measures. The detailed reductions allow management to identify organization changes, changes in services provided by service and support activities, and the consequences of such changes. Staffing reductions are identified in detail, and the personnel department can use its manpower inventory and job descriptions to shuffle personnel among operations to minimize layoffs and keep the best people.

The negative impact on motivation and morale can also be minimized because managers can see that the reductions made were in proportion to organization priorities and needs, with each operation's goals and objectives revised in accordance with the revised budget.

THE CONTINUOUS EFFORT TO IMPROVE OPERATIONS AND PROFITABILITY (OPERATIONAL AUDITING)

No budgeting or planning system can expect to solve all of management's problems, which may be long range or deeply entrenched. Although zero-base budgeting will not provide the immediate solution to all problems, the process does provide a great deal of data and analysis that should help to surface or highlight both short-term and long range problems, and force management to reevaluate operations that may have become obsolete or inefficient over the years. The zero-base budgeting process itself is confined within a period of one to several months, while management problems and efforts to improve operations and profitability are ongoing. The formal management effort to improve operations and profitability is sometimes referred to as operational auditing, and zero-base budgeting can play a significant role in this effort.

Operational auditing is a review and appraisal of the effectiveness and efficiency of operations and operating procedures. Its purpose is to complement the normal information and control systems by supplying top management with an appraisal of operations, with emphasis on assisting management in problem solving and increasing profits by recommending realistic courses of action. Operational auditing is often confused with financial auditing because of the term auditing in its title, but there is a decided difference. Financial auditing is primarily concerned with accounting, financial systems, and control, with the main benefit to the organization being protection of assets and verification of financial information. Where this traditional financial auditing is concerned with *verification* of profits, operational auditing is concerned with *increasing* profits; where financial auditing concentrates on the *past*, operational auditing concentrates on the *future*; where financial auditing stresses *fact-finding*, operational auditing stresses *problem solving*; and where financial auditing is normally limited to *financial and control* activities, operational auditing encompasses the *entire spectrum* of an organization's activities.

Operational auditing is not an organizational entity but is an ongoing method or philosophy of analysis by management. Operational auditing may be performed by several types of participants:

1. Internal to the organization

    *   Individual managers
    *   Management teams
    *   Internal audit departments
    *   Central analytic staffs

2. External to the organization

    *   Management service and consulting firms
    *   Public accounting firms

3. Combinations of the above

The nature of each audit and the internal capabilities of each organization dictate the participants required. Because of the ongoing nature of management's problems in today's dynamic environment, many large organizations are developing permanent in-house capabilities to perform operational auditing, which may be assigned to internal audit departments or centralized corporate and/or division analytic staffs.

The need for ongoing management analyses and operational auditing is created by the arm's-length management required by decentralization in medium size and large organizations, plus the general lack of control or management indicators to identify profit potential. Management obtains the information it needs to operate and control its business in many ways. Sales forecasts, quotas, and reports enable management to assess its marketing activities; operating budgets enable it to assess the cost effectiveness of its manufacturing department; and cost control and progress reports enable it to keep abreast of day-to-day operations. Yet, whether management realizes it or not, such information developed by the normal control and communication channels may be grossly insufficient to enable management to approach optimum profitability. Top management cannot always be sure that information received is accurate and complete, and management may not realize that past inefficiencies may still be reflected in current budgets and cost standards. Nor do any of these tools necessarily measure the performance of staff and support groups or help management keep abreast of changing technology and product development.

Zero-base budgeting goes much deeper and further into operations than do other such techniques to help solve some of the problems of arm's-length management. However, in many cases zero-base budgeting only scratches the surface of a problem area or indicates that a problem may exist. Management must then employ its analytic resources to investigate in detail and resolve the problem, with the investigation or operational audit taking place during the budget process or the operating year. For example, the zero-base budgeting analysis of maintenance may indicate rapidly rising maintenance costs, unfavorable trends of maintenance costs to production volume, or an unfavorable cost comparison between a maintenance activity in one plant and a similar activity in another plant. In a large or complex manufacturing operation, the maintenance activity itself can be large and complex and have a significant impact on the manufacturing operations that is not reflected in the maintenance budget or reporting system. To investigate and rectify any deep-rooted or complex problems, management must often assign additional manpower to the task since such problems may not be completely evaluated or resolved during the normal course of events or the budget process.

In performing an operational audit on the maintenance function, management might discover that the maintenance department has a large backlog of work requests that lacked any evaluation as to need or timing; that maintenance materials were not being adequately controlled, with the result that there were excessively high inventories of many spare parts—some of which had become obsolete; that the preventive maintenance program was not adequate or well controlled, with the result that there was increased downtime and production delays; that the more expensive maintenance labor was often used to supplement direct manufacturing labor, without adequate costing or reporting, so that maintenance costs were overstated and manufacturing costs understated; and that management was not receiving adequate information about job backlogs, job cost estimates, actual job costs, and actual versus scheduled completion dates.

Zero-base budgeting itself will not uncover such detailed problems, but additional investigation into such a problem area can result in the solution required and may alter the type of zero-base budgeting and special analyses required during the planning and budgeting cycle in future years to avoid the recurrence of the problem.

The Impact of Zero-Base Budgeting

Zero-base budgeting provides management with a tremendous data base of information and analyses and can be a significant aid to operational audits in two ways:

1. Identifying problems and determining areas of potential operating and profit improvement.
2. Improving the efficiency and effectiveness of the operational audit.

Since management does not have unlimited manpower resources, it must effectively identify problems and areas of profit potential on which to concentrate its efforts, and must be able to perform the audit efficiently and effectively.

Zero-base budgeting aids managers in identifying problems and determining areas of potential operating and profit improvement by providing managers with:

- Historical cost data and performance measures for each activity.
- Comparisons of similar activities across the organization.
- Identification of goals and objectives, organizational structure, and functional relationships among activities that may create or impact on a given problem.
- Alternatives (that were rejected by the operating managers who prepared the decision packages) that warrant further investigation, or obvious alternatives that were not identified or evaluated by the operating managers.

Zero-base budgeting is especially useful for centralized staffs in large organizations who can readily scan the decision packages and rankings from across the organization in their search for profitable audit areas, and can do it at a level of detail not usually available from any other source.

After management has determined the problem areas that warrant further attention, there are six steps that are usually performed in making the operational audit:

1. *Preaudit research.* Information gathering before the start of the actual audit to provide data about the area to be audited and the current state of the art, and to help determine the scope and procedures of the audit.

2. *Familiarization.* Information gathering to clearly establish the existing objectives, operating methods and procedures, operating problems, and relationships and constraints imposed by other activities or management policies.

3. *Verification.* Determining accuracy and completeness of reports, compliance of operations with existing procedures, and sampling and gathering of operating data to determine the effectiveness and efficiency of operations.

4. *Evaluation.* Determining what the operating objectives and procedures should be to produce the greatest impact on profits and operating effectiveness.

5. *Recommendation and reporting.* Summary of audit findings, specific changes recommended, and the anticipated impact of the changes.

6. *Postaudit analysis.* Follow-up to determine if the audit recommendations were implemented, produced the desired results, or require modifications or further investigation.

These basic steps will normally be followed by assigning an individual or group of individuals to evaluate and report on the problem area, with the exact nature of the effort varying with the nature of the activity audited and the background and expertise of the individuals performing the audit.

Zero-base budgeting can be a significant aid to the individuals performing the operational audit since it can impact all audit steps:

Audit Step	Impact of Zero-Base Budgeting
1. Preaudit research	Zero-base budgeting provides a ready-made reference library for managers undertaking an operational audit. The decision packages for a period of several years can be reviewed for the specific operation being audited, for similar operations in other parts of the organization, and for other activities that may influence or be influenced by the operation being audited. This research will include a more detailed evaluation of the information that led to the audit, and may indicate areas of additional research relating to specific practices, management or control techniques, and state of the art.

Audit Step	Impact of Zero-Base Budgeting
2. Familiarization	Decision packages define the objectives and interrelationships of the activities for the operation being audited, describe the nature of each activity, and identify costs and performance measures for each activity. This information provides a framework to which the auditor can add detailed information and operating procedures, and from which he can identify other meaningful performance measures not displayed on the packages.
3. Verification	Decision packages identify specific costs, benefits, and performance measures against which actual data can be compared at a functional level and detail not available in most reporting systems. The operational audit offers a separate and independent appraisal of operations and can be used to verify management reports as well as decision package information on which the budget was based.
4. Evaluation	Evaluation is a continuous process that begins when the auditor is looking for potential audit areas, so zero-base budgeting affects evaluation in the ways, already mentioned (such as comparing costs and performance of similar activities). In addition the data base provided by zero-base budgeting makes it easier for the auditor to identify operations outside his initial audit scope that are affected by any proposed changes in general policy and procedures, and to evaluate the impact that any recommended change in policy and procedures will have on all operations. Decision packages will sometimes identify excellent alternatives that were rejected by individual managers because they felt constrained by existing practices that they did not control. These practices can be challenged by the operational audit.
5. Recommendation and reporting	The decision packages and rankings provide a well-defined framework from which recommended audit changes can be explained to and evaluated by top management, changes in costs and performance can be compared, and any resulting cost and performance improvements incorporated into the budget and control systems.

Audit Step	Impact of Zero-Base Budgeting
6. Postaudit analysis	Zero-base budgeting offers a natural reporting and update process, with the decision packages in years subsequent to an audit reflecting changes (or lack of changes) brought about through the audit recommendations. Centralized audit staffs, or division or corporate managers, can readily keep tabs on many operations over a number of years.

Zero-base budgeting therefore allows management to perform a more effective audit by directing the auditor's attention to the most promising audit areas, and allows the auditor to be more efficient since he would be forced to develop much of the information and analysis himself that he is handed by the zero-base budgeting process.

CONCLUSION

Management is faced with the problem of coordinating a broad scope of dissimilar activities such as those illustrated in Exhibit 7. These activities must be balanced to ensure effective and efficient operations, which indicates the need for centralized coordination and direction. However, management is also faced with operating problems that are complicated by several factors:

1. Increasing size, diversity, and complexity of organizations.
2. Wide geographic dispersion.
3. Rapidly changing technology.
4. Increased sophistication and specialization of technology.
5. Diverse product lines or services rendered.
6. Increased need for specialized services in taxes, banking, health, environmental control, investor relations, purchasing, data processing, and so on.

These factors, as well as lengthy lists of problems specific to each organization, create the need for decentralized operations, with increased delegation of responsibility and arm's-length administration and control exercised by top management. Zero-base budgeting meets management's divergent needs for centralized coordination and direction with decentralized operations and all it includes. Zero-base budgeting is a top-down, bottom-up, top-down planning and budgeting process:

> *Top-down* because top management must determine the goals and objectives of each major organizational entity and establish the general operating guidelines and expenditure levels acceptable in achieving the objectives.
>
> *Bottom-up* because the operating managers responsible for each activity have the opportunity to evaluate their own operations and recommend a course of action to achieve the organization's objectives.
>
> *Top-down* because top management can take the recommendations and priorities established by the operating organizations, make any desired changes, and allocate the organization's resources accordingly.

Zero-base budgeting can aid management in developing a fully integrated control system that:

1. Establishes clear-cut goals and objectives.
2. Measures progress toward those goals and objectives.
3. Indicates positive action required if performance deviates from plan and budget.
4. Displays potential for further improvement.

Zero-base budgeting requires that macroeconomic goals and objectives be established for the organization, then proceeds to define the microeconomic goals and objectives for each activity. It provides both budget and performance measures as well as operating objectives, so management's control and reporting systems can indicate both budget and performance variances. These variances at the budget unit or cost center levels can be evaluated in detail by analyzing the several activities and series of decision packages from which the cost center's budget and performance capabilities were determined, and can therefore help pinpoint the specific action required that might affect only a few of the activities performed. The detailed evaluation of performance measures is especially important in the overhead, service, and support activities applicable to zero-base budgeting since budget variances for these operations are poor indicators of performance. Zero-base budgeting also aids management's operational auditing efforts by identifying problems and areas of potential operating and profit improvement as well as improving the efficiency and effectiveness of the operational audit itself.

Perhaps the greatest long-range impact that zero-base budgeting will have on improving management effectiveness will result when the basic philosophy and analytic procedures become ingrained in management's thinking, or psyche. Webster's dictionary defines psyche as "the mind considered as an organic system reaching all parts of the body and serving to adjust the total organism to the needs and demands of the environment." After going through the zero-base budgeting process several times, many managers will get in the habit of evaluating alternative ways to solve a problem, considering various levels of effort, and evaluating the relative importance and priorities of problems and needs competing for attention and limited resources—not only during the formal planning and budgeting process, but during the operating year as well, as they are faced with changing situations.

The purpose of this chapter has been to identify the significant operating tool and impact that zero-base budgeting can provide to all levels of management in both industry and government, and to identify the flexibility and adaptations available so that each organization can adapt zero-base budgeting to its own particular needs. We hope that the discussion throughout the chapter leads to the conclusion that:

Zero-base budgeting is a practical management process and a part of the psyche that extends beyond the range of typical planning and budgeting techniques to impact all segments of the management domain.

"The need for effective zero-base budgeting is increasingly obvious not only in industry but in government as well."   *Peter A. Phyrr*

CHAPTER 10

COST REDUCTION BEGINS WHERE COST CONTROL ENDS

JOEL L. ROTH

"Cost control utilizes standards as goals to attain. Cost reduction, on the other hand, continually challenges these goals in a relentless effort to achieve lower and lower costs."

In most of my memory industrial cost reduction efforts were limited to cyclical efforts by individual companies, generally in a crash, one-shot program that was later abandoned as the crisis passed or the need for publicity disappeared.

But in the last few years there has been a startling transition. Not only companies, but entire industries have become uncompetitive from a cost point of view. Two obvious examples in recent years were consumer electronics and textiles. And in fact, the problem of cost inefficiency or cost noncompetitiveness has gone beyond the cyclical or occasional stage. It has become a permanent and growing trend. In fact, we're approaching the point where entire nations have become noncompetitive in cost. Again a rather obvious example of this is what has happened in Britian in the last ten years or so.

This condition of cost noncompetitiveness has led to the many economic problems and policies in the United States' monetary revaluation, wage-price controls, volatile capital flows, and cost-push inflations. So we're talking about more than a one-country problem or a one-company program.

Most sizeable companies today probably devote considerable time and effort to cost accounting and cost control. But, unfortunately, in today's business climate the ability to reduce costs and not just control them has become absolutely essential in order to prolong product life and to maintain existing markets as well as to achieve new ones. For example, without the element of cost reduction, there probably would be no color television market as we know it today. And the initial success of the Ford automobile undoubtedly resulted from Henry Ford's ability to bring unit costs down to a level affordable to a large number of families. Similarly, convenience alone would not have caused the housewives in recent years to switch from cloth napkins and cloth towels to disposable paper ones, unless the cost had been reduced to make paper an attractive alternative. (It is noteworthy that recently escalating costs of such products may eventually reverse the trend for the same reasons.)

In order to distinguish clearly between the two terms—cost control and cost reduction—I'd like to redefine them. In classic terms control, according to the standard textbook definition, is the measurement and correction of the performance of subordinates to assure the accomplishment of your organization's or department's directives and plans. This control implies the existence of goals and plans. In the case of cost control, the plans are the operating budgets; the measurement is the accumulation of cost data through time keeping records, vouchers, and so on. Measurement is the comparison of operating costs against budget or, in other words, the generation of variance reports. That is the classic control definition that most are quite familiar with.

DISTINCTION BETWEEN COST CONTROL AND REDUCTION

Ideally control is forward looking. And the best kind of managerial control anticipates deviations before they occur. If that is not possible, the next best method is to detect variations as they occur and take immediate corrective action.

Cost control is concerned with maintaining costs in accordance with established standards, whereas cost reduction is concerned with reducing costs. It challenges all the standards and endeavors to reduce them continuously.

Second, the standards in the case of cost control are targets to shoot at. But in cost reduction the standards are suspect. Cost control emphasizes the past and present, but cost reduction emphasizes the present and the future. We usually limit cost control efforts to items that have standards. But in cost reduction we apply our efforts to every section of the business, whether or not standards exist.

In cost control we seek to attain the lowest possible cost under *existing* conditions. But in cost reduction we recognize no condition as permanent, since a change in conditions can result in a lower cost. (For instance, coal is once again becoming cost-competitive with oil and natural gas.)

In both cases, cost control and cost reduction, we have a state of mind. In this respect they're similar, although we're talking about a different attitude. And finally, cost control is never finished. It is a continuing function; however, cost reduction can be finished because it's essentially a project-type approach.

These, then, are some of the common distinctions between cost control and cost reduction.

Example of Cost-Reduction Approach

A company engineer using motion time analysis (MTA) set a standard for an eyelet press operations of 3 hours per 1000 pieces at a base wage at that time of $2.50 per hour. Under the cost control approach, as long as the direct labor costs for this particular operation did not exceed $7.50 per 1000 pieces, the operation was considered to be under satisfactory control. A cost reduction approach, on the other hand, might lead a change in the machine speed, manning, tooling, tolerances, or materials to permit the standard to be reduced to $2\frac{1}{2}$ hours per 1000 pieces or $6.25 per 1000. We now have a lower standard. And the cost accounting department, having adjusted the standard cost sheets, will remain quite satisfied as long as the direct labor costs of the operation do not exceed $6.25 per 1000 pieces.

Within this traditional cost control framework we're content to aim at this existing standard based on the past and present production method, namely the eyelet press. But in applying the cost reduction approach, we find that by putting the part on an automatic screw machine we can reduce our direct labor cost to $4.75 per 1000. Again the cost accounting department changes its standard cost sheets. However, those cost reducers never quit, and they're back for another look this year. And they find that the ±0.0005 in. tolerance on this part is overdesigned. It's tighter than required for product reliability. So we change the specs to ±0.005 in. and direct labor cost becomes $4.00 per 1000.

Going further still, the cost reducers look at another lower cost solution. They find that the part can be made as an injection molded plastic part in the plastics department at a cost of $2.75 per 1000. Let's suppose at this point that somebody fails to notify the cost accounting department—which happens. They are not aware of the change in method, and their standard direct labor cost remains $4.00 per 1000 pieces. Every week the plastics department variance report shows a favorable (or plus) variance against the recorded standard. And manufacturing supervision is happy. But the cost reduction team takes another look at the part, and finds it can be purchased from an outside supplier at a delivered price of $2.00 per 1000. We could carry this example ad infinitum, but the point is already evident. From a cost control viewpoint, we would have been satisfied with a direct labor cost of $7.50 per 1000 pieces. But the cost reduction approach would not accept that given standard, so the cost was materially reduced.

It's ironic that management has devoted considerable attention and resources to the problem of cost control. Such common corporate activities as general accounting, budgeting, cost accounting, industrial engineering, and even data processing, to some extent, have been devoted to the cost control methods and techniques. But in many organizations, comparatively little effort has been expended on cost reduction, particularly on a continuing full-time basis. Yet as we have illustrated, even the best cost accounting and cost control system can do no more than maintain the status quo. In today's economy, the status quo is just not enough.

In other words, a company with good cost control is not necessarily cost efficient. Starting with that premise, how do you determine where to concentrate your cost reduction efforts? Let's assume you have a given level of financing requirement—$2 million. Let's suppose, however, that you can find a way to squeeze some excess cash out of your operations. Conceivably you could reduce your dollar financing requirements even though the interest rate at this given point is a constant amount in the marketplace. You can reduce your interest costs by reducing your financing requirement.

Over the years my work has taken me into almost every facet of business activity. I have seen cost reduction successfully achieved in virtually every facet of business—from taxes to direct labor—from selling expenses to utility costs. However, the amount of cost reduction that can be achieved is related to the characteristics of the given cost, and to the amount of management effort devoted. Accordingly, a point of diminishing returns can be reached where the cost of additional effort outweights the potential savings. It's obviously unwise to concentrate on a relatively minor cost element while excessive major costs go unchecked. Therefore, it becomes essential to identify those areas where cost reduction efforts should be concentrated.

TWELVE IDEAS FOR SPOTTING COST REDUCTIONS

Now I'm going to discuss briefly some cost techniques that I have found to be quite useful over the years. This is not to say that these are the only cost reduction techniques, or even necessarily the best ones.

Major Versus Minor Costs

The first is what I call major versus minor costs. Any business organization, whether it be manufacturing, extractive, financial, or commercial has a distinctive cost structure or cost profile. Such a cost profile commonly expresses every cost element as a percentage of sales dollars or cost of sales. It's obvious that where we have labor and raw material costs aggregating two thirds of the total factory cost, it's rather fruitless to concentrate efforts—let's say on insurance, which is 0.1 of 1 percent of factory cost. The emphasis should logically be on manpower and raw materials. Many companies spend a lot of time and effort on minor items while excluding major cost areas.

Pareto's Principle

The second thing I find useful to keep in mind is the vital few versus the trivial many, more formally known as Pareto's Principle of Maldistribution, but which we commonly call the 80:20 rule. The economist Pareto observed at one point that wealth is distributed through society in such a way that a small percentage of the population controls a very large proportion of wealth. This principle can also be applied to a business organization in many different ways. For example, a small percentage of orders accounts for a large percentage of revenues. A small number of customers accounts for a large percentage of production. The same concept can be extended into virtually every department or operation. For example, most standard work can be attributed to a few operators, or a few machines. Most equipment maintenance can be attributed to a few machines. Most purchasing dollars could be attributed to a few materials, and so on.

Controllable Versus Noncontrollable Costs

The third concept for identifying cost reduction opportunities is controllable versus noncontrollable costs. At any given level of an organization the manager has control over certain costs, but no influence at all over other costs. Accordingly, he has to learn to distinguish between the controllable costs and concentrate on reducing those, rather than wasting his efforts on cost factors that he cannot influence.

I'm not suggesting that some costs are noncontrollable and, therefore, must be tolerated at their existing level. *It is axiomatic that every single cost element is controllable at some level of the organization.*

If the cost is not controllable by a manager at one level, then it's controllable by someone up the line. For example, a foreman can control and reduce downtime in his department, but he has virtually no influence over personal property taxes. But the controller or the treasurer has substantial impact over personal property taxes, but probably very little impact, if any, on building occupancy expense. The president can make an impact on building occupancy expense by deciding to relocate the plant to a lower cost area, or through some other similar management decision.

Every cost is controllable at some level of the organization, and it becomes important to direct management's attention at that level to the cost that it can control.

Fixed Versus Variable Costs

The fourth technique is recognition of cost behavior—fixed versus variable expenses. Managers generally think of variable expenses as controllable and fixed expenses as noncontrollable, and, therefore, they think of variable expenses as susceptible to cost reduction and controllable expenses as relatively irreducible. Actually, expenses in the fixed categories, which generally are regarded as not susceptible to cost reduction, can in fact, be made to behave like variable expenses from the viewpoint of cost reduction.

Let's take three examples of expenses that you would normally consider fixed, and see how they can be converted into variable, reducible costs. Building depreciation is generally included in factory overhead, and regarded as fixed at a given location. However, this expense can be regarded as variable with geography. The cost or occupancy cost for a given building can vary by as much as 100 percent between different locations.

Take a second illustration: maintenance labor. The maintenance department payroll for craftsmen such as millwrights, tinsmiths, riggers, plumbers, and electricians generally bears little relationship to production volume, yet these costs can be made to behave like a variable expense. For example, one of our plant managers complained bitterly about the high cost and low productivity of a nine-man painting group in his maintenance department. We found a reliable industrial contractor who was hired only when needed, reducing our painting crew to two men. Not only did we achieve substantial economics, but the painting contractor was willing to work on evenings and weekends, thereby removing any disruption from our production and office operations. Therefore, we took a fixed cost, the painting crew, and converted it to a variable expense.

A third example is general office clerical payroll. Office payroll varies even less in relation to production volume than does the maintenance payroll. Yet, here again, a fixed cost can be changed to a variable cost. For instance, one of the insurance companies instituted an "apron shift" that allowed local housewives to work at clerical jobs on an hourly basis. These ladies would arrive at 10 or 11 o'clock in the morning and go home at 3 or 4 o'clock in the afternoon, thereby allowing them to meet most of their family responsibilities. Not only did the office payroll decline with volume, but this approach also alleviated problems of a tight labor supply for full-time workers. And moreover, we found that these hourly workers, because they did work shorter hours, were substantially more productive during their shorter working day; again, a fixed expense was converted to a variable one.

Unit Costs

The fifth technique is that of unit costs, a phrase you've heard many times over the years. But it's one of the most useful indicators of cost reduction potential. Bear in mind that the fixed unit cost of a product, that is, the fixed portion of the unit cost, is variable with volume. And the variable unit cost is fixed with volume.

The fixed costs, since they are fixed, will vary per unit depending on the level of volume. The variable costs are constant per unit, by definition. What does that mean? Certainly it means that sound cost reduction is obtained when we can achieve greater productivity from an existing production unit, whether it be man, machine, or building, or when we convert unused productive resources to usable ones. Remember, as productivity goes up, the fixed unit cost will decline and the variable unit cost will remain the same. Consequently, the total unit cost will also decline.

Let me illustrate it with an example encountered a few years ago in a gray iron foundry, which had a bottleneck in the molding operations due to a lack of both manpower and space. It's very difficult to get mold-making labor, or any labor, to work in a foundry. Through an industrial engineering study of the flow and layout of the foundry, we were able to recover about 15 percent of the foundry area by storing flasks, molding boards, and other materials outside the building, and by changing pattern storage practices. Through an anlysis of product and customer mix, we found that small, intricate castings with a lot of core work took almost twice as much labor as large, simple castings with very little core work. Therefore, by reducing the amount of core work—the number of small, intricate castings—we found that we could convert a great deal of core-making labor and space to mold making. In doing so we freed substantial manpower for mold making, and accomplished two things simultaneously: first, we increased productivity, and, thereby, lowered our fixed unit costs of building and equipment because we had more revenue going through the building by a factor of almost 2:1. And second, we shifted our product mix toward higher margin business.

Static Standards

The sixth technique is static standards in budgets. A study of existing standard costs would generally reveal that there are some figures that haven't changed for years, or have changed very little. This often suggests that a particular cost or operation has not been closely scrutinized for some time and, perhaps, should be reevaluated. In one plant not long ago we found that a material standard on a rather volatile-priced material, had not been changed for five years. Obviously someone wasn't looking at the standards for that operation.

Budget Variances

The seventh point concerns excessive or continuing variances. Variances from standard, as shown in periodic variance reports or operating statements, can be significant indicators of cost reduction potential. For example, a continuing negative labor variance, if analyzed properly, can be traced, perhaps, to excessive overtime. This, in turn, may lead to the installation of new equipment, addition of more manpower, or a change in production scheduling techniques. It should be noted that a positive variance, or a gain variance, is just as important to analyze as a negative variance. If an operating manager has found a methods improvement, for example, and lowered his cost, that change may be applicable elsewhere in the company.

Profitability Analysis

Eighth is what I call a profitability measure of each business segment. It's continually amazing to me how few business managers demand or receive a regular income statement or return on investment evaluation of the various key components of their business. For example, how many sales vice-presidents get a gross income statement by branch, by distributor, by salesman, by product line, by territory, or by customer? My experience is that few get this, or request it. How many plant managers have a balance sheet or a return on investment measure of the major product lines going through their plant, where they produce a number of different product lines in the same plant? Again, an amazingly large number do not get or request this kind of information.

Illustrative of this is a forgings manufacturer who produced both standard or stock pipe fittings and nonstock or special pipe fittings. Both product lines were produced in the same plant on essentially the same equipment. We conducted a return on investment analysis of the two lines and found that the stock items accounted for over two thirds of the net investment in that plant including working capital, partly due to heavy slow-moving inventories, but less than one third of the pretax income. Conversely, the special items provided more than twice the profit on less than half the investment.

In another company that comes to mind there were five unrelated product lines aggregating $10 million dollars in annual sales. Although the company did not maintain internal product income statements, an estimate of product line performance was made. We found that one of the five lines had lost an estimated $3.5 million dollars over the preceding eight years. It also represented a disproportionately high amount of total investment. It seems to me that if you want to reduce costs, it's pretty important to know that. And, again, it's amazing how many managers don't have access to such information about their operations.

Make Versus Buy

Ninth is the make-versus-buy decision. Although this technique has been very well publicized, many companies just do not avail themselves of it. Too often management attempts to produce everything possible "in-house" in the belief that such a practice will increase burden absorption, when, in fact, it may be more economical to reduce the burden than to absorb it. I've always felt that putting maximum volume through a plant, for example, to maximize burden absorption is a very defensive approach to business. It's really going about the problem backwards. Why not reduce the burden, instead of trying to absorb it? I can think of a manufacturer, for example, of electromechanical products who maintained a sizeable production machine shop and other fabricating operations, even though they operated on an average of about 15 percent of capacity. He also maintained a sizeable parts inventory since the cost of a setup, in some cases, justified three years of production. We found that by having the engineers do minor redesign of many of their components to standard industry practices, many of these parts could be purchased directly from suppliers and distributors at lower cost. As a result the machine shop and the fabricating departments were virtually dismantled, and the parts inventories were cut sharply. Not only were costs lowered, but management is now concentrating on what its business really is—electrical products design, assembly, and marketing—and not trying to run a metal fabricating operation.

Standardization

Tenth is standardization. As in make-versus-buy decisions, the technique of standardization is well-known but not so often practiced. Any company that has numerous or lengthy bills of material, for example, is probably a condidate for standardization analysis. One example, perhaps the most dramatic one I can think of on this score, is a machine tool manufacturer whose models were designed from the ground up. This created tremendous burdens in design engineering, in delivery times, in manufacturing setups, in inventory levels, in parts replacement, and so on down the line. But a switch to modular or building-block design concepts, using standardized components and subassemblies, attained dramatic reductions in costs and improvements in service, which was equally important in this case.

In a different framework, a large commercial and consumer finance company negotiated separate automobile purchase loans every time a customer walked into an office. They developed unique contract terms and conditions on each occasion, eventually leading to 84,000 different automobile financing contracts. An analysis of these contracts suggested that every one of them could be handled within one of 12 standard contract conditions or terms. The result is a fantastic potential reduction in paperwork processing, in clerical labor, and in data processing costs.

Intracompany Pricing

The eleventh technique relates to transfer, or intracompany, pricing, otherwise known as "spare the sacred cow." Numerous companies, in an attempt to use the profit center concept, mislead or distort their internal operating results. Transfer pricing is often based on arbitrary or artificial management policies, resulting in depressed results for efficient profit centers and inflated results for inefficient operations. I can think of a metals mining company, for instance, where all of the mines were treated as a profit center, and all the concentrates from these mines were consumed within the company for its own mills and smelters. Mine revenues were computed on the basis of prevailing, comparable market prices. So long as the mines, in aggregate, showed a profit, management was well satisfied. But investigation showed that four of the mines in this company were extremely costly and inefficient, since the ores could be purchased on the open market far cheaper than they could be produced in these particular mines.

The management of a fabricated metal products company adopted a practice of selling from its plants to its warehouses at standard cost plus 20 percent. Thus the loss variances were transferred to the warehouse, and market discounts were taken at the warehouse, effectively insulating the high-cost plants from management view.

Competitive Analysis

The last point I'd like to make in this particular area of cost reduction techniques is that of competitive analysis. A great deal of insight can be gained from public and quasi public information about your industry or competitive companies within your industry. For example, many industry groups prepare operating ratio statistics and other data, as does the IRS, Dun & Bradstreet, and a number of other services.

To illustrate, a natural resources firm was spending about $3.5 million a year on research and development (R & D) with less than spectacular results. An analysis of their competitors' financial statements revealed that the company had a much higher ratio of R & D expense to profits than did other more successful companies in the industry. This led to a critical review of the R & D function. As a result, the budget was cut to a $1.5 million a year—less than 50 percent, and the efforts of the R & D laboratory were redirected. Perceptible progress in penetrating new markets was evident within a year.

A cosmetics company was losing money steadily. Analysis of the registration statements, prospectuses, 10-Ks, and other data available on some of the more successful companies in the industry quickly revealed that the company's cost of sales were in line with more successful competitors, as were their direct sales and administrative expenses. However, other selling expenses such as promotion, demonstrators' salaries, and other selling costs were double what other companies were experiencing. This led to a pruning of the customer mix, a revision of promotional allowances, and an alteration of trade channels.

I don't suggest that these 12 techniques for identifying cost reduction potentials are the only techniques we could discuss. You could perhaps list another 50 to 100 techniques. These are 12 of the more common and successful that I have seen applied. However, I believe that the number of techniques available for effective cost reduction is really limited only by your own imagination.

"In spite of the benefits to be gained from cost reduction, many companies deprive themselves of these benefits because their efforts are made on an intermittent basis."   *Joel L. Roth*

RETURN ON INVESTMENT—PROFIT PLANNING

The return-on-investment concept of measuring profitability is relatively new in terms of the number of years that accounting has been practiced. It came into more popular use within the last 25 years.

It seems surprising that widespread use of this type of measure should be so long in coming. There are several reasons contributing to the general adoption of the return on investment concept in evaluating business performance.

- Accountants no longer shun this measure in preferance to the traditional percentage of sales.
- The size of the investment has grown substantially since World War II.
- Stockholder pressure.
- Pressure from financial institutions who want to monitor the company's progress.

The major part of investment is made up of capital items, receivables, and inventory, which will be dealt with in the section on asset management. Although profit planning deals with making a profit on sales as well as managing assets, this section is intended to deal principally with the return-on-investment concept.

PROFIT PLANNING THROUGH COMPUTERIZED SIMULATION

Preparation of the annual business plan (profit planning), if properly done, is a major task requiring much time and a good deal of management attention. Generally, the "first cut" raises questions that require revisions to the plan. Questions that arise are due to new developments that have occurred and must be provided for, need for modification of facilities to accomodate the plan, or an indication that the plan is overoptimistic.

Making the necessary revisions to the business plan requires substantial clerical effort. The author makes the point that although computer technology has advanced greatly in recent years, it has not been utilized adequately in this very important area. Michael Tyran describes the steps to be taken in financial decision data development. He includes in his discussion not merely the computerization of the profit planning approach but also the building in of various action alternatives.

HOW RETURN ON INVESTMENT CAN BE IMPROVED THROUGH COST ANALYSIS

Measuring return on investment is one thing but providing the reasons for deviating from plan is an important adjunct to the control procedures. Leonard Kamsky, the author of this chapter, provides a series of graphs that demonstrate the development of manufacturing variances, earnings as a percent of sales, investment turnover, and return on investment. A recap summarizes the change in sales volume, profit margin, and return on investment, followed by an explanation of the reasons for deviations.

HOW AN INVESTMENT BANKER LOOKS AT PROFIT PLANNING

An investment banker can be helpful to a company needing additional funds by assisting it in obtaining capital at minimum cost. However, to be helpful, the banker must have a good "feel" for the company's business and its problems. The management of the company would be well advised to recognize this and work with the bank representative to give him the best possible understanding of the business.

Richard Hexter recognizes this need and goes further in other recommendations that will result in a better return on investment for the company. He speaks of underutilized assets and emphasizes the importance of overcoming this—a circumstance that is tantamount to overcapitalization. On the subject of acquisitions he notes that many companies acquire the new company first and then start their profit planning—when it is too late to reverse the decision to make the acquisiton.

SUMMARY

There are two variables involved in obtaining an acceptable return on investment. The first is the level of profitability through efficient operations. The other is the amount of investment in capital items, in receivables and in inventory. The first is usually given a fair amount of visibility while the second often is neglected. For this reason the next section concentrates on the important subject of asset management.

CHAPTER 11

PRESSURES ON MANAGEMENT FOR PROFITS

THOMAS S. DUDICK

"The professional manager of a publicly owned company is subjected not only to the normal competitive pressures of the marketplace—he is also pressured by the stockholder who demands an optimum return on his investment even though he may have unwisely purchased his stock at too high a price. This chapter reviews some of the steps that can be taken to improve return on investment."

Konrad Lorenz, the Austrian physiologist, in his book *On Aggression,* points out that the modern way of life is a kind of grotesque overdevelopment which violates Nature's laws by continuing growth patterns even though such growth can harm man. The hectic pace of modern men is really not necessary, for they could take things more easily—so goes the theory. Actually, though, slowing down the pace is virtually impossible. Konrad Lorenz further observes that economic and technical overdevelopment in our modern-day society causes many to be subject to the so-called "managerial diseases"—heart attacks, high blood pressure, ulcers, and neuroses.[1]

   The professional manager of a publicly owned company is particularly vulnerable to such pressures—not just because of the normal competitive forces, which in themselves are difficult, but because of pressures exerted by the stockholders for profits. This pressure becomes particularly strong at stockholder meetings when the results for the preceeding year are reviewed.

   Another facet that makes up the profile of the stockholder is represented by the group whose interest in the company is limited to the desire to obtain

---

[1] David C. Anderson, "Policy Riddle: Ecology vs. the Economy," *The Wall Street Journal,* February 2, 1970.

an optimum return on stocks owned. It matters little to this investor that he may have unwisely purchased his stock at unprecedented peak prices due to a temporary market advantage that the industry or company enjoyed. He still demands that the company meet dividend payments that furnish an optimum return on his investment on overpriced stock.

Since the number of stockholders is usually large, there is always a pool of available critics who voice dissent at stockholder meetings and apply unreasonable pressures on managements already preoccupied with problems created by the forces of competition (not to be confused with those who play a useful devil's advocate role). This stockholder unwittingly plays the role of distractor—thus playing into the hands of competitors by diverting the attention of management from matters requiring its undivided attention. As profits deteriorate, pressures on management increase.

THE POORER THE PROFITS THE GREATER THE PRESSURES

Each segment of management quickly becomes conscious of the importance of showing a good profit—not only for annual report purposes, but for interim statements, which become the measure of progress during the year.

Marketing managers strive to book a large order just before the figures are issued to reflect their efforts at making a contribution. Sometimes the large order is, in desperation, taken on a marginal basis—it increases the sales volume but does little for profits. As a consequence, competitors quickly respond with their own price reductions, so that subsequent orders must likewise be taken at depressed prices; fueling a cycle of price reductions that generate a downward trend of profits in the entire industry.

BORROWING FROM THE FUTURE

A fairly common practice is to work feverishly at the end of month to expedite the shipment of everything possible—even to the point of borrowing from next month's shipments in order to meet the budget commitment.

A new management, crusading to clean up the "mess" left by the previous management purposely overdoes the job of writing off costs in order to provide itself a "cushion" which can be drawn on to make the coming year look good. Actually, this can be a misleading ploy.

HOW PROFITS CAN BE IMPROVED

Managers will probably always be plagued by such pressures as:

- Stockholder demands.
- Competitive price erosion.
- Difficulty in obtaining firm sales forecasts to facilitate proper planning of production.
- Frequent interruptions of production schedules to accommodate changes requested by customers.
- Restrictions by the financial officer of the company that prohibit building of inventories during lull periods in order to reduce the peaks.

The nightmares that a professional manager experiences usually find their root in declining profits. Often the condition that caused the declining profits is entirely beyond the control of the manager; it may be a situation being experienced by the entire industry—overcapacity, for example. While there is little that can be done in such circumstances, there are certain positive steps that can be taken in many instances. The professional manager should focus his attention on:

- Proper product pricing practices.
- Equipment utilization.
- Control of inventories.
- Knowledge of costs.
- More realistic planning.

Because of their importance, each step is explored in greater depth.

PROPER PRODUCT PRICING

There is too great a tendency to substitute gimmickry for common sense—particularly in an important function such as pricing products. The marginal contribution concept, which determines how much of the sales dollar is left to cover fixed costs and profits, after accounting for the direct costs of a product, is a very useful analytical tool. But it can be badly abused when used for pricing.

The danger in using the marginal contribution approach in pricing products is that recovery of fixed costs in the selling price is arbitrarily determined—without regard to the actual investment in facilities required to make the product. The risk lies in the frequent assumption that these costs are there anyway so why bother to associate them with a specific product.

It would be far more logical to determine fixed cost recovery using the same assumption used in justifying purchase of the facilities in the first place. If a purchase of equipment was based on the use of a machine for two full shifts at 80 percent utilization, for example, then this is the basis that should be used in establishing the cost of the product.

In determining the material cost, the price used for purchased material should be based on economical quantity purchases. Spoilage, likewise, cannot be excessive. Labor, similar to material, must be reasonable efficient.

Market prices do not include a subsidy for inefficiency. Therefore, costs must be based on efficient operations. These costs should then be used as standards to measure performance. Variations from "standard" provide a guide as to how far actual costs are deviating from those costs used in setting the selling price.

IMPROVED EQUIPMENT UTILIZATION

The previous section referred to justification of the purchase of equipment if it could be used for two full shifts at 80 percent utilization. It follows, then, that there must be some monitoring of the actual number of hours the equipment is productive. In many highly automated operations, if equipment utilization is high, labor and material usage efficiency falls in line. In such instances it may not be necessary to maintain detailed records on labor and material.

There are four basic guidelines that should be followed in maintaining utilization of equipment and facilities at an optimum level. They are:

1. *Keep tooling in good condition.* Upon completion of each job, make certain that tools are inspected prior to placing in the tool crib. Any tool that requires sharpening should be sharpened before being placed in the crib in order to be certain that production won't be held up when the tool is required again. Don't try to squeeze through with an unsharpened tool to save time. You'll only have to rework the parts.

2. *Reduce delays in making first piece checks.* Have some backup

people available to make first piece checks when several machines are idle awaiting the results of the test. These can be employees drawn from other assignments at peak periods. Unless you do this, you are liable to have several expensive machines lying idle for hours.

3. *Monitor the quality of production closely.* Reduction of spoilage automatically increases equipment utilization. It reduces waste motion and thereby lowers costs. Spoilage reports should not be mere statistics accumulated for the purpose of making analyses at some later date. Properly prepared spoilage reports give a clue to the reasons for spoilage. Also, watch the returns from customers as a clue to inherent defects in the product.

4. *Keep material flowing.* Avoid bottlenecks in the flow of material through the processes—this always means downtime. Also, keep an eye on the backlog of material at incoming inspection. If there is a delay in processing these items, it could mean subsequent delays all through the plant.

KEEP INVENTORIES UNDER CONTROL

Inventory represents a sizable investment in most companies. Return on investment can be improved by exercising proper controls over inventories. Here are two guides:

1. *Make production changes wisely.* The general manager of one company had a habit of cutting off production of an item abruptly without letting the various parts on the floor be assembled into a finished product. As a result, a great many subassemblies and components had to be returned to stock—some never to be used again, some so fragile that they were certain to be damaged. The best rule to follow is to run everything through to completion. If this isn't feasible because the end product has become obsolete, then give serious consideration to scrapping all items not usuable in the near future.

2. *Integrate the accounting system with production control.* Frequently, accountants develop their own independent set of inventory records and reporting procedures. this results in a duplication of record keeping, which can be expensive and confusing.

Since the production control department is responsible for seeing to it that products are properly scheduled through the factory, their records should be used as the basis for accounting. Actually, the accounting department should place dollar values on production control records.

KNOW YOUR COSTS

It frequently happens that a company or division of a company operates for the first 11 months of the year at a profit only to find at physical inventory time that profits were only phantom profits because the inventory was not being properly relieved. This happens when input into inventory is based on actual costs incurred, but relief is something less than input because of unreported spoilage. During the months in which this underrelief of inventory was taking place, profits were being overstated. At physical inventory time, the required adjustment to the inventory meant that the overstatement of profits had to be adjusted—a circumstance that can be a nightmare to any production manager.

The recommended approach to correcting a situation such as this is to establish standards for the various items made. The input into inventory should be based on the net good production multiplied by standard values. Basing input on net good rather than gross production minimizes the possibility of a phantom profit that must later be corrected. The use of the same standard value for relief of inventory assures that input and output values match.

MORE REALISTIC PLANNING

Forward planning sometimes implies that the past is dead so why look back. Actually, it is characteristic of companies and managements to make the same mistake over and over again. A searching look at the past can frequently be quite revealing. Future planning can be directed to avoid repetition of certain experiences that have proved to be expensive in the past.

SUMMING UP

No human being can do his best work while under great strain; these strains, unfortunately, accelerate in direct proportion to the deceleration of profits. The manager of a business is therefore hard put to reverse the trend of profits. While there are admittedly some situations that he can do nothing about, there are some positive steps that can be taken. These are:

- Improve the utilization of equipment, thereby improving return on investment.
- Keep inventories under control. This reduces the investment and results in an increase in the return on investment, the favorite measure used by the stockholder.
- Make sure your cost system gives you correct costs, thus avoiding phantom profits.
- Profit by mistakes of the past. When you plan ahead, make sure you take a backward look.
- Don't resort to gimmicks in pricing your products. Base your costs on normal volume levels and efficient operations. If you do this, your prices should be competitive and you will be able to use these costs to measure performance.

"It is characteristic of companies and managements to make the same mistake over and over again. A searching look at the past can frequently be quite revealing."   *Thomas S. Dudick*

CHAPTER 12

PROFIT PLANNING THROUGH COMPUTERIZED SIMULATION

MICHAEL R. TYRAN

"Manual preparation of the company's business plan does not allow time for testing alternative courses of action—so necessary in our highly competitive business community."

Although computer and information processing technologies have advanced significantly in the past few years, appropriate management attention has not been accorded to its potential in the management decision making process. Manually prepared annual budgets and long-range planning data development still remain a horrendous clerical effort that is inflexible to the tempo of changing plans and the needs of management to effectively test their "what if?" and "what happens?" courses of action. A detailed annual budget or long-range forecast, however prepared, involves a mass of data needed to support an intelligible and valid plan that will fulfill the requirements of management's decision making as well as for future comparative reporting of actual results. It is a time-consuming effort, and many functional (grass roots) organizations are involved in the preparation of the projected plan of operation.

FINANCIAL PLANNING CRITERIA

The decision making process involves a number of considerations that will appropriately reflect the anticipated future operational environment. Examples of major planning ciriteria utilized in the forecasting process are listed below:

1. Level of effort
2. Market prospects
3. Sales risk
4. Economic conditions
5. Products/service sales
6. Investment
7. Profits
8. Performance
9. Break-even point

Projected sales volume would govern the level of effort to be required to meet the needs or, on the other hand, the level of effort could be the controlling factor in determining sales potential, particularly on cost-plus contracts or service function performance.

Dependent on the product and the known experience associated with it, performance would indicate the learning curve factors to be used or, in new product development, estimated learning parameters. Performance results of the past are the basic and logical references for projecting future anticipations, and market prospects are a significant criterion for predicting new business volume and sales potential.

A study of anticipated economic conditions is another guideline in the projection process, particularly when it can be associated with its direct effect on an organization's growth, stability, financing, profitability and return on investment.

A decision as to the type of product or service to be offered or exploited in the future plays an important role in an organization's planning operation. The decision could very well govern the requirement for different skills, equipment, facilities, location, financing, and other related considerations.

BASIC PROBLEMS

After the detailed data, based on premised ground rules, have been prepared and summarized into the primary financial schedules, they are forwarded to management for review and approval. More often than not, changes are required because of the following considerations:

1. New developments have occurred since the start of the planning and development process cycle.

2. The results generated often indicate that the projected manpower dictates a need for facility expansion or contraction, which may or may not be practical or desirable due to cost and financing plus other associated considerations.

3. The sales values might indicate that the manpower requirements are either too large or too small to accomplish the projected activity or that they may not be realistic in terms of anticipated business and/or economic conditions. The government budget spending or a competitor's new product development could also very well influence an organization's marketing position.

4. The profit from operations might indicate a too-optimistic outlook or, based on past experience, management may choose to make it conservative as a "hedge" on possible or anticipated future business conditions.

5. The generated overhead could indicate that changes are required due to competitive influences on the net income. Further, it could very well be a management decision to establish cost control goals that represent lower expense projections than historical experience has indicated.

Any and all of the above factors could very well influence management to make revisions of the projected plan. Under the manual environment, approval and implementation of changes were made at the summary level of the plan. But they were generally not reflected in detail until sometime later on a "time available" basis. This procedure can be aptly classified as the "cart before the horse" detailed plan implementation.

PLAN CHANGING PROCESS

Testing alternate courses of action manually is a tremendous task. It takes a considerable amount of time to rework the complete plan each time a change has been initiated and to have it reflected throughout the detailed projected data. Further, there is no capability for comparing a forecast development plan starting with manpower projections to cost and sales value buildup with sales projection translated into terms of the attendant costs and manpower requirements. In other words, the comparison of these two approaches cannot be readily reconciled manually to test the validity of the detailed data. If this capability were available it could provide a means for revealing certain major inconsistencies between the two development techniques.

WHAT SHOULD BE DONE

In order to improve and change the environment, it is necessary that organizations design, develop, and implement a computerized process for developing and improving their budget/forecasting procedures. Mechanization of the planning process is a necessity, particularly in the larger, more complicated organizations. This is not to imply, however, that smaller organizations should ignore this type of capability. Mechanization would provide timely, detailed, and summarized projections for analysis and for satisfying the revision processing needs. Flexibility and timeliness, also, are major goals for decision guidance, and the preparation of a financial and operating action plan. At General Dynamics, Pomona Operation, we are completing the development of a computerized forecast/simulator model that will provide capabilities for mechanical projections and a rapid means of testing alternate courses of action.

DESIGNING THE MODEL

In order to develop an effective and appropriate projection model, the usual considerations outlined below are common to most system designing efforts:

1. Data requirements
2. Manual procedures
3. Participating organizations
4. Degree of sophistication
5. Level of process
6. Organization structure composition
7. Assessment of historical data
8. Specific flow and data interface

Development Criteria

Exhibit 1 displays the considerations involved in a financial plan data flow and various interfaces that exist. In the development of a projection and decision making model, detailed flowcharts should be prepared in addition to the overview shown in Exhibit 1. This is necessary in order to determine the most logical approach to the development of data from its initial source to the summary levels. The model should provide for the following types of input:

1. Projected direct manpower levels by organization/contract.
2. Time phased hours by period.
3. Sales forecast of deliveries.
4. Lag timing of the invoice issuance, payment, cash receipt.
5. Projected other income and expense.
6. Indirect manpower forecast or projected percent indirect to direct by organization and contract.
7. Direct and indirect labor rates or a correlation formula.
8. Planned fixed asset acquisitions and depreciation factors.
9. Simple identifiers and location codes.

Computer Processing

Based on the input and program instructions, the computer performs the various mathematical requirements. If the direct and indirect manpower values are given, they are combined for a manpower loading schedule. If the indirect manpower is a ratio to the direct, then it is applied to the direct headcount to produce the indirect headcount and the total manpower requirement. The total manpower is then converted into hours through a projected hours per period application. An overtime factor is applied to obtain overtime hours both for the direct and indirect totals. The total of the straight time and overtime hours results in total hour expenditure.

The hours are priced through straight time and overtime rate application to obtain the total labor costs. The costs then flow to various accounts and processes such as overhead (indirect labor), earned payroll as an accrual and disbursement, as well as to inventory and cost of sales. The payroll dollars are also involved in the price of the sale, which, in turn, is reflected in the receivables and cash receipt processes.

Direct material can be projected by various means. It can be a direct input, rate per direct labor hour of effort based on historical data correlation, percentage of direct labor plus overhead, and so on. Exhibit 2 indicates some of the possibilities and how the data is processed in a forecast or "gaming" model.

Exhibit 1. Organization Financial Plan Data Flow

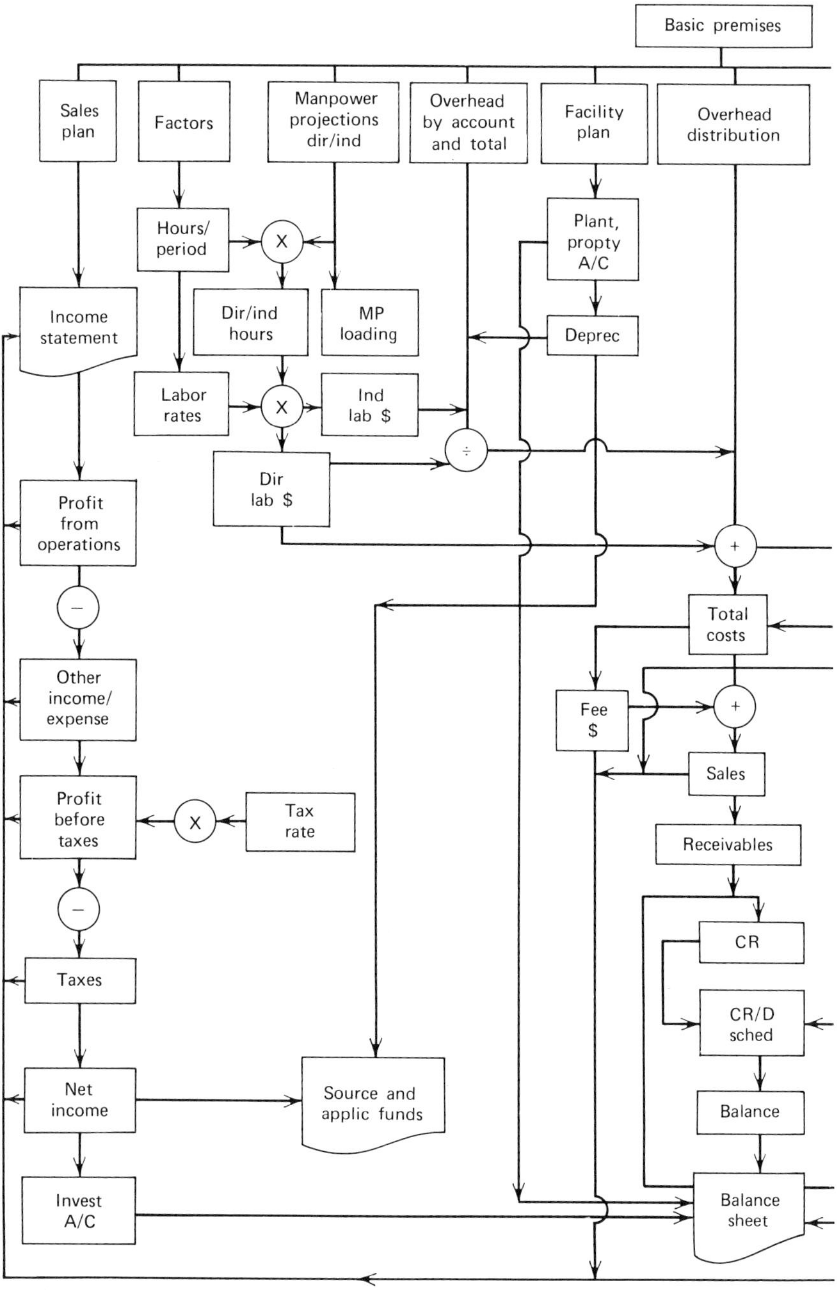

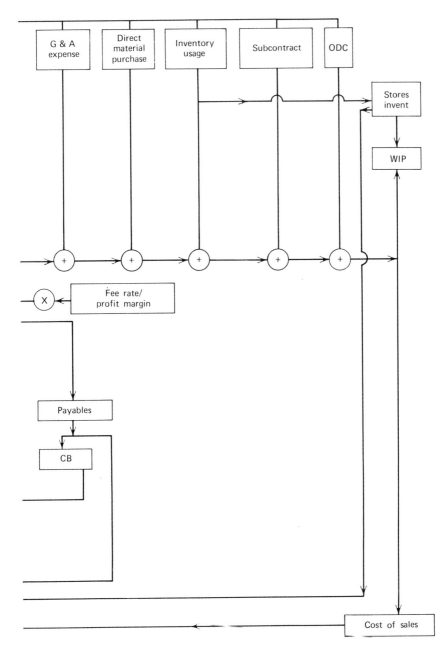

212

Exhibit 2. Direct Material Projection Model

A	Basic data by period
1	Total material by contract
2	Detail material by contract
3	Direct labor hours
4	DL/overhead costs
5	Sales value
6	Total costs

B	Factors/correlations
1	Material rate/DL hour
2	Percent LD/overhead costs
3	Correlation of material detail to total
4	Percent factor of detail to total (including S/C)
5	Subcontract as percent of sales
6	Material percent of total costs
7	Percent factor of detail to total (excluding subcontract)

Input

Manipulation

| A1 | Sum A2 | A3 × B1 | A4 × B2 | B7 | A6 × B6 | A5 × B5 | B3 | B4 |

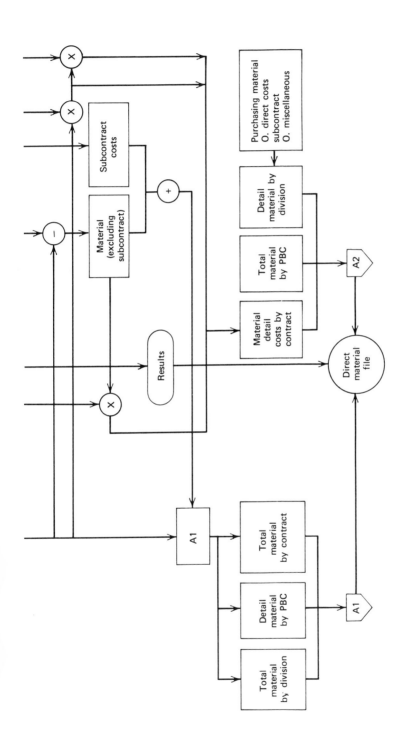

213

The method to be used is dependent upon the organization's knowledge of what is its most reliable projection criteria. In standard products, the material dollars are fairly accurately known from past experience of production costs. In new product areas, this element of cost is the most difficult to predict—at least initially. The subclassifications of overall material costs can be percentaged from the total or possibly derived through another means such as "subcontract costs" projection as a percent of total costs or sales volume, and so on. The material data is projected by contract and product line, organizational budget centers, and division totals.

Overhead costs can be generated through various means. If the overhead rate has been established by management, it is applied to direct labor hours or dollars to obtain the total overhead expense. The control account values can be a function of experience, data factoring or may be through the use of correlation formulae. For example, indirect labor can be generated from manpower projections as mentioned above. And fringe benefits are generally correlated to total headcount and an appropriate formula developed to be used in the mechanical process.

Supporting indirect supplies and material are usually associated with level of effort to be expanded. Direct labor or total hours can be used for the projection formula.

Travel and communication expense is based, as one alternative, on the headcount projections—the premise being that the more people you have, the greater expense is incurred in telephone costs, travel, publications. The testing of other related independent variable data will reveal the best correlation to be used.

Other business expense, which includes memberships, contributions, and professional services, is correlated to total headcount, although some of the specific detailed acounts within this classification could be a direct input based on past experience or planned expenditures.

Fixed charges are generally predeterminable. Depreciation is based on gross property owned and the facility projection plan, which also includes the depreciation method formula to be used. Taxes and rentals are based on past experience assessments and known changes to occur in the future relative to current actuals.

Total overhead has a definite correlation to direct labor hours or dollars. The regression analysis technique is typically used and it can be adjusted from period to period based on projected events in order to reflect unusual and anticipated deviations in specific time periods. The following formula can be used as a method for segregating the fixed and variable overhead values after the total overhead has been determined:

$$F = B - \frac{(A - B)}{(C/D - 1)}$$

where F = Fixed expense
    A = Maximum expense
    B = Minimum expense
    C = Maximum percent of activity
    D = Minimum percent of activity

A variable rate check is computed at several levels of labor values in order to prove the validity of the formula. If a reasonably constant variable rate per direct labor hour or dollar is not achieved, then the two remaining alternatives are direct input of fixed expenses or use of the regression analysis formula.

The general and administrative expenses are usually associated with rate per direct labor hour or dollar, or they are projected as direct input by the organizations concerned. This category of expenditure includes selling, advertising and miscellaneous administrative expenditures.

Disallowance rate per direct labor hour is predicated on historical experience and customer negotiations. It is reflected in government cost plus fixed fee contract projections. In fixed price contracts and commerical endeavors, disallowance type expenses are an ordinary reduction to income as a business expense.

FINANCIAL PLAN OVERVIEW

Assuming that the basic data has been developed as described above, the next consideration is to summarize it into logical segments of data for financial management reporting. Exhibit 3 illustrates a simplified flow of data to its subsequent utilization for fixed price and/or commercial business.

Consideration must be given to the segregation of data as to current "in house" contracts or sales orders, anticipated follow-on business, new product development, or potential sales and special projects. As shown on this exhibit, the costs are summarized into a finished product inventory. A gross margin percent is applied to obtain the profit amount, and this value totaled with costs represents the sales price. The sales price is associated

Exhibit 3. Overview of a Commercial Business Product Cost and Sales Data Flow

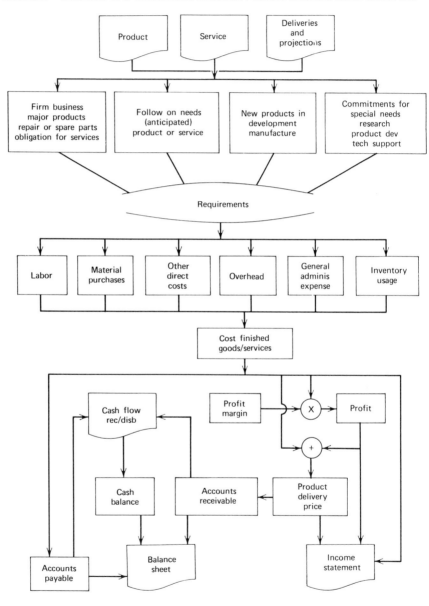

with units of delivery and an average price per unit is established. The flow of data affects various account classification values and schedules involved with cash flow, receivables, payables, and investment.

DECISION-MAKING PROCESS

When the projected plan is completed, it is forwarded to the responsible management for review, approval, and/or change. Some of the governing considerations used in making the overall evaluation of the plan are as follows:

1. Return on sales
2. Cash liquidity
3. Inventory turnover
4. Working capital
5. Age of receivables
6. Facility expansion/contraction
7. Backlog
8. Return on investment

Management must make a determination whether the sales volume is realistic in terms of supplemental knowledge of future events and projected backlog. Is the return on sales too high or low? Is the return on investment in line with past performance? Will the working capital be sufficient to fulfill the operating requirements? Will cash be a problem thus involving financing needs? Each organization undoubtedly has established what it feels are the governing criteria for the projected plan evaluation. These considerations are the result of management's judgment, experience, and the direction in which they decide to proceed for the projected period. The output from the forecast model would highlight, specifically, the summary data to be reviewed with a comparison to prior period actuals as an aid in the decision making evaluation process.

FINANCIAL DECISION DATA DEVELOPMENT

Exhibit 4 provides an insight as to how a "gaming" model would operate in the development of various data. As illustrated in the exhibit, there are four

Exhibit 4.   Financial Decision Data Development

		Input			
		Alternative A	Alternative B	Alternative C	Alternative D
a	Dir Manning	×	×	—	×
b	MP Hour Factors	×	×	×	×
c	% Ind/Direct	×	×	×	×
d	% Overtime	×	—	—	×
e	Wage Rates	×	×	×	×
f	Fee %	—	—	×	—
g	Overhead Rate	×	×	—	—
h	Disallowance %	×	—	—	—
i	Tax Rate	×	×	×	×
j	Cost of Sales %	—	×	—	×
k	G & A Rate	×	×	×	×
l	Oth Inc/Exp	×	×	×	×
m	Sales	—	×	×	×
o	Correlations	×	×	×	×

Input/Computer Developed Output

A	Manpower				
	A1 Direct	Input (a)	Input (a)	$B1 \div b$	Input (a)
	A2 Indirect	$a \times c$	$a \times c$	$A1 \times c$	$a \times c$
	A3 Total	$A1 + A2$	$A1 + A2$	$A1 + A2$	$A1 + A2$
B	Direct Labor Hours				
	B1 Straight Time	$b \times A1$	$b \times A1$	$C1 \div e$	$b \times A1$
	B2 Overtime	$d \times B1$	—	—	$d \times B1$
	B3 Total	$B1 + B2$	$B1$	$B1$	$B1 + B2$

alternatives in this particular model. However, it does not mean that these are the only alternatives that can be used. The main purpose of this capability is to provide management with the flexibility to test alternate courses of action mechanically, based on certain premises and/or changes to input or developed data. This exhibit indicates that the output is computer generated when an input is provided. These alternatives reflect the processing sequence involved with a given input and/or change to the initial projection.

The alternatives discussed are fairly representative of changes that concerned levels of management may want to make in order to finalize their

		Input/Computer Developed Output			
		Alternative A	Alternative B	Alternative C	Alternative D
C	Direct Labor $				
	C1 Straight Time	$e \times B1$	$e \times B1$	$E1$	$e \times B1$
	C2 Overtime	$e \times B2$	—	—	$e \times B2$
	C3 Total	$C1 + C2$	$C1$	$C1$	$C1 + C2$
D	Sales	$F + E$	Input (m)	Input (m)	Input (m)
E	Cost of Sales	$E1 + E2$ $+ E3$	$j \times D$	$D - F$	$j \times D$
	E1 Direct Labor $	$C3$	$C3$	$E -$ $(E2 + E3)$	$C3$
	E2 Overhead	$g \times E1$	$g \times E1$	$o \times E$	$E -$ $(E1 + E3)$
	E3 Matl/O Dir Costs	$o \times C3$	$E -$ $(E1 + E2)$	$o \times E$	$o \times E$
F	Gross Profit	$E - G$	$D - E$	$E - G$	$D - E$
G	General—Admin.	$k \times E1$	$k \times E1$	$o \times H$	$k \times E1$
H	Total Costs	$E + G$	$E + G$	$D \div 100\%$ $+ f$	$E + G$
I	Fee Dollars	$D - H$	$D - H$	$D - H$	$D - H$
J	Disallowances	$h \times C1$	—	—	—
K	Profit fr Opns	$I - J$	$F - G$	$F - G$	$F - G$
L	Oth Inc/Exp	Input (l)	Input (l)	Input (l)	Input (l)
M	Profit Bef Taxes	$K +/- L$	$K +/- L$	$K +/- L$	$K +/- L$
N	Prov for Inc Tax	$i \times M$	$i \times M$	$i \times M$	$i \times M$
O	Net Income	$M - N$	$M - N$	$M - N$	$M - N$
P	% Inc to Sales	$O \div D$	$O \div D$	$O \div D$	$O \div D$

financial plan. The data developed in this particular decision model is then reflected in the cash schedule, balance sheets and other appropriate reports. Changes in various inputs provide varying results in the Summary of Operations Schedule.

A general description and/or objectives of the varying action alternatives and what they propose to do is summarized below.

Alternative A

Given, primarily, the *manpower, overhead and G and A rates and fee* input, the major objective is to develop the *sales value* from *cost and fee buildup* and, in turn, reflect the data flow through the profit and loss schedule. Since *disallowances* are used in this alternative's input, it can be assumed that this procedure is primarily tailored to cost-plus-fixed-fee (CPFF) type of activity for developing a P and L schedule. Fixed price and/or commercial business do not reflect disallowances in the manner shown on this exhibit, but rather are considered as a reduction to profits.

Alternative B

Given, primarily, the *manpower, sales, cost of sales as a percent of sales, overhead rate and fee* input, the objective is to develop *total cost and its composition* by elements of cost. Since the fee rate is given, profit is "pegged" with the forced cost difference being reflected in the *material* cost value.

Alternative C

In this instance, *sales, fee rate, and cost correlations* are an input, and the objective is to obtain *total costs and the elements of cost* forcing the difference into *direct labor dollars*. The direct labor dollars are also mechanically converted to hours and manpower.

Alternative D

In this alternative, *sales, cost of sales percent, G and A rate,* and *correlations* are a direct input and the objective is to develop *fee dollars*. The *overhead dollars* are forced because of a developed and projected cost of sales value.

Another version of the decision model is reflected in Exhibit 5 which indicates the effect of changes as a result of revisions to manpower. For example, an increase or decrease in direct manpower would influence a revision probably to indirect manpower and, in turn, to overhead dollars, cost of sales, payables, and cash disbursements. It would affect the number of direct labor hours and dollars and labor costs that are part of the cost of sales and accrued payroll account. The return on sales and investment could very well be affected because of resulting changes in profit values.

In the same way, sales revisions could influence either costs or profits or both. Further, the effect of the change would be reflected in inventory, de-

Exhibit 5. Effect of Changes to Projected Data

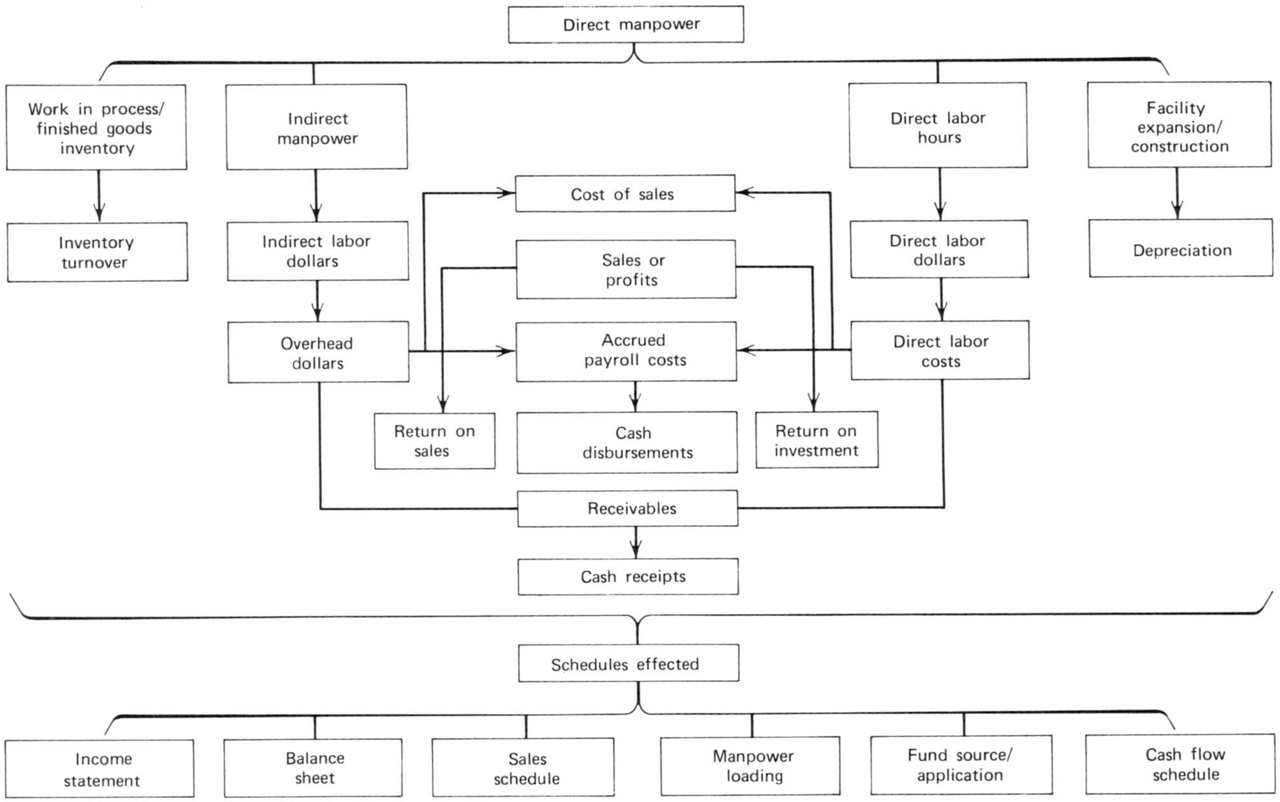

Exhibit 6. Overview of Data Interface

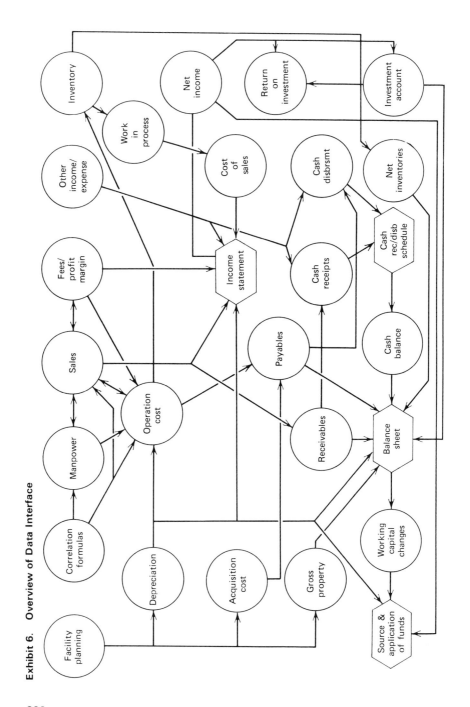

livery price, and, possibly, facilities. The specific financial schedules that would be affected by revisions are:

1. Income statement
2. Balance sheet
3. Sales schedule
4. Manpower loading
5. Fund source and application
6. Cash flow schedule

The interface of financial data flows shown on Exhibit 6 further demonstrates the need for establishing a forecast/decision model in order to take advantage of simultaneous multiple and reporting information updating, which can only be achieved by computerized processing.

CONCLUSIONS

In the discussion above, it has been indicated that a properly constructed forecast model can be used to develop mechanically the requirements of financial and operating projection plans. The decision table provides a capability for making changes and having this information reflected in various financial schedules.

This forecast technique provides the means to achieve the following benefits:

1. A rapid means of making projections with minimal clerical effort.
2. Detailed as well as summary information.
3. Improved accuracy in data development since it is all mechanically generated from one input source.
4. Opportunity for management to make various assumptions and to test alternate courses of action based on any change to the basic premises, with resulting data for finalizing the projected plan of operation.
5. The capability for management to change summary data and have the revisions reflected in the supporting detail.
6. A means for frequent interval up-dating of the plan resulting from changing business environment and/or management prerogatives of direction needs caused by internal and/or external influencing forces.

7.   An online "gaming" capability through remote terminal devices thus bypassing card and tape input, reflecting changes which delay output results.

"Although computer and information processing technology has advanced significantly in the past few years, appropriate management attention has not been accorded to its potential in decision making."

Michael R. Tyran

CHAPTER 13

HOW RETURN ON INVESTMENT CAN BE IMPROVED THROUGH COST ANALYSIS

LEONARD KAMSKY

"Cost accounting and financial analysis are closely related and can be of great value to the profit-minded executive."

The phenomenal growth of American industry during recent decades is in a very substantial sense the fruit of cost accounting and related activities. This is not idle boasting. Cost accountants perhaps more than any other professional business group have uncovered opportunities for profitable investment. But I am not interested in reviewing the past. I am more concerned with the future, specifically with means by which the tools of cost accounting can be more effective. This requires improved techniques and salesmanship. In both there is a need for a broader approach which will contribute more directly to management planning and action.

First, as to the techniques of cost accounting, these have been carefully developed over the years. We have had for some time now a scientific body of facts and procedures that enjoys a degree of acceptance hardly thought possible a short time ago. Standard costs and cost variances are a part of the operating executives' everyday vernacular. This acceptance places a very heavy responsibility on the cost accountant. He is the controlling force, from a cost standpoint, in the attainment of a satisfactory rate of return on the investment that the stockholders have made in the company. It is in this sense that the activities of cost accounting and financial analysis are closely related and can be of great value to one another. It is essential that a system be developed to integrate the results of a good cost accounting system into the financial analysis of the entire company's operations, and with respect to each of the company's major products, using a series of charts. I would like to examine the elements of such a system.

SIX USEFUL ANALYSIS AND TREND CHARTS

Financial analysis and trend charts have to be readily understood if they are to be of any value. Bearing this in mind, the charts must be presented in a nontechnical manner and should contribute to the principal concern of management, that is, return on investment. The subject of the first chart exemplified here is operations planning (Exhibit 1). This is the first step in selling a financial analysis procedure to operating managements. As can be seen, all the elements of operations are examined in relation to return on investment. Costs are analyzed as they contribute to profit margin which, in turn, related to investment turnover, yields return on investment. The relevant formulae are

$$(1) \quad \frac{\text{Profit}}{\text{Sales}} \quad \times \quad \frac{\text{Sales}}{\text{Investment}} \quad = \quad \frac{\text{Profit}}{\text{Investment}}$$

(2)   Profit Margin $\times$ Investment Turnover = Return on Investment

It is imperative that the financial group in a company draw attention to the interrelations portrayed on this chart. There is no danger of attaching undue significance to a cost variance in any category if, in our thinking, we follow logically through to the return on investment impact as shown here. The system provides the key to the way in which cost accounting can fulfill its broad objectives. Thus, in the analysis of variances, the cost accountant is clearly impelled to the examination of, not only the actual cost elements but sales and production volume and size of investment as well, leading to the very broadest concern with matters of production capacity, inventory control, production scheduling, and capital planning. Now let us take the formula and see how it applies in an actual case. The rest of the charts have been prepared to prove a point. They do not relate to any particular company but relate to specific operating problems found in many companies.

Exhibit 2, entitled Manufacturing Costs, is a charting of manufacturing operating variances. The straight line across the middle represents allowable costs at actual volume. Excesses over allowable are plotted as percent bars above the line and favorable percents in relation to allowable are plotted

Exhibit 1. Major Elements in Operations Planning

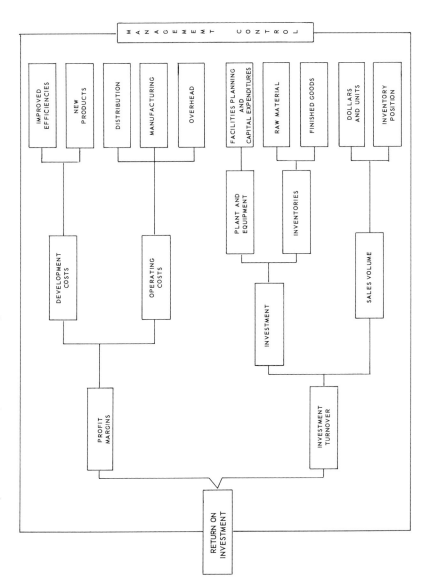

Exhibit 2. Manufacturing Cost—Actual Versus Allowable

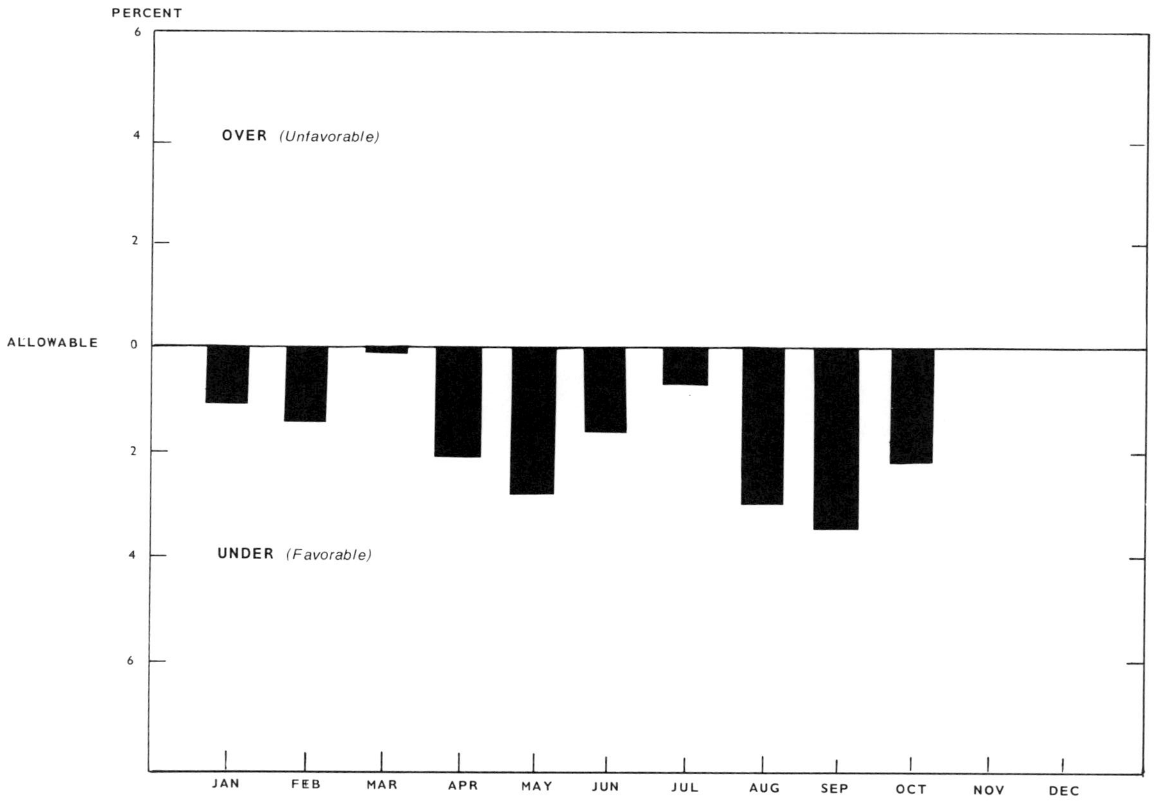

under the line. It appears that the experience every month of the year was favorable. Management had reason, certainly on the surface, to be proud of its performance, but the cost accountant will not have done his job if he stops here. Follow through another step in the system of analysis, to profit margin. Exhibit 3 shows earnings percent of sales monthly and on a twelve months moving average basis. Let us look at both lines—monthly to read current performance, the moving average to gain a better appreciation of the underlying trend. Both appear healthly and give reason for management to have a very real sense of satisfaction.

But now look at what was happening to Investment Turnover (Exhibit 4) while variances were favorable and profit margin was increasing. The sales-volume-to-investment-ratio was going down. In simple language, this meant that the company was paying a higher price for the business it was doing. Instead of $1.95 sales for each dollar invested, it was getting only $1.71. On balance, the combination of lower variances and higher profit margin but lower turnover, resulted in a less favorable position with a decrease in return on investment (Exhibit 5).

The Operations Review (Exhibit 6) sums it all up. For the first seven months of the year, volume was roughly $45 million which, considering the decline in general business conditions, was not considered unfavorable as compared with the same period the year before. At the same time, the profit margin increased from 11.1 percent to 12.1 percent. However, return on investment, the measure of operating success, fell from 21.7 percent to 20.7 percent. This resulted primarily from an increase in the investment base from $30 million to $35 million. In other words, with lower costs and higher profit on sales and with volume maintaining a relatively stable level, the result was unfavorable, because the company was not getting a satisfactory return from the extra $5 million that had been put into the business. Exploring the matter further it was found that both plant and working capital had increased.

INTEGRATING ALL PERTINENT FACTORS IN PLANNING AND CONTROL

There is nothing mysterious or complicated in the proposition that profit, sales, and cost savings must be measured in relationship but, in our modern age of specialization and large-scale operations, we sometimes lose sight of some of the most important and fundamental concepts. The danger is

Exhibit 3.   Earnings Percent of Sales

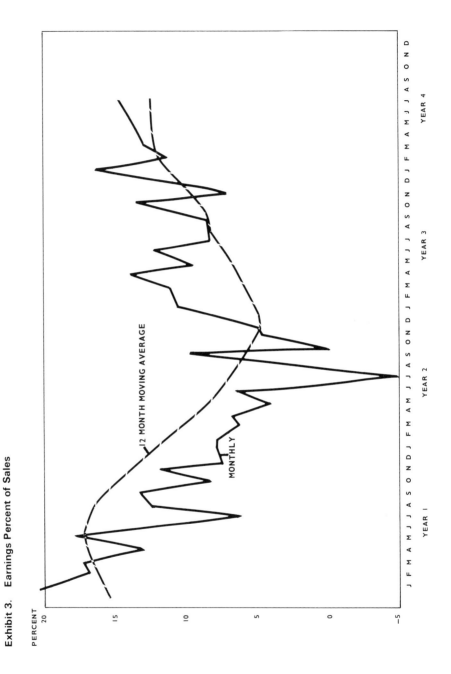

Exhibit 4. Investment Turnover

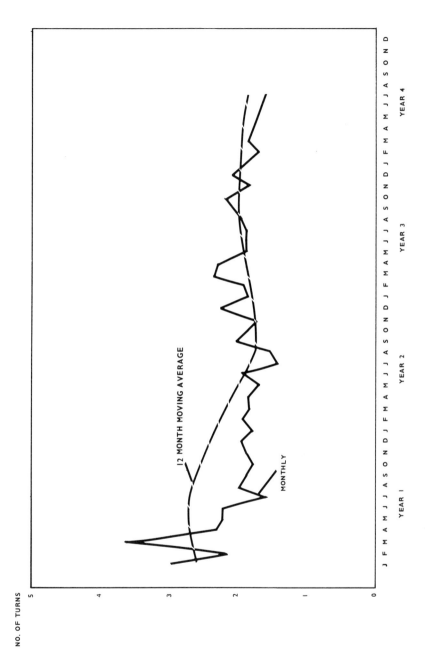

Exhibit 5. Return on Investment

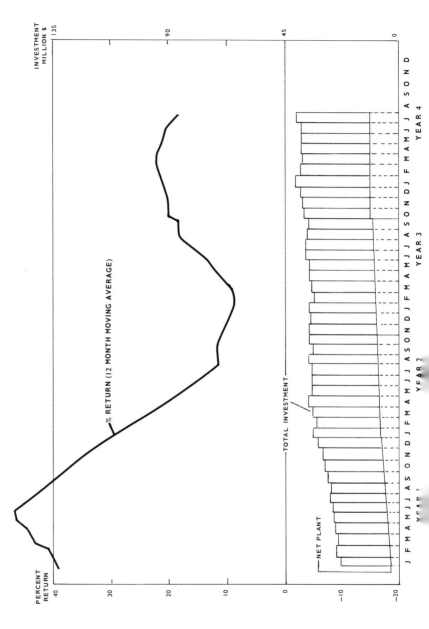

232

Exhibit 6

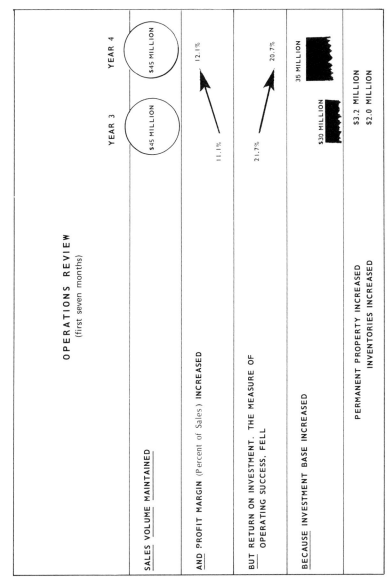

OPERATIONS REVIEW
(first seven months)

	YEAR 3	YEAR 4
SALES VOLUME MAINTAINED	$45 MILLION	$45 MILLION
AND PROFIT MARGIN (Percent of Sales) INCREASED	11.1%	12.1%
BUT RETURN ON INVESTMENT, THE MEASURE OF OPERATING SUCCESS, FELL	21.7%	20.7%
BECAUSE INVESTMENT BASE INCREASED	$30 MILLION	35 MILLION
PERMANENT PROPERTY INCREASED		$3.2 MILLION
INVENTORIES INCREASED		$2.0 MILLION

greatest with those of us who are essentially concerned directly with operations, unless we are continuously impressed with the importance of investment to the overall result. Line or operating management has the understandable tendency to regard investment as "something you get from the front or home office" and to give it little weight in appraising results. The operating executive is too often inclined to consider his responsibility to be solely one of producing at the lowest cost. It is clear where that can lead—to lowest costs associated with highest production volume and only indirectly and in a minor way considering the resulting inventories.

Low unit costs mean nothing if they stem from high production without correspondingly high sales. The lower costs can be more than counteracted by lower return on investment because of higher inventories. It is the cost accountant's job at the operating levels to keep management constantly impressed with the play of all forces. Here, as elsewhere, the cost accountant, using the tools of financial analysis, can supply the broad definitive information upon which sound decisions are made. In regard to inventories particularly, he must urge a policy that balances the compulsions of three areas:

1.   Sales department's desire for a wide variety of all types of products at all distribution points.

2.   Financial requirements of lowest possible inventories.

3.   Production objective of lowest unit costs through maximum and steady production volume.

So far we have covered cost accounting techniques as they relate to the analysis of current operations. In the development of yearly budgets and longer range plans, the interplay of cost and financial approaches is equally intimate. Cost accounting has the effect of assuring realism in planning. Cost standards, by definition, entail planning of activities in all areas of operation. Likewise, they require uniformity as to principle wherever applied. Above all else, they are set as a realistic probability and not as a theoretical possibility. Because they are all these things, cost standards act as a brake against visionary, unsubstantiated planning. The overenthusiastic manager is brought firmly to earth when ambitious growth plans are translated into resulting operating costs. By the same token, the overly cautious manager can be stimulated to take a bolder course. This aspect of the relationship between planning and standard cost accounting is generally understood and appreciated.

Not so clearly defined is the concern that cost accountants should have for financial performance when planning starts at the base, with the setting of the cost standards. In this, the tendency too often is to allow the determination of what is a realistic probability to rest on past experience. As a substitute for searching examination in terms of the impact on financial performance, there is the attraction of the easy way out, of simply trending past and current experience to obtain standards. It is extremely important, in this respect, that operating management appreciate the significance of financial analysis to cost accounting. Plans for attainment of return on investment in the financial sense can and should influence the construction of components on the cost side of operating projections. The additional fixed and working capital required in carrying out future plans must play just as important a part in the cost presentation as the fixed and variable elements of manufacturing and distribution costs. In this way financial analysis is applied as a positive force at the planning stage of cost control.

FROM PROBLEM IDENTIFICATION TO RECOMMENDATIONS

I mentioned earlier, as one of the aspects of cost accounting activity requiring attention, the matter of salesmanship. I was not thinking of salesmanship in the sense of high pressure tactics. On the contrary, some of the most convincing proposals in the field of improved controls, in my experience, have been made in presentations that follow the path of simple logic derived from painstaking study of the facts. There is one distinguishing factor which, more than any other, characterizes the analyses that have success in stimulating results. Let us call it management action projection. Stated simply, it is the quality of an analysis that hands management a ready action tool. The description of this quality as a projection is in recognition of the ability the analyst has shown in projecting himself mentally into the position of responsible management. If we are to sell cost accounting, we must assume the attitude of the individual who will buy. It is a bold approach, and it is one which pays handsome dividends in the form of follow-through and solid results. Here is an area ready-made for the partnership of cost accounting and financial analysis. The cost accountant must use the techniques of financial analysis if his efforts are to gain results where responsibility lodges, and that starts at the operating level. Unless cost analyses have a content of profit impact and unless they key into the return-on-investment concept, they can be of only limited interest and importance to general management.

The process of developing cost and other analyses that will get results and promote positive action falls into the following pattern. Identification of problems comes first. The cost accountant has a heavy responsibility for identifying problem areas before they become serious. It is an aspect of his job that requires initiative and know-how. His plants, products, and processes must be matters of intimate knowledge. He must keep informed as to changes in manufacturing techniques and their effect on the overriding profit and rate-of-return factors and their components, including inventory levels, sales volume, and capital expenditure requirements. For this, financial analysis techniques can be particularly helpful in applying the management-by-exception approach. Financial trends by products provide a handy method of selecting for special treatment, cost factors asserting themselves in end results. Every organization has problems requiring action. At a build-up stage it may be capital, requiring faster turnover of inventories. At all stages efficient lower cost operations are a continuing objective. The cost accountant must be alert to the shifts in emphasis and direct his efforts accordingly.

After problem identification come analysis and interpretation. The guide here should be to develop analyses to the point at which no questions of substance are left unanswered. The "why" of a condition must be foremost in the mind of the analyst. It is his business to provide answers, not to raise more questions. To do this effectively, again, the analysis must follow through to the significance of a problem from a financial point of view. Analysis and interpretation mean a great deal more than a statement of the problem involved and its cause. It means following through to the recommendation of a course of action. Especially on complex problems, this will entail the consideration of alternatives. Here the financial indications may well be determining. Weight must be given each alternative and a recommendation, with reasons, made for one course of action.

Presentation follows problem identification, analysis, and interpretation. The ultimate purpose, of course, of any cost analysis and problem survey is to stimulate action and bring about improvement. It is of great importance to the attainment of this objective that the facts, conclusions, and recommendations be presented in a forceful effective manner, whether the presentation is made orally, in the main, or entirely in writing. The attitude of operating executives toward reports takes many forms. Some understand and use charts extensively. Others gain no benefit from charts and may even respond negatively. However, there are two characteristics of good reporting that have universal acceptance. They are simplicity and clarity. Whatever the form of presentation, the chances of action results will be enhanced if it can be readily understood.

For example, in cost analyses, care must be taken to interpret volume variance in terms of the excess costs loaded on production by temporary unused capacity. Likewise, unfavorable operating cost variances should be presented as adversely affecting profit and return on investment. The analysis should project the effect on investment of failure to meet sales estimates, the resulting increased manufacturing variances, and build-up of inventories. In all of this, with the busy operating executive in mind, technical terms should be avoided to the maximum extent possible.

THE ENTIRE BUSINESS IS THE FRAME OF REFERENCE

This chapter has attempted to cover some fundamental principles and to illustrate their application with a few simple charts. Certainly there are many guides of this general nature that can be applied usefully to cost accounting. In summing up, I would suggest that in cost accounting, as in financial management generally, we apply a frame of reference that is as broad as the operation of which we are a part, keeping foremost in our thinking the difficult task of management groups in comprehending not only our own areas of specialized interest but the entire company. Toward this objective help is on the way. With new and faster computing and equipment, better methods of analyzing all cost, financial, sales, and other information on an integrated basis will be available. The stage of "push button" accounting and control is coming. This will not be a substitute for brains, but it will help human intelligence to do the job better and more efficiently.

"Line or operating management has a tendency to view investment as 'something you get from the home office' and to give it little weight in appraising results."   Leonard Kamsky

CHAPTER 14

HOW AN INVESTMENT BANKER LOOKS AT RETURN ON INVESTMENT PROFIT PLANNING

RICHARD M. HEXTER

"The role of the investment banker is important to companies seeking to improve profit performance. Among the functions served by the banker is minimization of the overall long term cost of capital."

Investment bankers often encounter the results of corporate profit planning, but much filtering takes place as to what it really is and who does it. I suspect the same filtering process occurs when corporate planners encounter the work of an investment banker. We have heard of one another, and seen the results of our efforts, but, as with taxidermists, philanthropists, and sewer cleaners, we may never have met one face-to-face.

INVESTMENT BANKERS DO MORE THAN RAISE CAPITAL

Since you are undoubtedly familiar with planning, let me begin by presenting my own definition of the investment banking function.

While investment banking is certainly a profession, the lack of licensing or meaningful educational requirements makes standards of performance difficult to establish. One focus of investment bankers, the underwriting of corporate security issues, highlights their importance in the capital raising function of corporations. Underwriting alone, however, fails to reflect the wide scope of services provided by firms and individuals who term themselves "investment bankers." Such services include retail brokerage, block trading, merger and acquisition advice, money management, and financial and strategic consulting for corporations.

This variety of functions suggests my definition of an investment banker as "one who provides services to corporations and institutions that lower their overall long term cost of capital." To oversimplify this definition, an investment banker strives to achieve, over time, the highest stock multiple and best credit rating for his client consistent with the basic fundamentals of his business. That consistency is important; a banker who has not taken (or been given) the opportunity to understand the basic fundamentals of his client's business may help to gain the wrong image for his client to the long-term detriment of both their reputations.

A good investment banker starts far back in the process—not just when his client has an immediate problem. He often serves as an interface between planning executives as the internal representatives of management and the investment and financial worlds. This chapter deals with the areas where our business worlds overlap.

We have at least three areas of common interest. These are financing, mergers and acquisitions, and market valuation of corporate stock. In discussing these topics in turn, we focus on what we've both done poorly together rather than on the more pleasant task of describing what we've done well.

PLANNING AS IT AFFECTS FINANCINGS

There are several aspects of financial strategy in which planning executives have a role to play but have not exercised that role as well as they might. The first concerns the question of long-range flexibility, an important development in financial fields after World War II. The concept of preserving one's options in financial planning somehow got lost in the 1960s when short-term considerations were emphasized by booming stock markets. Many companies raised equity in the early sixties and piled on more and more debt as the decade progressed. As a consequence some corporations today find themselves with funded debt that may well carry the highest interest rates of this century.

A certain herd instinct also seemed to prevail as successive industries came to market—airlines, real estate investment trusts, and nursing homes filled the marketplace to the saturation point and beyond. Investment bankers were sometimes guilty during this period of functioning solely as conduits rather than allocators of capital, but this "hot deal" philosophy involved as well the top management of many major corporations. In contrast, a few corporations raised debt in the early sixties and equity in the late sixties. Their current strong financial position is ample testimony to the value of planning for the future and anticipating its financial consequences.

An investment banker can provide top management with "market perspective," but such perspective is useless without a realistic assessment of the actual financial needs of the corporation. A crucial function of the corporate planner is to provide—and sometimes demand—that realism. We bankers often get the results of corporate plans in a rather condensed version. The probability and contingency aspects of a plan tend to be filtered out. Thus your conclusion that the corporation will need $20 to $30 million in new funds by 1975 may be simplified as a requirement for $25 million—today. As novices at running businesses, bankers have a tendency to accept such statements at face value.

What is really needed is a feel for the variables affecting a plan. Almost any kind of terms can be written into a financing arrangement if there is a precise understanding of what terms ought to be there. For example, if the $25 million needed today could actually be $20 million or $30 million, and the answer won't be known for two years, then the decisions between debt or equity, public or private, and a variety of terms and covenants are all affected. The trouble with this kind of sensitivity analysis is that it further complicates an already complicated planning process.

One of the greatest challenges in planning for profitability is to communicate probabilities and assumptions to top management (and thence, hopefully, to your investment bankers) in a way that sheds light on the risks in basing action on "the" answer.

A further comment in the area of financing concerns the idea "asset management." We adopted the term a few years ago only to find it soon misapplied as a substitute for portfolio management. What I mean by asset management goes beyond money management to include management of the whole collection of tangible and intangible resources that the corporation employs to do its business. One of the tasks of the corporate planner is to identify those corporate activities in which assets are underutilized or even misallocated. Despite its complexity, there is no substitute for the return on investment (ROI) criteria in identifying these areas of underutilized resources. A corporation that pays attention to its own cost of capital and allocates its internal funds to achieve the highest return will certainly minimize the need for external funds. And it must always be remembered—even in hot stock markets—that external funds must be paid for in cash or in a reduced ownership position.

THE PLANNERS' ROLE IN MERGERS

The second area of common concern to investment bankers and corporate planners is that of mergers and acquisitions. We find some companies who use planning well in this area and others not at all. In many cases, the planner is brought in to skin the tiger only after the hunt is over. In either example, bankers and planners offer services that should complement each other more than they often are allowed to do. Bankers are frequently qualified to evaluate such external factors as availability, economic forecasts, financial architecture, people chemistry, and aspects of legal and negotiation strategy. But it seems that corporate planners are uniquely suited to examine the real questions of operating business fit. Many a "synergistic" merger has floundered when it was later discovered that the compensation structure, marketing approaches, or accounting systems did not match. Planning executives have an important role to play in visualizing the kind of "Monday morning" questions of how two businesses will function together on a day-to-day basis. I want to emphasize emphatically that such visualizations are not just a numbers game. Corporate combinations almost invariably involve the most bizarre forms of human irrationality. A feel for the psychology of a combination is just as important as understanding its accounting consequences.

Corporate divestitures have recently become quite fashionable. There will be more divestitures in the future, and accordingly, more opportunities for acquirors as a result. People don't plan the sale of a business with anywhere near the thoroughness with which they plan an acquisition, however. Divestitures tend to be a one-shot, pessimistic kind of decision. If anyone could be found to assume the title, corporations could well utilize a "director of divestitures" to identify candidates for sale and go about the process of sale intelligently and aggressively.

A special reason for companies to involve themselves in the sale analysis is that such a study can be a useful benchmark for general corporate growth. If careful study indicated that a sale could be consummated today for more than the expected value on a "no sale" basis several years out, that result would certainly highlight the need for a rethinking of present plans. Further, even the most aggressive acquirer can quickly become a candidate for acquisition itself. Planning for that possibility in advance increases the chance that the proper decision and the maximum value will be attained.

Another thought in the area of acquisitions and divestitures concerns the value of contrary thinking. At times it seems to us that every corporate management wants to buy the most exciting, the most dynamic businesses available. In the 1966–1967 period, the business was leisure time. A year later it was educational publishing. In 1969, data communications became a sought-after talent. Those companies that persist in identifying their business opportunities at the top of the market are bound to get into trouble. The real challenge in corporate acquisitions is to find value where other people don't see it at the moment. Motion picture companies, in the early sixties, were hopeless investments until a few observers realized that they were goldmines in terms of assets because they had the product that other communications media wanted. Yesterday's sludge treatment dog is today's pollution control racehorse. The value received for anticipating, rather than following trends in acquisitions is higher than almost any other area in finance.

THE INVESTOR CARES ABOUT PROFIT PLANNING

The final point involves evaluation of the corporation's stock in the marketplace. Outside investors try to make some value judgments about the quality of management, the profitability of present businesses, and the soundness of growth plans. The price of a company's stock is determined by two elements—the earnings per share and the "multiple" placed on the earnings. The earnings component is a relatively simple determination. Investor confidence that the earnings stream will grow produces the multiple.

Confidence involves some feeling that the corporations' affairs are under control. One of the most important elements in evaluating management's control is its past success in meeting its forecasts. An ability to tell it like it is and will be, is rewarded in the marketplace much more than a mere reporting of how it was. To do this consistently requires good planning and good communication of those plans.

One of my favorite contrasts involves the operating records of General Motors and General Electric. Everyone knows that the auto business is highly cyclical and unpredictable, and that technology is a beautiful, solid growth business. In fact, the earnings records of GM and GE track quite nicely. In the latter case, someone has done a very nice job of planning and communicating to investors. This effort has been worth some $7 billion in market value.

LOOKING TO THE FUTURE

The ROI criteria should continue to gain in importance as an analytical technique. Consistent with this concept is the idea of expanding and contracting one's equity base to meet the available investment opportunities. It is entirely possible that a sound ROI analysis will indicate the most productive use for excess corporate funds is in the repurchase of its stock. The traditional notion has suggested that excess funds should be applied to the reduction of corporate indebtedness. In fact, many businesses have a stability and predictability that suggest that "permanent" debt is entirely prudent and beneficial. Rather than reducing this ratio by debt repayments, corporations might find it more profitable to expand or contract their entire capitalizations to match available investment opportunities.

In the area of business forecasting itself, I see an increasing need for developing competence in making midterm forecasts. We have grown reasonably expert in making one year forecasts, and we're all great at making ten year forecasts, but the midterm will assume increasing importance as the decade progresses. I expect that by the end of the decade earnings forecasts will be regularly included in prospectuses and annual reports.

Corporations will continue to deal with investment bankers, although they will almost certainly deal with fewer of them, if consolidation trends continue in our industry. While such experiments have not been successful in the past, it is certainly possible that some major corporations will begin to deal directly with investors in raising funds. The telephone industry, for example, deals with virtually every household in the United States on a monthly basis. The legal issues aside, one wonders about the consequences of a telephone company offering its customers 6 percent interest on any overpayments on their monthly bills. General Motors Acceptance Corporations has recently announced a plan to sell its securities directly to the investing public. Investment bankers will come under greater pressure to increase the scope of services offered, to become, in effect, a "one-stop" shopping center for financial services.

Finally, the 1970s have seen increasing attention being paid to what I call the "not-for-profit" area. A steadily increasing amount of our national assets reside in the governmental, educational, cultural, and health areas, and these all are in serious need of planning and financial services. Even the Russians are willing to admit that the notion of efficiency does not disappear when ownership passes from private to public hands. The rational allocation and efficient employment of this nation's limited resources is an area in which we all must make an increasing contribution. Investment bankers and planning executives alike have value to add to this growing segment of our economy. We can do it for profit and we must do it for our well being.

"A company that pays attention to its own cost of capital and allocates its internal funds to achieve the highest return will minimize the need for external funds."   *Richard M. Hexter*

MORE EFFECTIVE ASSET MANAGEMENT

Capital assets, receivables, and inventories, the three elements of the balance sheet that are dealt with in this section, account for 75 to 90 percent of total assets in many, if not most, manufacturing companies. The first two chapters deal with proper utilization of capital resources and making capital controls work. The next chapter is a case study of how a major company established better controls on its receivables. The final chapter deals with a more modern approach to control of inventories than that used by so many companies.

UTILIZING CAPITAL RESOURCES PROFITABLY

There are few businesses that are as capital intensive as a utility. According to Charles Ferris, five times as much capital investment is required to generate a dollar in revenue as is required for the typical manufacturing plant. Another important consideration is that construction must be planned far in advance to assure that the equipment is ready to serve subscribers just when it is needed—not too soon and not too late. This chapter also deals with the subject of plant obsolescence and modernization—circumstances that require additional capital expenditures unrelated to current ongoing projects.

HOW TO MAKE CAPITAL CONTROLS WORK

The author of this chapter, in describing capital controls for a manufacturing company, emphasizes the need for a return on investment approach (ROI) in justifying capital expenditures. John Rhodes emphasizes the need for program identification when making capital expenditure evaluations. He discards the piecemeal approach because this does not facilitate an ROI evaluation for the complete program.

The chapter takes a "how to do it" approach in demonstrating capital controls. It includes the basic paperwork required for justification of the expenditure, the program detail, and other data relating to reporting the savings and cash requirements.

HOW TO REDUCE RECEIVABLES TO MAXIMIZE RETURN ON INVESTMENT

At one time many companies maintained an arm's length relationship with customers who purchased merchandise on credit. The customer's purchase would be financed by a finance company and payments would be made to a third party rather than to the merchandiser. However, as credit buying became more popular and profitable to the finance companies, more and more merchandisers instituted a credit arm of the business.

The Singer Company was a pioneer in installment selling and has been successful at it. Leo Blatz describes Singer's MMM (Modern Merchandise Methods) program which has for its goal the reduction of the level of receivables, improvement of the quality of receivables, and accomplishing this without adversely affecting the level of sales. How this program was implemented and the results that were accomplished, is the subject of Chapter 17.

REQUIREMENTS PLANNING FOR BETTER INVENTORY CONTROL

At the factory level inventories can make up as much as 50 percent (or more) of total assets directly related to the manufacturing process. Inventories include not only the raw materials but also the direct labor and overhead that have been added to raw material to make up work-in-process and finished goods. A company seeking to exercise control over its inventories must not only schedule its material purchases properly but must also use good business judgment in the scheduling of production of components and subassemblies as well as finished products. Conventional statistical approaches that have been used by companies for many years rely on historical experience as a basis for determining inventory requirements. The author of Chapter 18 challenges the correctness of this approach. With the availability of the modern computer, he asserts that inventory controls should be established by breaking down the forecasted sales into raw material, component, subassembly, and finished product requirements.

SUMMARY

It should be evident from the viewpoints expressed in the chapters making up this section that capital expenditures and other major balance sheet assets must be kept under good control if a good return on investment is to be assured. Sales volume and cost efficiency are important, but the amount of investment being carried determines the amount of leverage applied to the turns of investment. Too much investment, in terms of utilization, can more than offset all the benefits of an optimum sales volume at efficient costs.

CHAPTER 15

UTILIZING CAPITAL RESOURCES PROFITABLY

CHARLES S. FERRIS

"Most utilities require about $2.50 in plant to generate $1 in revenue. The average manufacturing company requires about $0.50 in plant to generate the same $1 in revenue."

This chapter explains how the Bell System plans and manages its capital expenditures. Because of the nature of the telephone business, some of the procedures undoubtedly differ from those used in other industries. I suspect, however, that those of us involved in this facet of our respective businesses will find that what we have in common is far greater than our differences.

Any growing business that uses plant facilities in its operations has to deal with three principal capital considerations:

1. Plant expansion
2. Plant replacement due to wear and tear
3. Plant modernization

Before discussing these points let us consider some of the characteristics of capital intensive businesses.

CHARACTERISTICS OF A CAPITAL INTENSIVE BUSINESS

As a public utility the telephone company has an obligation to provide quality service in the areas served where the customer wants it, when he wants it, and of the type and amount that he desires. To do this we must constantly anticipate the communication needs of the public. If we understate or overstate these, we have not done the economical job, and eventually both the customers and the owners of the business will suffer.

Second, most of our plant is relatively long-lived. A substantial part of our plant has an average life of well over 30 years. Thus it is especially important that the design be optimum.

As a third point, most utilities are highly capital intensive. We require about $2.50 in plant to generate $1 in revenue. The average manufacturing concern requires about 50 cents in plant to generate that same dollar in revenue. You might say then, that we are five times as capital intensive as a typical manufacturing concern.

Because of the characteristics just described, our investment in new plant is running just below $10 billion per year. In the coming years we will undoubtedly find our capital needs to be even greater. These factors give evidence that the need is great to plan for and manage the capital programs in as efficient and prudent a manner as possible.

THE LONG-RANGE PLAN

The whole process of expanding or modernizing plant facilities starts with fundamental or long-term planning. This is planning that looks ahead 20 to 30 years, and provides the general direction that extension of the plant should take to meet the needs of the business in that time frame. In a broad sense, it outlines:

1.   The type and quantity of communication services the future will require.
2.   The scope of plant rearrangements and additions that will be needed.
3.   The optimum kind or type of equipment that will be required.
4.   And approximately when the additions to plant will be needed.

This kind of planning is done in each of the operating telephone companies, and provides a very necessary framework for all major additions to our plant.

As we approach the years when plant must be added to satisfy customer demands, the current planning phase begins. Here we are considering a much shorter time frame—the next 3 to 5 years. In the short range we must get quite specific about what we are going to do and when we are going to do it, because now we are reaching the stage of actual commitment of men, money, and material.

It is now that three basic questions must be answered for each project.

1. Has the time come when plant must be added?
2. Is the type plant to be added consistent with our long-term plans?
3. Are we adding the economic amount of plant?

To be more specific, I would like to cover how we go about this kind of planning in the telephone business, using as an example, an addition to a dial central office.

TIMING THE CONSTRUCTION

As mentioned earlier, our objective is to construct new plant so that it is available for service just when it is needed—not too early and not too late. Since it takes a certain amount of time to engineer, manufacture, and install dial switching equipment, we must make our commitment for central office additions in the order of 1 year ahead of the actual service need. Let's consider the timing aspects as depicted in Exhibit 1.

Exhibit 1.   Demand and Capacity Chart for Local Switching Equipment

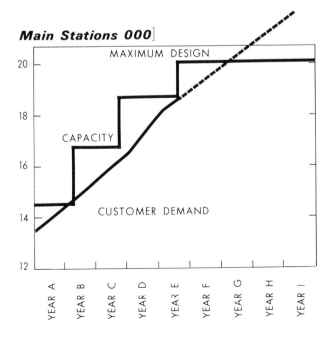

This is a tool we use to aid in "timing" central office additions. On the vertical axis are telephones, and on the horizontal axis, time. The line moving upward at about 45° represents the demand for telephone service placed on this office. The solid part of the line represents customers now being served, and the dashed part represents the added customers we expect in the period ahead. The straight stair-step lines represent the capacity of the office to serve customers. Each vertical line in the staircase represents an addition of equipment that increases the overall office capacity.

Out in Year G this office will exhaust, and very soon we will have to make plants for how the additional customers will be served. By keeping our forecast of demand for service always up-to-date, an examination of a chart such as this will clearly point out the timing required for the next plant addition.

Step two is to determine what to do. For the sake of illustration, assume that this dial machine[1] has reached its maximum capacity. By that I mean it is not technically possible to add more capacity to this unit.

With this constraint, we refer to our long-range plan for guidance as to where to locate a new machine. In this instance, the long-term forecast indicates continued growth in the entire area served by this office, and the right place for a second machine turns out to be in the same building as the first unit. Based on other data from the long-term plan it is possible to determine that the type of new switching unit should be one of electronic design. The long-term plan has thus helped us determine where the new machine should go and of what general type it should be.

EVALUATING THE ALTERNATIVES

The last of the basic questions that must be answered is, "How large should the initial size of the new office be?" There are many alternatives; we could, for instance, make the initial installation of our new machine adequate for 2 years of service. Or we could make it only large enough for 1 year, with a plan to add additional capacity after the first year.

This choice is primarily one of economics. If we provide 2 years worth of growth initially, we are spending more capital money in the first year than is absolutely necessary—a job lasting only 1 year would cost less. But, on the other hand, there are "getting started" costs associated with each job,

---

[1] The word "machine" used here is synonymous with equipment.

and for the same capacity during the second year the two jobs will cost more than the one larger job. Each time we confront such a situation, an economic study is made to determine which plan has the lowest "present worth of expenditures," with discounted weighting given to expenditures after the initial year.

As a matter of fact, this kind of study is made with considerable help from time-shared computers. We only considered two alternatives, a single 2-year job, or two 1-year jobs. The computer considers many other alternatives over a 4-year planning period, and quantifies the present worth of expenditures for each plan. (See Exhibits 2 and 3.)

With this last step completed, we now know *when, where, what,* and *how large,* and detailed engineering can begin. Planning projects as just described is done in each of the operating telephone companies. It requires the attention of engineers familiar with the forecast for demand for new service in the area served by that office, and with many technical details of that specific switching machine. This is not the kind of work that can be done best at a headquarters location. As a matter of interest, there are over

Exhibit 2.   Alternative Plans

Alt.	YEAR			
	1	2	3	4
1				
2				
3				
4				
5				
6				
7				
8				

Exhibit 3

```
- - - - - - - - - - - - - - - - - - - - - - - - - - - - - - - - - - - - - - - - - - - - - - - - - - - - - - - -


213-555  OFC EXISTING

MS CAP= 8220          LLF-N=24      CCS/LLF-N=1158     TLF=14
JCT PT= 9P            LLF-P= 0      CCS/LLF-P =   0


             213-555  OFC  COE  ALTERNATIVE PLANS
```

ALT	1	2	3	4	5	6	7	8
PW	855907	843068	845505	837999	827125	827348	839964	843741
SAVING	0	12839	10402	17908	28782	28559	15943	12166
YEAR 1								
C$	172400	172400	172400	172400	242870	313490	242870	396780
M$	0	0	0	0	0	0	0	190
FR	21	21	21	21	32	42	32	55
YEAR 2								
C$	89800	89800	253220	165740				
M$	0	0	210	0				
FR	13	13	36	22				
YEAR 3								
C$	98440	181600				181600		98440
M$	0	230				230		0
FR	12	25				25		12
YEAR 4								
C$	103650				103650		103650	103650
M$	240				240		240	240
FR	14				14		14	14

PLAN FUNCTION

10,000 dial offices in the Bell System, and each one of them requires the kind of planning just described.

BREAKDOWN OF THE CONSTRUCTION BUDGET

In addition to central office equipment, a number of other types of plant must also be added to provide telephone service. Cables to connect customers to the central office, telephone sets and PBX equipment at the customers' home or business, cable or radio to connect central offices to each other for long distance service, and of course, buildings to house both people and equipment. A typical breakdown of the components construction expenditures in the Bell System is shown below.

Land and buildings	11%
Switching and transmission equipment	38
Cables and supporting structures	23
Customer premise equipment	25
Data processing equipment, motor vehicles, and tools	3
	100%

When all these classes of plant are considered, each year literally hundreds of thousands of projects must be planned, receive management approval, be engineered, and constructed.

MONITORING THE PROGRAMS

Considering the large number of projects involved, how does the senior management of an operating telephone company assure itself that all these individual undertakings, with all the judgments that go into each one, constitute a sound capital program? To go one step further, how is the senior management at AT&T corporate headquarters assured that the System as a whole has a sound program?

This is accomplished through the process of summarizing relatively large amounts of data with regard to such things (1) amount of new service expected—new customers, and higher long-distance calling volumes, (2) amount of capacity added to meet this need, (3) material required to provide the capacity, and (4) dollars required to purchase and install the material. Once these data have been collected and summarized, they are used to analyze virtually every aspect of the capital program. Plant utilization, unit costs for capacity added, and progress toward reaching long-term objectives are all carefully examined. This kind of analysis is made in each operating telephone company, and independently at AT&T headquarters in New York.

In a broad sense, let me illustrate the way the dial switching part of a company's program might be analyzed. (See Exhibit 4.) Remember that the data in this analysis is the aggregate of data from thousands of individual projects.

Exhibit 4.   Broad Analysis Approach to Construction Budget for Local Switching

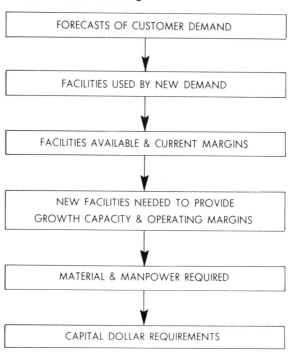

Variables in the adjacent steps are compared using regression techniques, tempered with as much sound judgment as possible. We begin with the forecast of customer demand, proceed to facility and material requirements, and end with capital dollar needs. The results are used to test the soundness of this portion of the total growth program. Other portions of the growth program for such things as cables, buildings, telephone sets, and so on are analyzed in a similar manner.

Expenditures for growth make up the largest part of the total program, 68 percent. Customer movement expenditures represent about 15 percent. These are the costs associated with relocating existing customers from one place to another. These expenditures are currently running well over $1 billion a year.

A smaller category is "plant replacement," which takes about 5 percent of the capital dollar. Expenditures are for replacing plant due to such things as storm damage, highway relocations, or just plain worn out equipment in some cases.

The last major category is "modernization." It accounts for 12 percent of the capital dollar and is now running in excess of $1 billion annually. Expenditures in this category are vitally important to the long-term health of the telephone industry. They are discretionary expenditures in the sense that they can be delayed from one year to the next without immediately jeopardizing service, but over the long pull they are not discretionary if the plant is to be kept modern and the System remain in a position to meet the nation's needs for communications.

PLANT OBSOLESCENCE AND MODERNIZATION

Many parts of the telephone plant tend to become obsolete before they physically wear out. An example is the open wire that once served individual customers and connected central offices. These are almost all gone. Cables, many of which are underground, and radio facilities have replaced these open wires. Automatic dial offices have replaced the old manual central offices where each call started with the operator's, "number please."

These older types of plant were removed for reasons other than being worn out. They were replaced because newer plant design could provide better service, and could provide it more economically.

Modernization of the telephone plant is still going on. The first generation of dial switching machines—many of which were installed prior to World War II—are being replaced with electronic switching systems. The reasons are the same as when manual offices were replaced with the first dial machines—to improve service and over the long term to provide service at the lowest possible cost consistent with financial stability of the business. This effort got underway in the late 1960s, but progress has been good.

A second major modernization project now underway in our business is the replacement of older cord switchboard positions used for long-distance service, with a new system that is computer controlled. The new system gives the customer better service. Calls requiring assistance from an operator such as person to person, credit card calls, and calls from coin stations can all be processed much faster. There is a real savings in operator expense when these new systems are installed. It's this kind of thing—constantly bringing the latest technology into our plant—that has made long-distance rates lower. Projects such as these two just described, and many more, make up the modernization portion of our budget.

PLANNING IS NOT A ONE-SHOT PROGRAM—IT IS CONTINUOUS

Construction budget planning is really a continuous operation in the Bell System. The budget is summed up three times each year. Each operating telephone company submits a budget to headquarters in April, August, and December of each year. We call each of these summaries a "view" of the budget.

The budgets are prepared and analyzed in each company, and after receiving management approval, they are sent to AT&T headquarters. Here the views are again analyzed, and put together to form a Bell System budget. Following review with senior management in both the companies and AT&T, further review is usually undertaken in each company. Very soon the process repeats itself with the next view. Each view of the program covers a 3-year period.

From the Bell System budget summaries come the very vital requirements for capital dollars, material needed, and manpower required for the provision of telephone plant needed to meet the constantly growing need for communications service in this country.

"The objective in a utility is to construct new plant so it is available for service just when it is needed—not too early and not too late."

Charles Ferris

CHAPTER 16

HOW TO MAKE CAPITAL CONTROLS WORK

JOHN E. RHODES

"A satisfactory system for any business must be tailored to fit the particular industry and company requirements. However, the control mechanism is basically the same for all industry, and it seems possible to take a common approach by first setting forth the policies upon which the program is to be based."

It seems safe to say that today no phase of business management is more important to the progress of individual industries and the well-being of the economy as a whole than control of capital expenditures. Our increased knowledge of the way in which the economy functions has made us acutely aware of the need for continuous expansion. However, this expansion must be planned to fit the population grow The specific control system on which this chapter is based undoubtedly has features in common with the program of many companies. However, it also includes special procedures which are necessitated by the particular position of the electrical-electronics industry. In short, generally accepted control mechanisms have been tailored to fit the specific requirements of a fast-growing industry.

This rapid growth has exerted tremendous pressure on the resources of the industry and has created an almost insatiable demand for capital. These developments were difficult to anticipate but certainly have highlighted the importance of sound planning.

A satisfactory system for any business must be tailored to fit the particular industry and company requirements. However, the control mechanism is basically the same for all industry and it seems possible to take a common approach by first setting forth the *policies* upon which the program is to be based. Some of the major items, indicative of the points that must be resolved before a program is formulated, are given attention in the paragraphs immediately following and are succeeded by consideration of programming particular projects.

POLICY FOR RETURN ON INVESTMENT AND INVESTMENT PROTECTION

This is a basic question—perhaps the most important of all business policies. It belongs at the head of the list in any business discussion, and it reminds us of our common objective, regardless of specific differences in the nature of our business. In a sense, we are all in the investment business. We all take monies from the same sources—stockholders (common, preferred), long-term loans (bonds, etc.), short-term loans, open accounts payable, sale of assets, lease backs, and so on. We all put the monies to work in about the same general way (buy productive equipment, labor and material, and sales and distribution talent). We all try to turn the money over as often as possible with maximum margin of profit on each turn. The process goes from cash to inventories to receivables and back to cash. The object is to get enough cash to pay monies back to original sources plus dividends and still have a residue for expansion. So, all firms have a common objective, a common prime policy, that is, satisfactory return on investment.

One philosophy holds that an investment in capital assets, particularly if for expansion, should provide a return equal to or greater than present return on investment. Otherwise, the earnings rate of present owners or stockholders is diluted. This conclusion is controversial because it could seriously impede progress and jeopardize earnings. "The old wheel turns," for profitable industry or products of yesterday may be only a memory today, and less profitable new ventures of today may be our mainstay tomorrow. To protect future return, it is frequently necessary to sacrifice or dilute some portion of the current return. In establishing a philosophy on this point and determining the satisfactory percentage of return, it is essential to consider firm policy on investment protection.

It is assumed, of course, that investment protection policies will include procedures and insurance to protect against dishonesty and various disaster possibilities. What I particularly want to cover here is the risk factors involved in running a successful progressive business. While return on investment is generally recognized as the motivating objective of business enterprise, the first responsibility of fixed capital management, from the financial manager's point of view, is to retain intact the capital originally and sub-sequently invested. If the capital investment is dissipated, there can be no return because there will be no business left. So, it is obviously important that operating plans and other policies of the business be in harmony with the policy on investment protection. However, in establishing this policy we must recognize that, in a large measure, the degree of protection will be directly re-lated to the desired return on investment. Generally, we cannot expect higher than average return without assuming greater risk. On the other hand, if we swing 100 percent to the financial manager's viewpoint, and demand positive protection of investment, we must be satisfied with a minimum return, and should have put our money in the savings bank in the first place. So, return on investment policy is interrelated to the policy on investment protection. Se-lection of a balance point is an individual matter for each business, depending somewhat upon the type of industry and the attitude of the owners or stock-holders.

Because of the variation in circumstances, there seems to be no good rule of thumb that can be applied universally, so I merely make the point that business is a gamble, and there is always some risk. To survive in the future, it is essential to keep up-to-date in your field, even though it means sacrifice of some portion of current earnings. To formulate other operating plans and policies intelligently it is essential to first establish management philosophy on these two basic policies, return on investment and investment protection.

POLICY FOR REPLACEMENT FUNDING

This does not go into the whole broad subject of business financing because that subject alone would require many chapters for adequate coverage. In fact, we refer here only to a financing plan for replacement of existing assets. Actually, this is closely related to investment protection policies in the sense that a plan to provide funds for replacement of assets may also be a plan that ensures the constancy of fixed capital. To accomplish both, it is necessary to retain in the business each year cash, securities, or other assets at least equal to the amount of depreciation of fixed assets. This means "true" deprecia-tion. So, in establishing the minimum needed to meet this requirement, book depreciation cannot be used unless it takes into consideration the difference between depreciable and "true" life, possible obsolescence before life expira-tion, and possible higher cost of replacement either because of inflation or new improved machinery or facilities. Actually, many variations from straight line depreciation do make corrections for some of these factors.

However, we should not rely completely upon any mechanical formula to solve the problem, because failure to establish a realistic policy giving proper consideration to all factors can result in dissipation of fixed capital, which may ruin or seriously handicap any business when replacement of worn out or obsolete facilities becomes necessary. There is the simple case of dissipating depreciation reserve by cash distributions representing return of capital, known to some as "milking the business," but perhaps the most tragic awakening is experienced by the fellow who has religiously set aside funds represented by depreciation, but did not take into account higher replacement costs brought about through general economic inflation. Even though the Internal Revenue Service will not allow depreciation based upon replacement cost, it is essential to consider this factor before declaring dividends, part of which could in reality represent a distribution of working capital needed in the business for future replacement of fixed capital assets. This may explain the retention of 50 percent of earnings by most corporations. Even those who do not plan on expansion should retain liberal amounts to cover higher costs of replacement. The best policy, of course, is to make calculations of inflationary effects each year and set aside the correct amount to cover.

After the determination of an adequate amount to be set aside, there are several alternative methods of retaining such assets in the business. Some of the basic ones include:

1. Paying off long-term or other business debt. The safest investment you can make is to buy up your own obligations.

2. Establishing a replacement fund in cash or gilt edge securities. This is safe but the yield is poor, so the effect may be idling cash at low interest rates.

3. Reinvesting funds in the business within limits indicated by long-term replacement and financing estimates. More risk is involved here but it represents a reasonable compromise for it provides an opportunity for good return on cash invested. Using this plan, it is well to adjust the net worth section of the balance sheet to deduct from the "undistributed earnings" account, and show separately the amount held in the business to provide for excess replacement cost.

PROGRESS, CAPITALIZATION, AND PROJECT APPROVAL AS POLICIES

There is usually no third choice. A business either moves ahead or falls back. In most fields we cannot expect to maintain the *status quo*. One danger is that stagnation frequently produces greater profit for a short period. Those who fall into this trap are milking the business and are bound for ultimate failure. Progress means keeping up-to-date or ahead in your field, or expansion by increased volume or additional lines. It may be either or both of these. The policy decision in this area requires familiarity with developments in the industry and business generally. Proper choice of financing method is important to either kind of progress. Such may be by means of issuing capital stock, borrowing, or using retained earnings. The problem of whether to capitalize or expense an expenditure is difficult but a general guide somewhat along the following lines may be appropriate:

Capitalize	Expense
Additions	Maintenance and repair
Replacements	Insurance
Renewals	Property taxes
Betterments	Interest
Original installation	

Starting from this general division of expenditure, it must be recognized that accounting and tax rules are both flexible and indefinite. There are some specific regulations but much is left to judgment of business management. Generally, as a practical matter, we should expense every dollar within legal tax limits. This minimizes taxes and preserves cash. To get maximum tax and cash advantage we would (1) expense items of doubtful use or life, such as experimental and development items, (2) expense physically small or delicate items if possibility of theft or breakage is high, (3) on capital items, consider physical life in terms of satisfactory quality and efficiency as well as possible obsolescence of either equipment or product and, of course, use the shortest time indicated by any of these factors, and (4) select depreciation on the sum of the digits, declining balance, or some other method that would give us the highest depreciation allowance. This approach will result in maximum write-offs on a current basis.

But we may not want maximum write-offs. There are some considerations on the other side of this picture. Under the following situations, maximum write-offs may not be desirable:

1.   No taxable income anticipated in current year or immediate future, for reasons such as new business, heavy expansion or research program, recession forecast, and losses of prior years to be carried forward (offsetting current profit).
2.   Anticipated increased tax rate.
3.   Impact on financial statements. Public reaction (or private banking reaction) might affect future or immediate financing. This would not be a factor in privately owned and privately financed business.
4.   Danger of overpricing product.

All factors must be weighed carefully, but I repeat that, generally, it is practical economics to expense to the legal limit. Speculation in tax rates is not our specialty, and probability of extended periods of loss is not likely if we plan to stay in business. One last point in determining policies on capitalization versus expense is the importance of making good initial decisions, because they are likely to be binding on future transactions. Basic to this system of capital expenditures has been a philosophy of maximum decentralization of control. Authority and responsibility for planning and carrying out operations have been delegated to division and plant managers, but central management is equipped with the minimum controls necessary to assure results. Exhibit 1 is indicative.

DEVELOPMENT OF CAPITAL OUTLAY PROGRAMS—THE IDEA OF "SEARCH"

After the basic policies have been established, we are ready to examine the process of setting up a programmed control system to implement them. As the first step in presenting the capital controls system, I should like to offer a definition of a program. There are certainly various good definitions but, for our purpose, I have defined a program as "a summary of related expenditures of proposals covering a specific integrated plan." This seems to be an adequate definition of any good overall operating program that is properly integrated. But the overall program is not really properly integrated if it unwittingly forces future expenditures not included as part of the approved operat-

Exhibit 1. Capital Expenditures Control

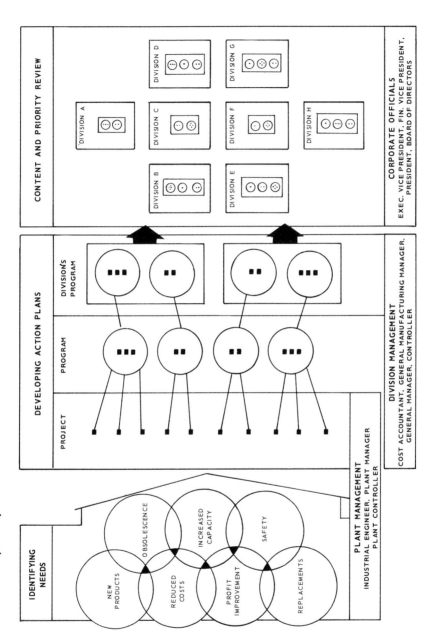

ing plan. For example, sales estimates may indicate that, two years from now, the volume of our profitable products will require ten more manufacturing machine units than we have now. If it takes 20 months to build these units, we must get immediate budget approval and place construction orders for the machinery (and, of course, the treasurer plans cash availability to pay for this equipment). But what a shock he gets if the first three new units delivered completely fill our present building facilities and the manufacturing boys hastily submit a requisition for purchase or construction of a new building and other facilities to accommodate the remaining seven new units. To avoid these surprises, we need a proper planning job, and to insure this the total overall program or budget is composed of many individual projects or programs, each one in itself being a "summary of related expenditures or proposals covering a specific integrated plan." An item cannot get on the list if it is not associated with one of these projects (or programs, as we call them) unless, of course, it happens to represent a complete program in itself. A program will not get approval without including or indicating all of the capital or expense items involved, now or in the future.

Next, let us review the preparation procedure. The first question is, "Where do we get our facts?" That is, "What is the source of information?" Obviously, we have to conduct a search by means of market research, engineering research, and cost analysis. I do not believe the aspect of search in relation to capital expenditures can be emphasized too strongly. We encourage this search in a number of ways. First, we are constantly reviewing our sales position by product lines, forecasting five years ahead, and scrutinizing our competition to make certain we are holding our own or better on volume. Market research plays a prominent role. It gives us much better estimates than we would get by relying solely upon past experience. Second, through engineering research we are developing entirely new products. These may entail outlays for new plants, complex equipment, and, from the financial standpoint, losses over a considerable period until starting-load costs are absorbed. Third, continuous cost analyses identify areas in which greater efficiency is required to meet and improve upon competitive prices.

After assembling this information, the next question is "How do we evaluate it?" As a result of the information stimulants, more investment proposals are submitted than available capital can accommodate. This is an indication of a healthy attitude on the part of division and plant personnel in uncovering opportunities. However, it then becomes one of top management's most important jobs to select the proposals that will be of greatest benefit to the company. To aid in this selection, each division must indicate the relative importance of each program in relation to other proposals the division has submitted. These proposals are subjected to qualitative and quantitative evaluation.

EVALUATION AND APPROVAL OF CAPITAL EXPENDITURE PROGRAMS

Qualitative criteria that apply in selecting capital programs and establishing priorities are in the nature of "urgency" evaluations. The ranking is about as follows:

1.   Legal and safety requirements and necessities of a similar nature. These rank very high regardless of profitability factors.
2.   Replacements of worn out or obsolete equipment.
3.   Completion of projects for which we are already substantially committed. These are ordinarily carry-overs from the prior year's program.
4.   Expansion or improvement necessary to retain our market position. As probably is done in most companies, we are constantly assessing our position in relation to that of the industry on all major products. Maintenance of industry position plays a big part in determining in what we invest.
5.   Cost saving items on present operations (two years or less for repayment).
6.   Expansion programs with high return.
7.   Expansion programs with average return.
8.   Cost savings items on present operation (over two years for repayment).
9.   Expansion programs with intangible or long-term advantages (such programs may provide us complements to an existing line of products).
10.   Others.

By way of quantitative evaluation, a rate of return on the investment can be computed. Much has been written on methods of gauging investment profitability or return on investment. A drawback in some methods is the complexity that often accompanies a high degree of accounting refinement. Admittedly, the method described strikes a compromise, but it is a compromise that gives management a practical measurement in relation to the company and the industry. Stated simply, return on investment is the percent of additional profit to additional investment. Each capital expenditure proposal should include this computation of the basis if the proposal is economic. The form in which it is worked up is indicated by Exhibit 2. Another important quantitative consideration is the availability of funds, so, on all profit improvement programs or requisitions, we can also calculate the cash payout period, that is, the length of time it will take to get the cash back in to the till. Cash return is quite different from book profit. This is calculated by adding back to book profit (after tax) the depreciation figure, because depreciation does not represent a cash outlay. This information on cash payback is essential to the treasurer in planning future financing requirements. To summarize our evaluation process, the qualitative listing establishes priority on the basis of urgency and the quantitative evaluation indicates (1) rates of additional profit to additional investment, and (2) time required to get the actual cash back into the business.

To complete the program preparation procedure, after gathering the information and evaluating it, the proposals or programs are prepared and

Exhibit 2

SUMMARY OF ANNUAL ADDED PROFIT		
____Division	P.P.R. No.____	
	Additional Expense $	Savings or Additional Income $
1. Net Sales		
2. Cost of Sales:		
Raw Materials		
Direct Labor		
Overhead Labor		
Overhead (Out of Pocket)		
3. Distribution Expenses (Out of Pocket)		
4. Administrative Expense (Out of Pocket)	_____	_____
5. Total	$	$
6. Added Annual Profit Before Depreciation & Income Taxes		$
7. Additional Depreciation Expense		_____
8. Added Annual Profit before Tax		$
9. Estimated Federal Income Tax		
10. Added annual profit before depreciation after Income Tax (6–9)		$

presented for approval. This approval procedure follows the course that has been indicated by Exhibit 1, with program preparation normally starting at the operating level at which capital expenditure is required and calling for step-by-step approval at each higher level of management. The procedure requires that in November each division or major department submit to the corporate office its expenditure plans for the next two years. This is proposed on a form entitled capital expenditure program summary (Exhibit 3), used to record the key control facts on each individual program, identified by consecutive numbering. It places capital expenditure forecasting on a continuous two-year basis. Supporting the summary are individual outlines covering each program in sufficient detail to enable management to review for approval. The outline of each program generally states (1) when it is anticipated that the program will be started and when it will be completed, (2) the cash outlay needed for the program and when needed, (3) additional working capital required on completion of program, (4) special expense items required by program, (5) whether or not a certificate of necessity has been issued or will be requested, and (6) the additional earnings or savings expected, (if any).

In general, then, assurance is provided that the proposal is the result of careful analysis of all factors, backed up by specific details supporting the improvements and profits claimed. The program outlines are reviewed by top management and presented to the board of directors with an appropriate summary for their overall review and approval. In many instances, the outlines list major items of equipment. However, control by top management is exercised by program total, and not by specific items. Division and plant management can and does change the specific equipment needed to complete programs as long as the scope of the program is not altered without prior corporate approval. So control on specific items within a program is delegated further down the line, to the divisions or plants or departments more familiar with the detailed requirements necessary to put over the program.

Finally, upon board approval, the president notifies the division and major department heads, and it is on the basis of this approval that the next major step in the system can be initiated, the expenditure procedure, which starts with the Permanent Property Requisitions (Exhibit 4). Approval of programs does not give approval to spend money. Expenditures must be authorized in accordance with the permanent property requisition procedure.

Before describing the requisition procedure, I want to emphasize one point in particular concerning the approval process and that is flexibility. Because of the volatile nature of the industry, we have to be prepared to shift attention

Exhibit 3

TWO YEAR CAPITAL EXPENDITURE PROGRAM SUMMARY
(000 Omitted)

Priority Rating	Program No.	Title of Program	Requisitions Already Approved	Amounts Already Spent		
				UP & WIP	Capitalized	Total
			1	2	3	4

Cash Outlay Needed to Complete Program

For Approved Requisitions	New Money	19__ Total	19__	Beyond	Total	Total Expense Required	Working Capital Required	*Total Cost of Program	Savings or Profit Improvement	Return on Inv. %
5	6	7	8	9	10	11	12	13	14	15

Notes:

1. *Total cost includes all funds spent or to be spent, necessary to attain earnings or savings.
2. Leave every fifth horizontal line blank to assist in reading schedule.
3. UP—Expenditures held in unfinished plant.
   WIP—Expenditures held in work in process.

Exhibit 4

PERMANENT PROPERTY REQUISITION

Division_____ Plant_____ Date:_____ PPR No:_____

Program_____ Program No:_____Plt. Req. No.:_____

1—DESCRIPTION OF ITEMS

SUPPLIER_____Expected DELIVERY DATE_____

2—REASON FOR EXPENDITURE

WAS THIS REQUISITION INCLUDED IN APPROVED PROGRAM? ___

3—COST   **TOTAL**

Plant or Equipment	$_____
Transportation and Installation	$_____
Cost to be Capitalized	$_____
Less: Salvage Value Obsolete Equipment	$_____
Net Capital Outlay	$_____
Plus: Non-Recurring Expenses (S.E.R. Required)	$_____
TOTAL COST	$_____

4—PROFIT IMPROVEMENT

Annual Added Profit $

Cash Pay Out Period:

$$\frac{\text{Total Cost} \quad \$}{\text{Annual Added Profit} \quad \$} = \text{———Years———Months}$$

5—EQUIPMENT OBSOLETED

Description and Disposition   Tag No:_____

First Cost   Reserve   Net Book Value

6—EXPENDITURE SUMMARY	Allocated	Previous Requisitions in Process and/or Approved	This Requisition	Unrequisioned Balance
TOTAL PROGRAM				
19__				
19__				
TOTAL DIVISION				
19__				
19__				

7—APPROVALS   **DIVISION**   **CORPORATE**

Industrial Engineer	Operating Vice-Pres.
Plant Mgr.	Financial Vice-Pres.
Cost	President
Gen. Mfg. Mgr.	Board of Directors
Purchasing	Approval Date
Controller	
General Mgr.	

and resources rapidly from one direction to another to keep pace with changes in the state of the art and changes in market factors. It would be unrealistic to consider that we had, at any time, an unalterable investment plan. For an example, in the early years of television marketing, sets ranged in size from the 5 to 7 to 12-inch picture tube. The industry had moved fast and looked for a period of stability at about the 12-inch size. But it had only a momentary pause until it was off again to the 14, 16, 19, and 21-inch tubes. Our company planned ahead and geared up not only for 21s but for 24s, and 27s. Color then entered the scene and there was the added uncertainty of smaller versus larger color sets, with stiff price competition from black and white sets. This is just one example illustrating the need for flexibility and continuous review and revision of the programs submitted in the annual summary. To provide for this situation, the operating divisions submit revised programs in the manner already described for regular programming. At the normal programming time each year, complete program outlines for the following two years, incorporating all revisions, are submitted to enable management to reconsider approvals in the light of the current financial situation of the company and general economic conditions.

Essentially, the capital expenditure program summaries and revisions provide a basis for broad operating and financial planning. The permanent property requisitions serve as a review and basis of control over actual expenditures. These requisitions must be prepared and approved before any commitments are made for capital expenditures. The requisition serves to identify the expenditure in terms of its specific items which, of course, may vary from the content of the program as originally submitted. The requisition provides the final evaluation before money can be spent. Also, it serves to identify any equipment obsoleted and indicates its value and method of disposal. Many times one permanent property requisition will cover a group of related individual items, or even all the items involved in a particular program. The method of processing requisitions depends upon the size of expenditure. Naturally, executives at the corporate level should not spend time reviewing individual requests for which the amounts involved are not substantial. The cut-off point for division versus corporate approval has to be established somewhat arbitrarily. There are dollar limits for approval at three levels: division manager, corporate officers, and finally the board of directors. In no case, can items covered by a permanent property requisition be changed without review and approval. Also, the estimated cost can not be exceeded by more than 10 percent without resubmission. Any overrun of $5000 or more regardless of the percentage involved, requires the same approval as the original.

PROGRESS REPORTING, AVAILABILITY OF FUNDS, FOLLOW-UP OF PROJECTS

Next, to tie all the pieces together and to review the overall activity, each division prepares a monthly report on division expenditures called permanent property program detail. (Exhibit 5.) This summarizes program authorizations, permanent property requisition approvals, expenditures, and unexpended funds. The division schedules are consolidated to provide a company-wide summary which is included in the monthly financial statement. This summary shows rate of cash authorizations, commitments and expenditures or, in other words, the overall progress in carrying out the capital expenditures plan. Finally, no system of controls would be complete without a reliable method of determining the amount of capital currently available for investment and what can be anticipated in the months ahead. Therefore, we instituted a cash forecast report, the form of which is illustrated by data on

Exhibit 5

PERMANENT PROPERTY PROGRAM DETAIL

STATUS REPORT FOR MONTH ENDING_____

Title of Program_____

Program Number	Approved PPR's	Capitalized to date	Unfinished Plant & WIP	Total Spent (2 + 3)	Approved not Spent	Authorized Cash Outlay	Authorized not spent (6-4)	Authorized not apprvd. (6-1) or (7-5)
1	2	3	4	5	6	7	8
	$1,000,000	400,000	100,000	500,000	500,000	1,150,000	650,000	150,000

capital expenditures program (Exhibit 6) and the purpose of which is to provide financial staff with this information far enough in advance to permit sound planning. It informs management of the current estimate of cash availability versus expenditure requirements. On the basis of this comparison, action is initiated to obtain additional cash, or to ration cash outlays or step up investment plans, as the case may be. Short-term forecasts are submitted by each division, each month, indicating future requirements by months up to 12 months. Long-term forecasts supplement the short-term by projecting cash availabilities three years ahead. These are prepared annually. Essentially, the cash forecast balances anticipated disbursements against estimated receipts, but entries on the cash forecasts report for permanent property outlays are made only on the basis of permanent property requisitions that have been approved. Thus, central management can use the forecast as a starting point in measuring the impact of additional capital expenditure approvals on our cash position. And, of course, whenever the forecast indicates an impending cash shortage position, expenditure approvals can be slowed down or plans can be made for additional financing, far in advance of requirements. In this respect, the cash forecast has been of enormous importance to the maintenance of our forward drive.

Exhibit 6

DATA ON CAPITAL EXPENDITURES PROGRAM

Program Title: Program No._____

Purpose and Description of Program: Priority Rating_____
Anticipated additional earnings or savings:
Program is estimated to start:_____Program is estimated to be completed_____

CASH REQUIREMENTS

Year   Capital Amount(a)   Expense Amount   Working Capital   Program Total

19__
Total

Capitalized against program in   *: $
Requisitions already officially approved for program and still open**: $
Expenditures against these requisitions:* $ 19__ $ 19__
Cash needed for these requisitions: $ $
New cash for capital requisitions: _____   _____
Total Cash for capital requisitions (a): $ $
(a) Each year amount in both places must agree. * Estimate as of 12/31. ** As at date
    of submitting budget.

There remains one other important phase of the subject of capital expenditures. This is the follow-up appraisal or postaudit. As a part of our controls system, we have made provision for follow-up of programs to assure results as originally proposed. This is important for a number of reasons. Foremost is the need to develop and maintain a high sense of responsibility among those submitting capital expenditure proposals. This can be assured by the knowledge that a follow-up will be made. Also, we have learned a great deal by comparing results against the plan and have applied this knowledge in formulating later projects. For example, it may be found, on examination of a proposal, that all the facts are clearly and thoroughly supported and that the return on investment is projected at a satisfactory level. However, on postaudit of the program, it proves to have been unsatisfactory because the high annual return on investment extended over only a short number of years, after which equipment became obsolete. It is important to maintain awareness of this possibility and, by review after the fact, to keep informed.

The follow-up takes the form of internal auditing and repetitive and special analysis. Up to this point, nothing is said about the role of internal auditing. This department operates independently of any division or plant personnel and, broadly stated, its function on this subject is to see that specific policies established by the company have been adhered to with regard to all capital expenditures. Particular emphases are placed on the determination that competitive bids were obtained before expenditures were made; that proper accounting for capital versus expense items, including installation and other costs, was made; that correct asset classifications and depreciation rates were used; that the disposition of obsolete equipment was made in accordance with company policy (accounting, competitive bids, etc.); and that approvals for expenditures were obtained in all instances, particularly in the instance of expenditures in excess of the original approvals. The internal auditing function also includes a postaudit of investment profitability when new plant, new equipment, or replacement equipment is in full operation. This audit phase includes a comparison of projected versus actual figures. The investment for plant, equipment and working capital items are examined and compared with the projected amounts.

Top management does not examine detailed reports on internal plant operations. However, at both corporate and divisional levels, we watch trends on the key factors (cost, return on investment, investment turnover, and earnings), as compared to the standards established when the project was approved. These investigations are made each month until it is certain that the investment profitability will be realized as originally projected or until other corrective moves are indicated. With the exception of the internal auditing processes, the follow-up procedures are conducted entirely within the framework of our decentralized organization. Division management, in most instances, provides the basic data from which the special analyses are made, and division and plant management is encouraged to develop its own analysis program.

THE ENDS IN VIEW

The contents of this chapter have been about equally divided between consideration of policies that relate the purposes of capital expenditures to the conduct of capital expenditure programs and particularization of the accounting tools through which an individual company in a fast developing industry gives effect to these policies in pursuit of increased profitability of operations in the near and not-so-near future. It will have been noted that, although the application incorporates certain mechanics, that is, procedures, it is not mechanical in character, but rather flexible and adaptable and, above all, responsive to managerial needs and changing circumstances.

"The overall capital control program is not really integrated if it overlooks future expenditures that are really part and parcel of the same program."
John E. Rhodes

CHAPTER 17

REDUCING RECEIVABLES TO MAXIMIZE RETURN ON INVESTMENT

LEO G. BLATZ

"The Singer Sewing Machine Company is a pioneer in installment-plan sell-
ing. Periodic credit crunches forced Singer, like so many other companies,
to take steps to reduce the amount of outstanding receivables. How this was
done is discussed in this chapter."

The Singer Company has come a long way since its organization as a sewing machine company in 1851. It has expanded both in size and in number
of products produced. In recent years it has diversified so widely that its
activities today cover five major business areas—consumer products, industrial products, aerospace and marine systems, business machines, and
education and training products.

Total sales for all areas exceed $2 billion.

To manage this broad range of business activities, the company is organized into eight operating groups. Each of these groups is a good sized
business in itself. The company's planning process is directed by a Corporate Staff Department which has the responsibility of setting broad directions for the operating groups and for monitoring the planning processes of
the groups to ensure that they are consistent with the company objectives
and in harmony with the planning of other groups.

The International Consumer Products Group, while principally concerned
with household sewing machines, also sells industrial sewing machines,
household knitting machines, and a variety of other consumer durable
products depending on local business opportunities.

The International Consumer Products Group does business in some 100
countries. In many of these countries, Singer was the first American company to be there—80 to 100 years ago. The company's products are bought

by both consumers and artisans. The sewing machine has been a very vital product in the development of societies from primitive forms to the varying stages of civilization that we see today. Singer has helped to make this development possible. It has provided product distribution in areas of the world that were previously considered inaccessible, augmented by education and instruction so that people could beneficially use the company's products. Perhaps most importantly, the company has provided consumer financing in parts of the world that had known only a cash or barter economy. Needless to say, being a pioneer in installment-plan selling was both an opportunity and a risk. But the lessons have been learned well, and Singer has grown proficient in managing the financial side of its business.

The International Consumer Products Group has annual sales of approximately $250 million. There are some 22,000 employees in the 100 countries, and a staff organization in New York.

Certain of the smaller countries are combined for management purposes within regions so that one reporting location may comprise several countries, such as the islands that make up the Caribbean area. Each reporting location has a Controller/Treasurer who is responsible for the financial aspects of the local business. The consolidation process is done in New York from reports cabled in from the field one day of each month.

The Group is furnished with corporate objectives by the Corporate Planning Department. Using a computer facility, projections are prepared covering five years of income statements for each reporting location in the Group as well as a consolidated projection for the total Group. These projections are then compared with the corporate objectives. When the Group projections indicate performance better than the corporate objectives, it is an indication that the Group is on the right track. On the other hand, if Group projections fall short of the objectives, there is a planning gap. Then objectives must be reexamined. If it can be agreed that the objectives are realistic and attainable, it is up to the Group management to devise strategies and plans that will bring the attainment of these objectives.

Budget guidelines are compared to the business plan, and if they are found to be acceptable, they are given to local management. It is possible to communicate with local managements in a series of three meetings at various locations around the world. This tends to minimize the amount of travel by local managers. It also permits dealing with people from fairly homogeneous areas of the world in each meeting. Well in advance of these planning meetings, each local manager receives a copy of the budget guidelines for his country. He comes to the planning meeting prepared to give a brief presentation on how his management will achieve budget guidelines. If he feels that he can not accept the budget guidelines, he must offer alternative targets for the coming year. Where disagreements exist, they are settled in private negotiations, and each local manager leaves the meeting with an agreed set of targets for his budgeting process. In due course, the local budgets are prepared and sent to New York for the final consolidation and presentation to the corporation. This kind of a process ensures a minimum of last minute surprises and forced budget changes.

In other words, Singer is a classic case of a decentralized, international company where each unit in the field has considerable autonomy.

In addition to the five-year business plan and the annual budget, the company employs a quarterly forecasting technique which is, in essence, an updating of the budget objectives for the current year. The Group also prepares each month a brief rolling forecast of the coming three months. This has proven to be a very valuable management tool at the local level and it enables management to react quickly to impending unfavorable developments.

On the philosophical aspects of budgeting, the Group has established certain basic rules:

- The budget must establish goals. These goals should be attainable but challenging.
- The budget should be realistic.
- Every location should budget for improvements.

On the other side of the coin, we recognize that a budget is sometimes more than a control and planning tool. There are times when a budget becomes a political document. The following are some of the types of budgets that have been identified as being unacceptable.

The "low-ball" budget is one where all of the targets are set unrealistically low and improvements are either understated or nonexistent. The intent is to provide a comfortable assurance that when the actual results come in they will look good relative to budget. Submission of this kind of a budget is a good way of insuring that the budget will be done twice.

There is another type of budget that can be called an "impossible dream." This is the budget that predicts an unattainable performance. This kind of budget has obvious short-range benefits. It also can lead to a long-term disaster.

Now with this system, painstakingly worked out over nearly 100 years, what happens when the entire process and approach have to be changed suddenly? That is exactly the situation we faced recently.

In setting corporate objectives for a recent year, the management recognized that American business was experiencing a credit squeeze. Large, reputable companies were having serious problems of liquidity. Hence, the planning objectives given to the operating groups for that year called for vigorous efforts to reduce assets and improve cash flow, without jeopardizing income from operations. The results of the planning exercise within the International Consumer Products Group indicated that they would be barely able to meet the corporate objectives by doing things as they had done them in the past. There was no margin for error, and the management was not at all comfortable with the idea of running the business for a year on that basis.

Clearly, it had to achieve a very delicate balance between the kind of aggressive and expansive selling practices that would maintain sales growth on the one hand. And, on the other hand, management needed conservative, cash-oriented practices that would provide the desired reduction in consumer accounts receivable investment.

Obviously, the company had to guard its cash position by reducing investment in installment receivables. Equally obviously, this represented some change in direction in a business that had been built over the years on an extension of credit.

One thing was certain, the job could not be done in the corporate offices in New York.

Here was a situation where the top level management of the Group knew what it wanted in terms of performance, asset utilization, return on capital, and so on. But on the firing line, where it really counted, that is, the clerk in the shop, the canvassing salesman visiting a prospect's home, things were not happening in ways that would bring about achievement.

After considering many different approaches to the problem, the Group management found what it believed to be the answer.

For many years the training of employees has been an integral part of the company's business. Here was the perfect vehicle for getting the message to the employees. What was needed was a program to redirect and invigorate the training activity. Hopefully, if this could be done, the employees themselves would carry out the new program.

One of the first requirements was a name for the program—one that would catch people's fancy and suggest something much more than the same old thing—even though that's what it really was. And so was born MMM—Modern Merchandising Methods.

To be successful, a program must have goals. The Group defined its goals as the following, not necessarily in the order of importance:

- Reduce the absolute level of receivables.
- Improve the quality of receivables.
- Accomplish the foregoing without seriously impacting the level of sales.

To reach these goals, it was decided to deal with averages. In other words, the salesman would not turn away the customer who had to have 24 months to pay, but he would concentrate on those customers who could afford to pay in less than 24 months.

Thus, the terms of reference became:

- Average level of cash sales.
- Average percent of down payment.
- Average length of contract.

Before assigning objectives to the individual countries, Group management tested the sensitivity of the various measurements agreed upon. The results of the sensitivity study brought out very clearly the size and difficulty of the task management had set out to accomplish. At the outset of any program to improve installment receivables, there is on the books a body of existing contracts that will be collected over a specified future time period. There is very little that management can do to change this. Therefore, a change in the average length of contracts sold from 24 to 22 months results in a reduction of investment of only 2 percent at the end of one year. It is only after two years that the mix changes significantly between new contracts and old contracts, and at that point the investment is reduced by 8.1 percent. With down payments, the effect of a rather drastic change from an average 10 percent to an average 15 percent is to reduce investment by 3.6 percent in one year and 4.0 percent at the end of two years.

To carry this message to the field organizations, the Group organized a series of regional meetings. By holding meetings in Caracas, Mexico City, Singapore, and Istanbul, it was possible to bring the message to the people who had to do the work in a relatively short period of time. Each meeting was attended by a group that operated in roughly the same kinds of marketing conditions.

On the first day of a regional meeting, the country's receivable status was presented to the audience in the form of charts that had been prepared at Group headquarters. These charts depicted cash sales, average down payments, and average length of contract. The MMM training was presented by the Group's Training Director. It was a thorough review of all the basic rules of selling, including those that directly affect the level of receivables and those that do not.

The motivation portion of the first day's agenda was devoted to various types of salesmen's compensation plans. The basic aim of these compensation plans is to provide the salesmen with an incentive for doing what is best for the company. Thus, a higher commission is paid on the sale of a sewing machine as opposed to a product that is not manufactured by Singer. A higher commission is paid on a cash sale than on a credit sale. A higher commission is paid on a sale with a short contract than on a sale with a long contract. In cases where variable commissions are not practical, bonuses are used to achieve the desired results.

Next, the program objectives and means of measurement were introduced to the people at the conference. The conference leaders outlined in a general way how they thought a typical MMM program should be organized at the country level. Essentially it is a pyramid-type training program where the training message is passed, starting at the very top of the organization, down the various levels by each supervisor to his subordinates.

On the second day of the meeting, representatives of each country presented to the Group an outline of their detailed program for accomplishing the objectives that had been set before them on the previous day. The level of enthusiasm generated in the first day's session was such that country representatives worked long into the night to prepare their program for presentation on Day 2. A real spirit of competition developed with each country endeavoring to present the most effective program.

After the conference, representatives from each country returned to their homes and began implementing their local MMM program. Each country was required to submit a progress report after 30 days. The results of the programs were monitored at Group headquarters.

The follow-up of MMM programs is a continuing function. In the second half of the year, the Group entered a stage that could be called "fine tuning." They found that some countries had gone too far with MMM with the result that their sales were affected adversely. In these countries they recommended some relaxation of the objectives, but only for a specified period of time and in the form of a sales promotion. For example, in one country, they authorized a 30-day promotion based on a 5 percent down payment. However, the salesman was trained and motivated to point out the advantage to the customer of making a higher down payment. As a result, the average down payment during the period of this promotion was 10.1 percent.

RESULTS

The program is now in its third phase, wherein Group management has analyzed a year's performance and identified those locations that exceeded their objectives and those locations that did not make their objectives.

It is now tailoring specific programs for the problem countries as a follow-up to the MMM program of the previous year.

The all important question is, of course, how did it all turn out? For last year, the Group came within 1 percent of meeting its sales commitment. Management is convinced that the sales they did not get were the problem sales that they really did not want. Group net income commitment for the year was not only equaled: it was exceeded! The Group ended the year with a lower investment in receivables compared to the prior year despite higher sales. Receivable turnover ratio improved by 10 percent over the year before, and this was even better than the objective. Installment arrearage as a percentage of gross receivables improved by 2.4 points. The cash flow budget for the year was exceeded, and turnover of capital employed increased significantly. These results were achieved because the management of the Group made the effort to direct its attention in an organized way to the basics of sensible selling and good management.

This then has been one experience in taking the steps that come after the planning process. They might be summarized as follows:

1. Develop the program.
2. Communicate the program to every level of the organization.
3. Follow up on the results.
4. Adjust the program when required.
5. Never lose sight of the basic objectives.

"Adoption of the Singer plan can result in a lower investment in receivables even with increased sales."   *Leo G. Blatz*

CHAPTER 18

INFORMATION SYSTEM FOR MATERIALS MANAGEMENT

D. LARRY MOORE

"Materials management may well take on the status of a profit center in the near future."

One of the principal measurements of the success of a corporate enterprise and its ability to attract capital is profitability. Return on sales, return on stockholders' equity, and return on investment are the typical expressions of this measurement. Return on investment (often used interchangeably with return on assets) receives the greatest emphasis in most organizations, since the owners of the enterprise are interested in the ability of management to generate earnings in relation to the assets with which they are entrusted.

Return on investment can be influenced, to a much greater degree than is generally recognized, by the effectiveness of a group of closely related functions that fall under the heading *materials management*. The effect of these functions on profits can best be viewed by looking at both the assets portion of the return-on-assets index and the earnings portion of a large company's annual financial statement.

Inventory usually represents the greatest single portion of assets, and is also the most controllable. Plant and equipment expenditures are not easily altered over the short run; and accounts receivable, which generally follow industry trends, are not capable of significant compression. However, it is here that effective inventory control, through material management, offers the greatest opportunity to provide a flexible, profit-yielding asset base.

The following chapter describes an information processing and control system developed and applied by Sperry Flight Systems Division. The primary function of the system—processing information about materials—relates directly to return on investment. The inventory control portion emphasizes control of assets, while the procurement, work-in-process, and customer service subsystems emphasize the planning necessary for cost-of-sales control. One of the most critical aspects of a total materials management concept depends on the integrity, timeliness, and innovation of the information provided. The information systems described here are an attempt to assume that challenge. While not all potential applications have been explored, the system is advanced in its degree of integration.

THE INTEGRATED SYSTEM

The concept for the integrated information system began seven years ago at Sperry Flight Systems Division, with the established need for more effective and timely planning and control. To fulfill this need, three major information subsystems (Exhibit 1) were designed and implemented.

Initial emphasis was on the upstream (inventory control) functions of materials management:

- Material requirements generation
- Material netting
- Scheduling
- Determination of order points and lot sizes
- Procurement control
- Receipt and disbursement of materials to manufacturing areas

This major subsystem is called the Sperry/UNIVAC material system (SUMS).

The next phase concentrated on the downstream functions:

- Customer order administration
- Customer allocation
- Physical order processing
- Shipping Control

This subsystem is known as forecasting, order administration, and master scheduling (FOAMS). The final phase linked the first two via a work-in-process subsystem for control during the manufacturing cycle and is appropriately termed the work-in-process (WIP) subsystem.

Exhibit 1. The Integrated Materials Management System Includes Three Major Information Subsystems: SUMS, Upstream Inventory Control; FOAMS, Downstream Order Functions; WIP Links the Two, Emphasis on Cost

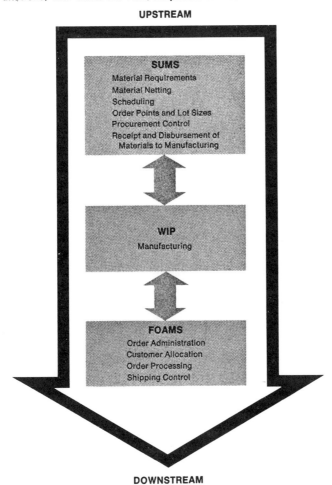

UPSTREAM

SUMS
Material Requirements
Material Netting
Scheduling
Order Points and Lot Sizes
Procurement Control
Receipt and Disbursement of
Materials to Manufacturing

WIP
Manufacturing

FOAMS
Order Administration
Customer Allocation
Order Processing
Shipping Control

DOWNSTREAM

SUMS—UPSTREAM INFORMATION SUBSYSTEM

The first subsystem developed and put on an operational basis was SUMS (Exhibit 2). Its objectives briefly stated are accuracy, minimum reaction time (both for customer and internal processing), minimum manual intervention, growth potential, and, as a byproduct, functional measurement. Since SUMS

Exhibit 2. Sums—Upstream Information Subsystem

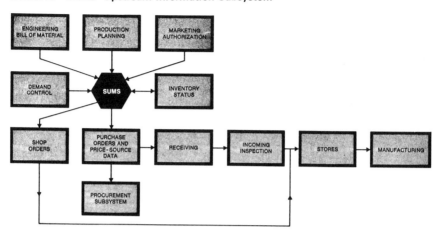

was implemented manufacturing output tripled, with no modification required to handle the expanded volume. Virtually all production programs are handled by SUMS.

With the broader data base, it is now possible to store 40,000 part numbers in 13 master computer files, with some 200 action reports available as required.

The first building block of SUMS concentrated on inventory control. This control was achieved by replacing manually updated card files with a computer storage bank (capable of recording up-to-date engineering requirements) thus creating the bill of material file. Responsibility for maintenance of this file is on engineering, since all material ordering decisions and actions are now based on the computer file instead of the data on a blueprint or list of materials.

The bill of material file serves a myriad of ancillary applications, such as "where-used," parts associations, matrices, and standard cost. An additional application that is somewhat unique is cost estimating; product requirements are compared to price and source history to generate cost estimates through mathematical projections. Approximately 15 types of information reports are developed primarily from bill of material manipulation for various users.

Requirement control is the main action loop of SUMS and involves the determination and generation of material requirements. Input requirements, held to a minimum, are quantity and the shipping schedule for the end item. The first stage of the computer processing results in an explosion that establishes gross material requirements. These gross-scheduled requirements are then run through an inventory-availability status file for netting. Here, gross requirements are compared to the availability of a specific part. Ordering action is not based on the amount on hand, but rather on the amount available. The basic formula is as follows:

On order + on-hand + in-house = availability + total open demand

On-order and on-hand are self-explanatory; in-house refers to that quantity received but not inspected and in stores.

The ramifications of using an availability base system for reorder determinations are quite different from using an on-hand quantity order point, for example, availability can be on-order with suppliers but not physically in the building. The availability also represents potential risk if additional requirements are not forthcoming. If an order point (or negative availability) is reached, an economic order quantity (EOQ) determination is necessary.[1] A subroutine determines the eligibility for EOQ ordering. However, if the requirement is a one-time order, or if the design stage suggests high susceptibility to revision, an EOQ is not used. When the part is eligible for EOQ, the order quantity becomes the EOQ amount, or multiples thereof, until the negative availability is cleared. If not eligible, a scrap factor is applied, using a one-year scrap history versus usage, and a learning curve is applied for future ordering determinations.

The final scheduling for the netted requirement is subjected to logic which adjusts the frequency of shipment. If the value of the order is within certain parameters, it will be scheduled for one-time delivery, monthly increments, or every two weeks. One of three types of orders is issued by computer printout: a shop order for internally made parts (with separate documents for each set-up), a purchase requisition, or a purchase order for vendor-supplied material. If purchasing has predetermined a source for given components via a purchasing agreement or other forward planning action, the computer will produce the complete purchase order, including delivery date, unit price, and terms. The order requires only a buyer's signature to be issued.

If the source is not predetermined, a purchase requisition is produced, along with the request-for-quote forms, and the price and source-history record for this item. Open requisition status is maintained until purchasing negotiations are complete, at which time the purchase order information is fed back to the computer, relieving the requisition file and opening a purchase

---

[1] Economic order quantity has been discussed in greater detail in the *Sperry Rand Engineering Review*, Vol. 23, No. 1, 1970, pp. 10–14.

order record. During this time, the various computer files such as purchase order status, shop order status, and so on, are updated continually as shipments are received from the suppliers or from internal sources.

It should be noted that processing from production planning initiation to generation of all scheduled orders is an overnight procedure. Daily updates are made on all major files with most status reports available on a daily basis. The UNIVAC 1108 computer system which processes SUMS, has real-time capability; however, with overnight processing available, real-time updating is not planned. Real-time inquiry of the data base, however, is felt to be advantageous and economically justifiable. Real-time inquiry has been implemented using UNISCOPE^{Tm} 100 CRT terminals and DET 500^{Tm} line printers, thus making most files accessible. The advantage is twofold: reduce hard copy reports where the number of interrogations is high, and reduce information access time.

The capability of the computer to simulate action is employed in the release cycle of parts to manufacturing. Prior to the physical issuance of the components to assembly, production planning simulates a release to secure complete information as to status of each component that is, on-hand, in-house, or purchase order and buyer information for further follow-up. This eliminates the need for additional storage space which was necessary when a staging concept was used to physically collect the components and place them in a "staged" area awaiting further receipt. The need for accurate computer records is again illustrated. If the simulation is to be useful, the parts must be on hand or short as indicated, or significant time is wasted. Audits of several fields of information in the major files are continually performed to achieve the desired accuracy levels and to correct out-of-control situations as they may arise. These audits may either compare the computer output against a predetermined output based on the inputs, or may be a physical check of the stock stated to be on hand.

Production planning makes as many simulated releases as necessary until a decision is made for an actual release. Another bill of material explosion is then performed to determine the specific level of assembly to be released. The computer then issues picking tickets and back orders for stores. Again, accuracy is controlled to the point where the back-order documents are prepared based on the computer information prior to the physical discovery of a shortage by stores personnel. Fewer than 2 percent of the predetermined back-order issuances are subsequently reversed.

Cost and Asset Reduction

The primary objectives of SUMS in relation to cost reduction are to provide the procurement function with the visibility, measurement, and controls to permit a more effective purchasing decision (Exhibit 3). One of the most effective cost-pressure techniques in procurement is the use of long-term purchase agreements. Historically, savings in excess of 10 percent have been experienced when commodities are first subjected to this technique. In addition, administrative and clerical time is reduced through the use of computer-generated purchase orders. Suppliers also benefit by having a known base of business, elimination of continual quoting activity, and so on.

Consistent with the potential in this area, SUMS services cost-reduction decision making in various ways. Forecasts of commodity and component usage are computer-aided, and status reports on forecast versus actual usage are available. Effective analysis of a multiyear, several-hundred-component agreement involving ten suppliers would not be possible without the system reports on price advantage, effect of set-up cost, savings per supplier, and benefits of clustered pricing. Analysis techniques based on SUMS-generated data have high priority in determining cost and asset reductions (Exhibit 4).

FOAMS—DOWNSTREAM SYSTEM

Information control from final test and acceptance of a product to shipment to the customer is the major concern of FOAMS (Exhibit 5). Generally, since products are made to customer requirements, a large, finished-goods inventory is not necessary; therefore, the objectives of the FOAMS system do not include any appreciable degree of asset control. The emphasis is on customer service. The ability to accurately quote delivery to customers based on previously committed production schedules is a prime objective.

Competitive lead times in the industry do not allow the luxury of passing on the full make span of the product to the customer. Therefore, anticipation orders are released to the manufacturing areas for literally thousands of different variables for hundreds of end items. The probability of accurately and currently monitoring the planned production rate versus customer requirements would be very low without computer assistance.

The main objective of the FOAMS system is to report on complete de-

Exhibit 3. **Sums Cost Reduction Objectives**

Type of Information Provided	Results
Status reporting	Shrinks the time-consuming area of vendor follow-up, allowing buyers to concentrate on cost potential. Since the introduction of SUMS, a 40 per cent reduction has been achieved in the time required for this function
Workload trends	Alert management if an out-of-control or potentially out-of-control situation exists
Delivery and quality ratings	Provided to purchasing for each vendor on a current and six-month moving average basis. Adds a degree of objectivity to purchase decisions
Commodity and vendor volume	Helps insure that the effort spent on forecasting and source development is consistent with the potential return
Commodity long-term price trends	Used in conjunction with quantity-based learning curves. This information is critical in pricing future customer orders and in providing a measurement base for material cost standards

livery status through shipping of all customer orders.[2] Active visibility and control are also provided for problem items such as export licenses, prepayment, and shipping information. To meet these objectives, the FOAMS system is composed of two segments. One segment controls assembled items while the other controls piece or spare parts.

Control of Assembled End Items

Based on past order patterns, marketing forwards an authorization order to manufacturing. This information is maintained by end item and delivery

[2] A secondary objective was to comply with the Air Transport Association's computerized system of ordering. Several airlines throughout the world are operating on a system whereby orders are transmitted by punched card to the supplier, who, in turn generates acknowledgments, invoices, and shipping papers in machine-readable form.

Exhibit 4.   Sums Asset Reduction Objectives

Type of Information Provided	Results
Accurate bill of materials file	Obsolescence and costs incurred for engineering changes have been reduced considerably
Accurate inventory records and audit control procedures	Reduced inventory adjustments and overall inventory
Dollars of availability	Reviewed continually by production planning for corrective action
Damage control by authorization order	Aggregate demand against any component can be viewed separately
Level-by-level setting and scheduling	Assures that schedules in inbound material are consistent with production requirements, obviating the need for large safety stocks

date. Each customer order enters the FOAMS system, thus reducing the "available for sale" amount. Information of net availability is then given to customer service so that in any time period for any product a customer's inquiry can be evaluated as to shipment date. Emergency orders are processed outside the FOAMS system because production capability must be investigated. Customer report data includes a six-month profile of required, acknowledged, and shipped-unit information; current and future order-status schedules; and specific customer order numbers, terms, and so on. Tracking of the order and items continues through shipment.

Control of Piece and Spare Parts

The piece and spare part segment of FOAMS is mechanized to process machine-readable orders. Acknowledgments are automatically made after the required schedule, amount on hand, amount on order, and availability are reviewed by the computer system. Manual intervention is required only if the computer logic determines that an acknowledgment date is inconsistent with customer requirements. The emphasis here is on quick turnaround, volume, and accuracy of transactions.

Both segments of the FOAMS system are committed to customer servicing

Exhibit 5.   FOAMS—Downstream System

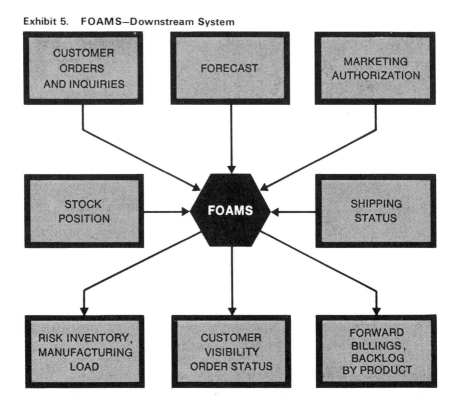

and specific status tracking after the manufacturing cycle. Value is measured by customer responsiveness, on-time delivery, ability to acknowledge the required schedule and staffing levels required to maintain the desired degree of responsiveness. The system has improved the operation in all these areas, but primarily in the quality of customer service.

WIP—MIDSTREAM INFORMATION SUBSYSTEM

The function of the WIP subsystem (Exhibit 6) is to provide information and control over a final assembly and test operation. Basically, WIP is a cost-improvement information system, with the emphasis on assembly cost and material shrinkage. The "make" phase of most products in the WIP cycle is six weeks or less; therefore, the work-in-process inventory is not subject to the degree of control necessary in finished component parts. The main objective

Exhibit 6.   WIP—Midstream Information Subsystem

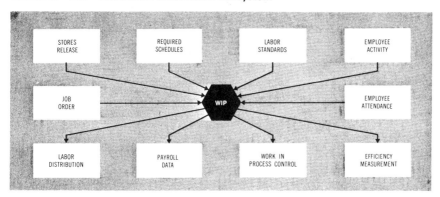

of the system is to collect accurate labor-expended information, work measurement and standards information, and payroll input.

Output from the SUMS release cycle becomes input to the WIP subsystem.[3] To keep track of the material released from SUMS, magnetic tape data collectors are positioned throughout the assembly and test area for easy accessibility to all production employees. Operators report work completed on each job and such nonstandard types of labor as generation of scrap and idle time. From this data, the status of the subassembly, assembly, or end item is determined. Hours expended are compared with predetermined time standards to highlight job or operator problems. These problems can then be summarized by product area, product line, or job order, as required for revision.

CONCLUSION

The impact and leverage that the numerous functions of materials management have upon profitability and growth are being recognized by many organizations. The systems approach to management, together with advances in computer technology, are forcing this recognition and making it possible. Dean Ammer, writing in the *Harvard Business Review,* suggests that materials management may well become a profit center concept within the near

[3] It is important to note that all fabrication areas such as wire harness manufacturing, machining, printed circuit boards, and encapsulated modules are covered in SUMS since all those items return to a central stores area for final disbursement.

future. It even seems possible that as high a return might be earned on a company's investment in material as on the assets it has tied up in marketing or manufacturing.

At Sperry Flight Systems Division, materials management is a concept where the entire function is monitored at a lower level organizationally; this, by contrast to the traditional procurement-production-shipping concept, which funnels relevant information directly to the chief executive. Since the system was introduced, it has experienced wide acceptance and utilization by operating personnel. As a result of this broad-based interchange of information, productivity has shown a significant increase.

"Because inventories represent a significant segment of a manufacturing company's assets, good inventory management can greatly impact the return on investment."   D. Larry Moore

CHAPTER 19

LET'S GET THE USER AND THE COMPUTER TOGETHER

PAUL MARANKA

*"User involvement in the development of a computerized materials manage-
ment system is a full time effort. It starts at the feasibility stage and ends only
when the user is satisfied that the system is meeting design objectives."*

Most companies installing new materials management systems are doing so
because their present method of controlling production and inventory are accomplished on an informal basis. The informal system leads to inefficiency of
men, materials, and money, and although the production goal may be met in
any given month, it is done so with much effort and grief. These inefficiencies
occur because the previous formal system addressed itself to a static environment and did not provide the timely information needed to run that business
in the dynamics of change. To avoid the problems caused by reliance on an
informal system, the materials manager must know the principles that un-
derlie his organization's operation and then assume the responsibility for
systems development to assure these principles are a part of any new system
designed for his benefit.

User involvement in the development of a computerized materials management system is a full time effort. It starts when the feasibility of the system is
being decided and it ends when the user is satisfied that the system is meeting
design objectives and that he can run his business with a formal system significantly better than he could before. It is not enough to be involved as a part
of a committee that decides what kind of information is necessary to run the
company, listen to some application and technical discussions about what
other companies are doing, and then turn the systems development over to
computer people for them to implement what they think is wanted or what
they think is needed.

This chapter is directed to the materials manager in a manufacturing organization. In general, he is responsible for purchasing, production and inventory control, receiving, storerooms, and the traffic department. His responsibility is to have material available on time and in enough quantity so that a product can be manufactured and/or assembled and then to ship the finished product to a customer or control its storage for later shipment. Characteristically, the demand for finished product is usually independent of any other demand and must be forecast. However, once the manufacturing build schedule is established, dependent demand for component assemblies, parts, and raw materials can be established by exploding bills of material. The formal system used by the materials manager to fulfill his responsibility is the scope of this discussion, and specifically, the chapter defines the role of the materials manager as he is involved in the systems development.

Let me illustrate the problem usually encountered in a discussion concerning the relationship of user involvement and systems development. Systems people often make the statement, "For the new system to be a success, we must have user involvement." Rarely do they suggest how the user is to be involved or exactly what he is supposed to do. Aggressive involvement in systems development is not generally an inherent trait of production and production control people. It takes a dedicated effort along with some knowledge of the systems development problem. It's analogous to a well intentioned golfer advising another golfer that to hit the ball well, he must keep his head down. Those who have attempted to hit a golf ball know there's more to keeping your head down than just doing it. In fact, keeping your head down is the natural result of the proper *execution of golf fundamentals* that are required for the set-up, take-back, and execution of the swing. In a systems development, everybody generally agrees that the system user must be involved; but what are the fundamentals of systems development and implementation from the viewpoint of the user that guarantee his participation such that he doesn't "look up" or execute his responsibilities improperly?

USER INVOLVEMENT IN SYSTEM FUNDAMENTALS

There are seven elements of systems development in which the system user should be involved:

1. Feasibility study
2. Systems design

3. Development of supporting procedures and system documentation
4. Education of users
5. Writing and testing computer programs
6. Conversion
7. Postconversion operation

In defining these elements, Dr. Joseph Orlicky's book, *The Successful Computer System* was used for background material. His book is a good, practical reference for most of the relevant factors necessary for a successful computer system. By design it does not contain discussions of specific applications. This chapter discusses the user involvement factor that Dr. Orlicky emphasizes in his discussion of system fundamentals and specifically relates them to the elements of materials management system development. My thesis is that the materials manager and/or his department representative must be involved from the beginning through the implementation of the system and that the manager must have an understanding of the principles in materials management and a desire to operate his function using a formal system. The less he is involved, the more nonusers will dictate the system characteristics and the more chance there is for the system to be nonrelevant to the actual needs of the manufacturing function. Irrelevancy will promote the use of an informal system to accomplish the goal of the formal system. An assumption is made that the system is computer based and large enough in scope to warrant the full time involvement of someone from the materials organization. With this assumption, what kind of individual would make a good user representative?

PROFILE OF AN IDEAL USER REPRESENTATIVE

Recognizing the possibility that only 1 in 100 companies may have someone who has all of the ideal characteristics, it is useful to have a benchmark. While some of the traits are inherent, others can be learned, and it is important that the individual at least have the potential to satisfy all of the requirements.

Ideally, the individual will have been a supervisor in one of the departments of the materials organization. He will have had enough contact with each of the other departments so that he understands the overall flow of material and paperwork and also understands the successful aspects as well as the problems of each area. He should be logical in his approach, analytical in mind, and progressive enough in his thinking to realize the potential benefits from a new system.

It is desirable that this individual have some experience with a computer, but this is not absolutely necessary. Computer specialists will be assigned to the project task force—this is discussed later. It is easier and less expensive to teach the user about computers than it is to teach the computer people about the application.

It may be appropriate that an individual with all these qualifications be appointed the task force leader. He must possess organizational ability to handle this successfully, and in possessing all of these qualities, he is also most likely to be a very important man in the current day-to-day operations of the department. As Dr. Orlicky has stated, "Departments whose jobs will go on the computer should . . . free up their top talent to represent them on the system development task force." He goes on to say that too many operating department heads fulfill this obligation by, ". . . releasing whomever they can spare with the least inconvenience." If taking the chosen individual out of day-to-day operations doesn't handicap the materials organization somewhat, then it is likely the proper individual has not been chosen.

This is what "user involvement" is all about. The materials manager can rationalize this requirement in various ways. He may decide he doesn't have an individual who approaches the ideal or if he has, he cannot afford to let him go for an undetermined amount of time. Alternatives open to him are:

1. Lead the project himself and allocate part of himself and part of a number of other people to the project. Under this form of organization, the systems design will tend to default to the systems people or the system implementation will be delayed because the resolution of current production problems will come before important systems decisions and decision follow-up.

2. Assign a systems analyst to the project with materials management experience and trust that the analyst will consider everything that needs to be considered and ask the user the appropriate questions at the appropriate time. This substitution can work with the proper analyst, but the materials manager has really abdicated his responsibility to the systems people. Consequently, technical considerations are prone to be given more weight than they otherwise might justify as well as causing unintentional omissions in the systems design because of a lack in understanding of all of the real problems faced by the particular using organization.

3. Specify an individual but do not free him from his current tasks. The individual in this position will find it difficult to do either job effectively and a

conglomeration of people and responsibilities will emerge whose probability of success is low. This approach will be inefficient and will waste human and machine resources as well as money.

Each one of these alternatives will enhance the chances of the informal system taking over when the formal system is implemented because each lacks the full time dedication on the part of the system user to achieve a successful system. Prior to discussing the seven systems elements listed above in more detail, we should note the role of a task force used in system development.

USER INVOLVEMENT IN THE TASK FORCE

Due to the many diverse concerns involved in implementing a materials management system, it is highly desirable to form a task force to represent the most important of these concerns. The task force will generally take two forms. The initial phase will develop into a form of steering committee that has technical, financial, sales, and user application knowledge present. The feasibility study, development overview, and implementation evaluation will be its primary objective. The materials manager will be a member of this group, and his most important contribution will come at this time. As mentioned previously, defining user requirements for a materials management system is the responsibility of the materials manager, and he must know the principles involved and how they relate to the environment in which he is managing.

The second form of the task force, which is responsible to the steering committee, will be the actual development and implementation people. Technical expertise is provided by one or more systems analyst from the computer department. The application representative(s) will be the individual described earlier and named by the materials manager. Others may be included on a full or part time basis as warranted by the particular system being developed.

The systems analyst(s) is responsible for translating the user's system requirements into terms computer programmers can understand. It is very helpful, if not absolutely necessary, for the systems personnel to have practical experience in the application being systemized. He will be better able to ask questions and make suggestions concerning the actual processing of the system data. Also, errors in the system specifications due to a lack of communication between the computer people and the user will be minimized. The level of practical experience required by the systems analyst is inversely proportional to the application knowledge and ability of the user representative assigned to the project.

Assuming that task forces will be formed that include computer and user representatives, let's look at each of the systems elements listed above and indicate where the materials manager or his representative will play an important role and where systems people will be involved.

FEASIBILITY STUDIES

At some time prior to the feasibility study, a master plan of overall information systems needs should have been developed for all of the departments in the organization. Priorities should be established and goals or objectives specified over a period of time. Major emphasis should be on the goals themselves, not necessarily the method for achievement. The *feasibility study* is the time to decide how big a bite of the overall goal the new effort will take. Because of the large potential payoff from a good materials management system, it is generally given a very high priority.

In short, three fundamental questions will be asked in the feasibility study:

1.   Technically: Is this application possible within the limits of available computer technology and our own resources?
2.   Economically: Will the system yield an adequate return on investment?
3.   Operationally: Will the application department use it or revert to an informal system?

The materials manager must be fully involved in the answers to these questions. This is the time to establish the minimum results that the system must achieve. He can thereby assure himself that those things most important to the smooth operation of the materials department will be included. He is also in the best position to know what systems compromises will least affect the performance of his department. As a result of this effort, some master plan for system implementation should emerge with a formal system for listing objectives and monitoring the path toward those objectives.

In summary, the materials manager must insure that the new system will solve his real problems. His strong involvement in the feasibility study represents the best way to obtain that insurance.

SYSTEM DESIGN

Having participated in all aspects of the feasibility study, the materials manager, using his representative, is now in a position to assure that detailed systems specifications remain consistent with his understanding. One of the materials department responsibilities in this phase is to define the input of the system to the level that it will be fed to the data processing service department. This input may be a new or existing form that will be used as a keypunch document, such as a new receiving form; or a piece of computer sensitive data output from another system, such as punched cards from the labor payroll systems; or a turnaround document from the system being designed, such as pull-cards used to issue assembly parts to the line and to relieve the balance-on-hand in the computer system.

The user must also decide what pieces of the input information will be retained to constitute the system files. As an example, he must be sure data other than inventory information that is relevant to the materials management function are included on the inventory records and that adequate data changing capability is provided. He should also specify the data necessary for establishing an order on the open order file and an allocation in the material allocation file if allocations will be used in the system. Some sort of part expediting information must be available even in the best operating circumstances.

All data validity checks should be specified by the user as well as any special data manipulation required or calculations performed as a result of a specific user requirement. Any edits, data manipulations, or calculations required as a data processing expedient are excluded from the user's control.

The user is also responsible for all reports or data inquiries that the system is to provide. The systems analyst may actually draw the detailed report layouts; however, it is the user's responsibility to know where each piece of data on the report originates, why it is displayed, and how each calculation is performed.

In order to assure himself that the detail systems specifications remain consistent with the initial systems design, the materials manager must maintain a heavy review of this phase. Trade-offs will be made and he must review these decisions so that the final systems specifications define a system that is operationally sound from a user point of view.

When systems design is complete, the user is in a position to work on supporting procedures, documentation, education, and systems test data in anticipation of the systems test when programming is complete.

DEVELOP SUPPORTING PROCEDURES AND SYSTEM DOCUMENTATION

The user is in the best position to develop and write supporting manual procedures for the new system. A detailed flow chart of the computer system will be a part of the system design phase, and using that as a basis for using input requirements and output availability, each of the existing written manual procedures must be reviewed. If they do not exist currently, this will be an excellent opportunity to put something in writing. If they do exist, new procedures may have to be written or existing procedures revised. New special forms that are required will have to be designed and ordered from a supplier. The reader should note that procedures are differentiated from computer system documentation in this section heading. User procedures are a step-by-step guide for performing a particular function external to the computer. It may include steps that indicate certain documents will be input to the computer or certain reports will be available for analysis and data resubmitted to the system.

User computer systems documentation refers to the computer system functions, capabilities, input descriptions, and output descriptions. It defines all of the data in the system, contains a flow chart of the major systems components, the input transaction editing rules, their functions, any special internal calculations and functions, and all output reports with field definitions. The user representative, with assistance from the systems analyst, can provide this part of the documentation. He is in a position to know in which format the information would be most receptive to the specific users.

In essence, the user procedures tell what to do and when to do it and the user computer system documentation describes how to communicate with the computer as necessary for those steps outlined in the procedure.

One other area of documentation needs to be discussed. The original systems specifications from the user's viewpoint will not be detailed enough, in some areas, for detail program coding. This function must be provided by the systems analyst in conjunction with the programming department. In my experience, I have observed systems specifications written in such a way that with a little modification, they can become a major part of the user documentation. This can help to reduce the cost of the documentation and aid in keeping the technical specifications consistent with the user's manual.

At the time of design, it is not always known exactly what the programming requirements will be. If the situation arises that a programming consideration must alter a systems specification due to some cost consideration or problem in technical feasibility, the specification can be changed. Of course, this is done only with the full knowledge and concurrence of the materials manager and his representative.

EDUCATE USERS

User education is the responsibility of the user. The effort so far should have provided the materials department with a representative familiar enough with the system to educate the specific people who will use it. To make the education process true training rather than orientation, some hands-on experience with the system input and output by the people who will use the system must be provided. This can best be achieved during presystems implementation by having the class participants create test data and run it through the system against the test files. For best results, the timing and completion of other phases of the implementation to this point would have to be fairly precise. In many cases, and realistically so, actual training is left to the conversion effort and the initial phase of the implementation process. A pilot operation approach lends itself to this quite well. Conversion and implementation is covered in more detail later.

If some form of system simulation by the users prior to the actual implementation of all or part of the system is not performed, then the best that can be achieved toward education of the users is a degree of system orientation.

The primary orientation medium will be classroom lecture and discussion. A valuable technique, where possible, is to compare what the users have been doing to how it will be done in the new system. This can be done in conjunction with the discussion of the procedures and system documentation that will be used. Since education is the initial contact of the users with the new system, it is of utmost importance to have the procedure and documentation available for the education sessions. As a side benefit, explaining the procedures and system requirements generates questions and may show loose ends that have not been considered.

The user's documentation must be reviewed thoroughly during the education process. It will be a heavily used reference in the initial stages of the system implementation and a very valuable reminder as the use of the system continues. Each input transaction must be explained relative to how it will be completed by the user as well as how the system will use the data. Each report must be explained and any action required by the user must also be covered. In general, anything the user needs to communicate with the system, input, output, or processing, must be thoroughly reviewed.

Consideration must be given to timing the education effort. If the user is exposed to detail too early, retention is decreased; waiting until just prior to conversion may not allow enough time to do a proper job if comprehension is slow. A suggested approach would be to start education sessions one to two months in advance of system conversion, depending on the time available from other workload. Initial sessions would be short and general and progressing to longer and more detailed sessions during the final week before implementation.

User education goes on while the computer programs are being written and tested.

WRITING AND TESTING COMPUTER PROGRAMS

The systems analyst involved in the project is responsible for assuring that the computer programs are in fact performing to system specification. Systems test is a phase of the development cycle that the user may delegate if he has participated extensively in the systems design and has confidence in the ability of the systems people to specify and program according to the system design. I have found, however, that there are some tangible benefits in having the user construct a set of test data and follow it through the entire processing cycle. These benefits are described as follows.

Gain Familiarity

In developing the procedure that will be used to test the system, the user (in conjunction with the systems analyst) will need to discuss certain technical aspects of the system. Questions such as, "Is all the data input at the same point in the system or are there diverse entry points?" "Why must the build schedule be submitted in a certain precise format?" "Why does the requisition writing procedure have to change?", will be appropriate at this time. Recognizing technical considerations will allow the user to understand why some current practices will have to change or be modified.

Assure Understanding of Basic Requirements

When the systems analyst creates test data, he will put something in each of the fields on the input transactions. In some cases, the numbers may be illogical or irrelevant, but he will be mainly testing data editing, data format on reports, accuracy of the calculations that were specified, and proper connections between the various parts of the system. As the user creates test data, he should attempt to place himself in the circumstances that will be encountered when the system is in operation. At this time, he may find that he omitted a piece of required data or that a significant procedural change is required to obtain a particular piece of data. He will also have an opportunity to review the output reports to be sure that they, in fact, contain the information in the format he wanted.

Provides Time for Changes

As the user notices discrepancies and omissions, there is still time for corrections to be made and implemented in the relative calm of the testing atmosphere rather than at the implementation and conversion time. It is axiomatic that no matter how well thought out the initial systems design, certain omissions or desired changes will develop. Careful systems design initially will minimize the omissions and early user exposure to system ouput should make implementation and conversion relatively painless.

Attain a Degree of Comfortableness

Organizations that have had bad experiences with systems developments and even those who have had no automatic data processing, tend to be very cautious about a new computer system. Those that have not had experience of their own, have often heard about the catastrophies that have occurred in other organizations.

This normal fear is based on the thought that some critical systems function will not work when the system is implemented and manufacturing lines will shut down or customer shipments will otherwise be missed. It is implied that the system cannot be tested well enough to assure that a disaster will not occur. My contention is that the system can be adequately tested. If the user participates in this testing he will attain a degree of comfortableness with the system and its level of reliability. When problems arise, he can concentrate on their solution without fear the system will collapse. Knowledge breeds confidence and lack of knowledge breeds fear, suspicion, and distrust. Systems test provides an excellent opportunity for the users to build their knowledge and confidence in the system.

In Depth Check to Declare System Ready for Implementation

It is the user's responsibility to declare the system ready for implementation. This point is the most important reason for the user to participate in the testing of the system. If he has not participated in the test phase, he must rely on the judgment of the systems analysts. It has been stated previously that the system test is the responsibility of the systems analyst and that it must be "adequately tested." He assures that it is performing per specification. There are certain phases of every materials system that are crucial to the operation of a materials department. Where requirements generation is involved, the bills of material and component part explosion logic must be accurate. Stock replenishment orders must be properly added and removed from the open order file. Receipts, disbursements, inventory count, and inventory record change transactions must be updating the inventory file properly. Certain reports must be available and the data accurately displayed. The user can test these functions adequately and assure himself that disaster is not imminent. He can relegate the problems that will occur to areas that can be cured by rerunning a given set of data or spending extra man hours outside of the computer system. The point is that the users must be dedicated to the new system to a degree that they will want to devote their full efforts to making the new system work. The key to the successful computer implementation is not to implement until the system *and* the user are ready. The user, from a people education viewpoint, can generally determine if he is ready by using parallel processing or a pilot operation; and by participating in the testing, he can be sure in his own mind that the system is ready. Systems test time, not live implementation time, is the time to assure yourself that the system *does* perform to design specifications.

CONVERSION

The conversion effort is another area where the materials manager will need to become directly involved. This is a vital point in his progress toward goal plan mentioned earlier, and a great deal of planning should go into the conversion effort. The materials manager and his representative should participate in the establishment of an Implementation Action Plan (IAP). Specific procedures need to be developed detailing how they will monitor the conversion and insure that each of the plan elements are, in fact, carried through.

The IAP as initially established should be flexible and a generalized list of all events required for the conversion should be foreseen prior to the first one being implemented. Dates need not be assigned to specific events more than two weeks to one month away. Each week, the next two weeks' specific objectives can be established. Previous commitments can be reviewed and rescheduled if necessary. Computer processing required should be reviewed at this time and file conversion and special processing will be considered. Working on weekends may be required by the user personnel and for computer processing of large file conversion efforts; therefore specific user people need to be committed at this time.

With this kind of planning, the user representatives will be able to monitor the important and critical aspects of the conversion process. The kind of conversion effort required will vary depending on which method is used. In Dr. Orlicky's book he indicated that conversion approaches vary from complete parallel operations to what he calls "cold turkey." If parallel processing is involved, the materials department representative must insure that it is occurring, but his primary responsibility is for the new formal system. Someone else (who is designated by the materials manager) must be concerned that the old formal system is being adequately maintained. This is a very important point because it is very difficult for the production and inventory control people to concentrate on the new system when the product they control is being manufactured using old system information and probably, a corresponding informal system.

In my opinion, every effort should be made to minimize or eliminate altogether parallel operations of a new and old materials management system. Parallel processing confuses the issue, both in direction of manpower resources and commitment to the new system by the using people. It works well in the precise areas of banking and accounting where the numbers should be the same regardless of how they are obtained. The very nature of a revised materials management system suggests that the system environment will change so that inaccuracies in the old system should be eliminated and the two will be different by definition.

A pilot operation approach, should be utilized whenever possible. This will involve the users sufficiently and together with an adequate testing program, should make the conversion effort relatively painless.

POSTCONVERSION OPERATION

Several postconversion details should be resolved before the materials department representative can be released from his systems duties. When the system is in operation, it will be noticed that certain data available in the system is not being maintained properly. It may be data previously available in the old system such as lead time for purchased parts, or it may be new data such as material and labor costs provided by the accounting department. The user representative must assure that cleanup effort is initiated for all data in this category and that the proper maintenance procedure will be followed.

The user representative must review all data flow and report inadequacies that were not detected in the design or testing phase. He must suggest desired changes based on the results of the system operation so far. Also, because of his involvement in each of the implementation phases, the user representative is in a position to declare when parallel processing (if implemented) is no longer required.

This part of the development will again come under the close scrutiny of the steering task force as they evaluate the system implementation. They also will review the results they have witnessed and suggest changes or improvements where necessary.

CONCLUSION

The previous paragraphs have attempted to describe what a materials manager must consider as he becomes involved in the development of a new materials management system. Every detail cannot be covered in a single chapter, but by assuming the responsibility for all phases of the development of his new management system, the materials manager will be a giant step closer to running his business with a timely and formal system that is accurate. Concomitantly, the users will not be inclined to resort to an informal system to perform their daily tasks. Since the manager is responsible for the formal system and believes in it, he will make it work. User involvement brings understanding and knowledge to the using organization, understanding encourages acceptance, and acceptance will be the foundation for the user's commitment to the success of the system.

"Aggressive involvement in systems development is not generally an inherent trait of production and production control people. It takes a dedicated effort along with some knowledge of systems development problems."

Paul Maranka

MAKING ACQUISITIONS FOR IMPROVEMENT OF PROFITABILITY

One of the characteristics of American business in the past has been a pattern of unrelenting growth. Business literature is replete with examples of new industries that started with hundreds of competitors vying with each other for an increasing share of the market. As a result of competitive pressures, prices were continually reduced. To accomplish these reductions it was necessary in many cases to invest in expensive automated equipment and a more complex overhead structure to support the increased volume of business.

Because many companies experienced difficulty in their attempts to finance growth from within, acquisitions and mergers became increasingly popular. This permitted not only a pooling of capital but a sharing of management know-how.

BASIC GUIDELINES FOR EXPANSION OF CLOSELY HELD COMPANIES

Chapter 20, which relates exclusively to privately held companies, discusses the philosophy and thinking of the owner of a family business who may be sought after for merger or acquisition.

Although some private companies are blinded by the glamor of becoming big, many others enter into a "marriage" through necessity. This chapter discusses some basic guidelines for the many mergers and acquisitions involving privately held companies.

THE TEN COMMANDMENTS FOR ASSURING PROFITABLE EXPANSION

This chapter also concerned with growth—both internal and external—and describes a case history of an actual company (fictitious name used) whose general manager and successors were instructed to pursue certain goals for growth. These goals were followed with little regard for proper foreplanning and preparation.

Internal and external growth were scheduled simultaneously even though there was a shortage of certain skills in the labor market; production was transferred from a newly acquired company to the parent location with incomplete bills of material, and a new addition was constructed with floors that were not sufficiently strong to bear the weight of the equipment. These circumstances, which many would refer to as a "comedy of errors," occur often. This chapter not only discusses the various problems but also describes the actions of a new manager who took firm steps to correct the situation. As a result of these steps, he put into effect his version of the "Ten Commandments for assuring Profitable Expansion."

CHAPTER 20

BASIC GUIDELINES FOR EXPANSION OF CLOSELY HELD COMPANIES

THOMAS S. DUDICK

"Many companies—public as well as private, large as well as small—violate these basic guidelines to growth, simple though they may be."

One need only reflect on such names as Rockefeller and Ford to realize that United States industry was founded on the concept of the family business. Through growth from within and numerous acquisitions, many small family operations have become the giants of today. It is appropriate, then, that this chapter be devoted to the privately held company.

The concepts covered in this chapter apply to publicly held companies as well as privately owned. Private companies, like publicly owned competitors, must, in their long-range planning, consider the future. Should they embark on a program of acquisition for growth? Should they remain the same size? If they are in need of capital, should they go public or should they become candidates for acquisition? While no one can furnish specific answers to these questions, the listing of considerations can be helpful in arriving at the answers.

DIFFERENCES BETWEEN PRIVATE AND PUBLIC COMPANIES

When economic considerations foreordain what must be done, there may be no alternative than that dictated by the circumstances. But when these are not a factor, the following considerations usually dictate the course of action that a company will take. These might better be referred to as advantages and disadvantages.

Private	Public
You are your own boss.	There can be numerous bosses—not only the new management—but the stockholders as well.
You have a personal identity.	Relationships are less personal—the larger the company the less personal.
Comfort of confidentiality.	You live in a fish bowl. Private information must now be published for all to see.
You expand or do not expand. If your choice is to expand, you can be selective.	Often there is a relentless push for growth. This can result in continuous turmoil. and uncertainty.
You are free to employ various members of the family.	Family hiring is limited; in some companies it is not permitted at all.
Perquisites such as automobile and insurance are available at the owner's own discretion.	Company policy generally dictates what perquisites will be allowed.

Private companies can range from the "Ma and Pa" type that are satisfied to merely make a living, to the substantial companies along the lines of Block Drug, Levi Strauss, Gates Rubber, Readers Digest, and Leviton Manufacturing Company.

EXPANDING THE PRIVATELY HELD COMPANY—INVENTORY OF STRENGTHS AND RESOURCES

Proper profit planning begins with an inventory of strengths and resources, which when properly done raises such questions as:

What are the capabilities of the management and where does its expertise lie?

What kinds of knowhow does it have—where are the areas of greatest strength?

If we are to expand, what are the products that have the greatest potential for expansion?

Is our growth limited to only one region?

How good are we at marketing our products?

How good are our manufacturing capabilities?

Do we have a plant that has excess capacity?

Is the company's marketing structure properly developed?

Is the company properly attuned to the economics of the business?

How about our capabilities in the research and development area?

Finally, what are our financial capabilities for expansion?

Although these questions apply with equal force to publicly owned companies, let us consider, for illustrative purposes, several of these points.

Management Expertise

Many companies whose management expertise is adequate in a small company environment will find themselves lacking as managers in a larger entity. The owner who is accustomed to running a "one-man show" and who personally oversees every function may hinder the growth of his company after it has expanded beyond a certain point.

If the management of a company is highly production-oriented and lacks marketing and engineering skills, this may also place a limitation on growth. In such a circumstance, the management must acknowledge its lack and bring in the necessary know-how to supplement its shortcomings.

Marketing Capabilities

A company that is strong in one regional area may find that in order to grow it must expand its marketing effort into new areas. Sometimes, if such growth is not implemented, it can mean failure for the company at its present size. This was evidenced in recent years by regional beer companies that could no longer compete with their national rivals.

In a different way, some radio and television manufacturers went through a similar experience. Their share of the market was limited because they did not have an entire line of appliances to sell. They did not have the refrigerators, washing machines, and air conditioners, for example. Naturally, the dealer favored the companies who could supply him with the entire line.

This is where selective acquisition and merger could correct the deficiency.

Economics of the Business

Frequently, established businesses find that sources of supply have changed radically—requiring material that was previously close at hand to be hauled great distances. One company, faced with this problem, recognized the basic economics of the business and took the required remedial action:

Company A was a manufacturer of wood products. Because of its need for a large supply of lumber, it was located by the founder near a large forest area with numerous sawmills in the vicinity. After two generations, the forest was depleted, the sawmills moved out, and the company had to have its lumber shipped from a distance of 2200 miles. Realizing that it could not compete as well as in the past, the decision was made to move the facility near a good source of supply. This move meant that the waste pieces and sawdust, which represented about one third of the total weight of the actual lumber used, also were no longer shipped 2200 miles. The total saving in freight amounted to several hundred thousand dollars each year.

Research and Development

Some companies are heavily endowed with innovative ability right from the start. Thomas A. Edison and Land of Polaroid are examples. More recent examples are the numerous semiconductor manufacturing companies that have been formed by engineers who have left the larger electronic companies.

All companies do not start with research capability, however. There are many instances in which the closely held company has little chance to compete when the "name of the game" is good research capability. Take the case of the small chemical manufacturer. The chances of successful research, as compared with the large chemical companies is slight. In Chapter 1 of this book Paul Elicker, Chief Executive Officer of SCM, refers to much scurrying on the part of many paint labs trying to find something that will make paint dry as fast as a lead drying agent. The probabilities are that one of the larger companies, with good research capabilities will come up with the answer.

The company seeking to grow should evaluate its position with respect to its research and development potential. Some companies, lacking the necessary expertise and capital requirements, have sought other alternatives—such as copying the design of others. This has been done through licensing agreements.

The privately held company wanting to expand should seriously review the foregoing considerations and evaluate its opportunities for growth very honestly. If it cannot make an objective appraisal of its own, it should not hesitate to seek outside advice uncolored by subjectivity. In addition to an objective overview, the company should . . . .

"EXPECT THE UNEXPECTED"

"The things we worry about most seldom happen" seems to be a truism when all is going well. But when everything seems to be falling apart, Murphy's Laws of Random Perversity take over. These can be summarized as follows:

- There are times, in any field of endeavor, when anything that can possibly go wrong, does,
- When this happens, look for things to go from bad to worse.
- If there is a possibility of several things going wrong, the option that is most damaging is the one that will most likely occur.
- Nature seems to side with the hidden flaw. (Nature is not only niggardly—it is ruthless)[1]
- If everything seems to be going well you may not be seeing the whole picture.
- If you toy with something too long, it will surely break.

The best defense against these is defensive profit planning based on sound guidelines. These are discussed next.

GUIDELINES FOR GROWTH

One of the prerequisites for growth is a management that understands risks, is ready to take such risks, and is capable of managing the program that it has undertaken. Naturally, it is necessary to have capital in sufficient quantities to support such a program.

Stay within Areas of Proven Skills

When a company is being enlarged, it should remain in the areas of its proven skills if it is to succeed in its goals. The Stanford Research Institute made a study of companies that had expanded either internally or through acquisition. The purpose was to correlate successful growth with the basic business of the company. As might be expected, those companies that stuck to their

---

[1] Parenthesized portion supplied by the author.

areas of expertise were more successful than those that simply grew willy-nilly without consideration of their abilities.

Evaluate the Economic Climate

Growth should be planned against all kinds of business and economic conditions. Many companies interested in making an acquisition have borrowed short-term money for long-term purposes. Their intention was to make a public offering and repay their short-term debt. However, they never came to market because there was no market. It is important to plan in a way that resources are going to be sufficient to weather hard times.

In planning for growth, the impact on earnings can be planned to some extent. On the one hand earnings can be reduced in the short term, or they could be left on a par with what they were prior to the expansion program. For the cautious and conservative management, growth plans can have as their goal adding to the prior earnings so there is an improvement in profits. And finally, the planned program might accept peaks and valleys in earnings until it begins to mature.

Monitor your Progress through Operating Statements

Quite frequently during a growth period companies find, after say two years, they need more money. It is important at that time to be able to prove that you have a well thought out plan for growth, supported by comparisons of actual results with what has been planned for recent periods. You must be able to demonstrate to the investment community that you have good fiscal management and an ability to improve earnings on an annual basis. Should you want to sell or merge the company two, three, or five years later, you will have a much stronger case if you can demonstrate a pattern of consistency. This is not a recommendation to sell or merge at that time—some companies are neither going to go to the public nor merge for many years.

The Top Executive Should Get Involved

Searching out the right company is sufficiently important to involve the top executive in the company. If the president can't be involved, then someone should be selected with the authority to negotiate the terms of trade and act as spokesman for the company.

Sources of Leads to Acquisitions

The sources are numerous. Among them are Moody, Thomas, Dun and Bradstreet, the banks, accountants, and attorneys. If the company is a manufacturer, it might consider an association with one of the competitors making similar or related products. The management personnel of the company, particularly the sales people, can be helpful in this regard.

Look for Businesses that Fit

It's not enough to have a certain expertise related to technology alone; "fit" applies to the application of the technology. A company with expertise in a certain area dealing with specialized custom products that are produced in short runs can be very efficient, because it also has the ability to move quickly from one job to another. It may also have the associated skills required in making inexpensive jigs and fixtures to substitute for intricate automated equipment that its high volume competitors would be inclined to use. Such a company could be treading in rough waters if it embarked on an acquisition program to get into the standardized high volume type of business unless it carefully assessed all the factors and recognized that it was actually getting into a different business, even though the basic technology was similar.

Examine the Prospective Acquisition Carefully

There are enough problems associated with an acquisition without gratuitously introducing more. The importance of looking behind the obvious can be illustrated by some examples.

Company X purchased a small company run by one man, who didn't believe in paperwork of any kind. He therefore had no formalized drawings or bills of material of any kind. His foremen instructed the employees how the product was to be made. When changes were required, the foremen made the decision as to the nature of the change. No written record was made. The company decided to move this new acquisition to the parent's location where it had excess capacity. When the move was completed and the new employees started to make the product, problems came thick and fast because of the lack of written information. Efficiency dropped in half, and rework increased tenfold. Obviously, the problems were not resolved until all the required information was gathered and recorded on paper so that new foremen and other employees could find a central source of data.

Company Y bought a company that was working on some government contracts in addition to commercial business, but never took the trouble to investigate the nature of these contracts. After the purchase was completed, it was found that there was a large fixed price contract that was destined to have over several hundred thousand dollars in overruns, at the minimum, before it was completed. Because of the magnitude of the overrun, the new acquisition could not become very profitable for several years. Company Y wanted very much to get into the commercial product line of its new company because it complemented its own products. However, the price that was paid was excessive because of the loss contract. Some careful investigation could have resulted in tighter bargaining and undoubtedly a lower price.

Company Z found a potential acquisition that appeared to be highly desirable. It was achieving gross margins that were almost 5 percent higher than its own, after adjusting for differences in classification of costs. The acquisition was made without too much further investigation except to note that inventories were somewhat high. After the negotiations were completed, and several months went by, the newly acquired company's gross margin shrank to about 1 percent less than that of Company Z. Investigation revealed that the newly acquired company had been building inventory for the past two years prior to purchase with the result that it was inventorying a good deal of its overhead. When Company Z decided to reduce production and sell off some of the inventory, profits were adversely affected because of the reduced volume of production. The obvious moral to draw from this company's experience is that the financial statements of potential acquisitions should be carefully studied to determine whether the profitable operations were reflecting profits from high production rather than from profitable sales.

Too Much Knowledge can Backfire

An important caution to follow when investigating a company that has a product covered by a patent or secret process, is to avoid seeking too much information relating to that product. An example of what can happen was illustrated by the case of a soft drinks manufacturer who wanted to add a new soft drink to his line. It seemed more expedient to buy an existing company rather than develop the new product through extended research. Accordingly the owner started looking. He located a company that seemed to be very desirable (at the right price). In the course of negotiations, he was shown the ingredients and formula to make the soft drink in which he was interested. Although all else looked good, negotiations were broken off because agreement could not be reached on the purchase price.

The soft drinks manufacturer, instead of looking for other possible acquisitions decided to have his own chemist come up with a formula. When this formula was market tested, it proved to be very popular. Six months later, after the marketing program for the new drink was underway, he was sued by the company he had been interested in purchasing. The claim was that he had used information contained in the secret formula that was shown to him.

CONCLUSION

The effort expended toward growth, like any other function in a business must have proper balance. All functions of the business must also be properly balanced with each other. There are extremes—some companies planning for their growth in a very haphazard manner; others being so involved in acquisitions that other facets of their business are neglected. The company that is lackadaisical in its approach to growing may fare out, but it may not remain competitive; it will be guilty of an error of omission. The very aggressive company, on the other hand, that neglects its other functions could be guilty of errors of commission. It may grow very rapidly, but it if ignores the guidelines for sound growth it may well take three steps forward and two backward.

"Searching out the right company is sufficiently important to involve the top executive. If the president can't be involved, then someone should be picked with the authority to negotiate the terms of trade and act as spokesman for the company."   Thomas S. Dudick

CHAPTER 21

THE TEN COMMANDMENTS FOR ASSURING PROFITABLE EXPANSION

THOMAS S. DUDICK

"When sound business policies are subordinated to rapid growth, profits suffer and liquidation of past gains is the inevitable result. This chapter describes a pattern that has been typical for many companies, and it recommends a set of guidelines for orderly growth in the form of "ten commandments for expansion."

The desire of management for bigness can be the by-product of a desire for a place in the sun. The bigger the company, the more important the executives of that company become in the business community. Bigness, in this case, is a matter of pride coupled with aggressiveness and ambition.

The needs for bigness can also be ordained by the forces of competition continually squeezing out the marginal producer who does not have the resources to keep up with the growth of technology. This competitive situation forces companies to do more forward planning than they might otherwise do.

It is fortunate that the importance of forward planning is attracting so much management attention. However, because of the emphasis on looking into the future, there is a tendency to discount the importance of past history. This is unfortunate because history frequently contains a wealth of information on past errors in judgment, which can be minimized in future planning.

THE CASE OF THE DURARD COMPANY

Take the case of the Durard Plastics Company whose products consist of plastics molding, metal stamping, and related hand assembly operations. The product line includes such items as push buttons for radios, plastic knobs for appliances, plastic bottles with caps, electric shaver parts, small radio cabinets, and a variety of metal parts used in the appliance industry.

The management of this company wanted to increase its share of the market. It planned to achieve this goal through the purchase of established companies as well as expansion from within. As each acquisition was digested, the plan was to move the operations to the town of Durard, for which the parent company was named.

The management of the company was disappointed in progress—and changed general managers three times during a six-year period. The chronology of events leading to management dissatisfaction follows.

- *Purchase of Acme Plastics and expansion from within.*   Acme Plastics became a part of Durard in August of the first year—as indicated in the pictorial diary represented by Exhibit 1. This acquisition resulted in a substantial increase in sales volume, as well as profits. Since plans called for all Acme activities to be moved to Durard, a building expansion program was undertaken. This was completed in the spring of the second year, and the move was made. Concurrently with the completion of this move, 12 injection molding presses were purchased and set up in the expanded plant. The combination of the Acme move and the establishment of an injection molding department proved to be "too big a bite." Since only key supervisory personnel of the Acme Company were transferred, critically needed skills such as setup men and die and mold repairmen were in short supply. Utilization of equipment, which had normally been running at 95 percent, now dropped to an average of 45 to 50 percent. The new injection molding presses ran less than 25 percent of the time for several months following installation while "bugs" were being taken care of and operators and setup men trained.

Naturally, these problems reflected themselves in reduced sales volume as well as reduced profits. As a result, the second year ended with a loss.

Sales slipped throughout the second year because of the company's inability to make shipments to customers. Some improvement was experienced during the third year. Utilization of the equipment transferred from Acme increased to 75 percent—somewhat short of the desired 90 to 95 percent. The newly purchased injection molding equipment still lagged at 65 percent rather than at the desired level. The company anticipated it would take from six to nine months more before utilization of the equipment could

Exhibit 1. Durard Company Actual and Projected Sales for Ten Year Period

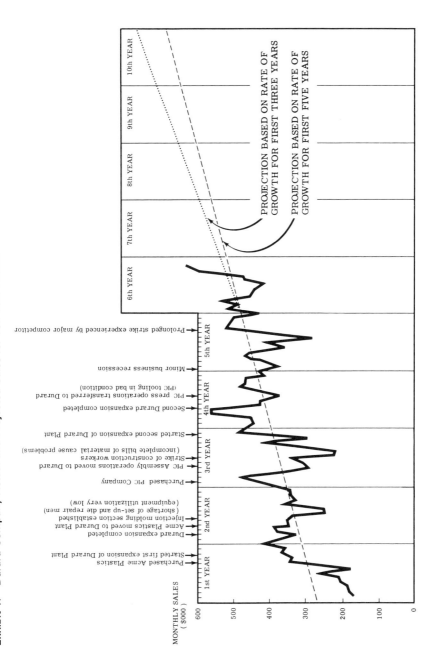

MONTHLY SALES ($000)

600 — 500 — 400 — 300 — 200 — 100 — 0

1st YEAR — 2nd YEAR — 3rd YEAR — 4th YEAR — 5th YEAR — 6th YEAR — 7th YEAR — 8th YEAR — 9th YEAR — 10th YEAR

Purchased Acme Plastics →
Started first expansion of Durard Plant →
Durard expansion completed →
Acme Plastics moved to Durard Plant →
Injection molding section established →
(shortage of set-up and die repair men) →
(equipment utilization very low) →
Purchased PlC Company →
PlC Assembly operations moved to Durard →
Strike of construction workers →
(incomplete bills of material cause problems) →
Started second expansion of Durard Plant →
Second Durard expansion completed →
PlC press operations transferred to Durard →
(PlC tooling in bad condition) →
Minor business recession →
Prolonged strike experienced by major competitor →

PROJECTION BASED ON RATE OF GROWTH FOR FIRST THREE YEARS

PROJECTION BASED ON RATE OF GROWTH FOR FIRST FIVE YEARS

327

attain optimum levels. The profit outlook still was not good, but improvement seemed in sight. Because the Durard Company was in sound financial condition, it was able to weather the storm. Under similar conditions other companies would have failed.

- *Purchase of the PIC Company.* The general manager, who had been with Durard two years, had been released and replaced by a new man. The new man was advised of the company's interest in growth and of the recent problems that had been encountered.

Shortly after taking over the new general manager learned that the PIC Company, which was in financial straits and losing money, could be purchased at a bargain price. This purchase would permit Durard to immediately get into another related product line and pick up PIC's customers. With the Acme move out of the way, the decision was made to purchase PIC and to transfer the operations to Durard as soon as possible.

Within two months, the unprofitable hand assembly items were moved. It was felt that the high labor rates paid at PIC's present location made profits out of the question. The substantially lower rates in the Durard area should help considerably. Although the rates were lower, management miscalculated on two other counts:

1. Purchasing and production scheduling personnel were unfamiliar with the new product line. Bills of material were incomplete because PIC personnel had kept this information "in their heads" rather than on documented records.

2. The Durard plant could not accommodate the PIC press operations. The trouble was not lack of space but the wrong type of floor construction—PIC's heavy presses required heavily reinforced floors.

PIC press operators and tool shopmen were leaving as soon as they could find other employment—knowing that their tenure was limited. Downtime on presses, because of shortage of skilled personnel, increased astronomically. Plans for the second Durard expansion were hurriedly made, but actual work could not start because of an unexpected strike which closed down all construction in the area. Finally, with the settlement of the strike, construction began late in the year. Durard made a small profit that year, but its working capital was becoming strained.

The second expansion was completed late in spring of the fourth year.

Production schedules were firmed up and certain PIC items were now running at high volume. But then problems began to mount again. The tools used at PIC were of a poor quality—no longer meeting the tighter requirements of the industry, which had greatly increased the use of automated assembly equipment. As a result, many fabricated parts that did not meet the greater tolerances required had to be scrapped or reworked. It was obvious that a substantial retooling program was required. In the meantime productivity dropped and production schedules had to be "juggled" frequently to satisfy specific customer demands. The tooling program would require from 15 to 18 months before it could be completed. In the meantime production output continued to drop with the resultant slippage in sales and profits. To add to the problems, a business recession developed near the end of the fourth year during what was normally a high volume production period. Although the recession was relatively mild, productivity continued to slip while the company frantically tried to find competent toolmakers to speed up the retooling program. At this point the general manager was relieved of his responsibilities and still another new man brought in.

The new general manager (let us call him Norm Bayard) was somewhat surprised to learn that his predecessors had such short tenures. He realized that if he mechanically picked up the reins, without some deeper investigation, he might fall victim to the same problems that resulted in the release of his predecessors.

In his "get acquainted" interviews with the members of his staff, he decided that he would attempt to determine exactly what the problems were and how they might have been prevented—or at least greatly minimized. He sensed that some of the staff would undoubtedly, in the role of "Monday morning quarterbacks," apply the 20/20 vision of hindsight to impress the new boss. To avoid being misled Norm double-checked all statements that were made. When he was told that bad tools had been at fault, he asked such questions as:

- Were the tools poorly designed or were they merely worn out and in need of maintenance?
- Could better maintenance have prevented the problem?
- Is it possible that only some of the key high volume tools were the source of the problems? In that case would the availability of a duplicate set of tools have allowed for the needed maintenance?

By asking questions such as these, statements could be pinned down to more factual data. Without being obvious, Norm gradually accumulated a "bank" of information which was correlated with past sales. To this he added the data accumulated during his own tenure. Exhibit 1 was then prepared. Since growth was being emphasized by the company, two projections were made for the balance of the 10-year period. These were based on:

- Rate of growth for the first three years.
- Rate of growth for the first five years.

The first three years would project the trend if the high rate of sales increase experienced in the first three years could be duplicated. The five-year period, however, was a more conservative estimate because it reflected the problems incident to the PIC move and the effect of a business recession. The favorable effect of a major competitor's strike, which occurred in the sixth year, was not included because this was considered to be a nonrecurring "windfall."

A PERIOD OF CONSOLIDATION

Corrective programs instituted by Norm and his predecessor gradually began to take hold. Although production volume continued to slip, defective production was reduced considerably. It was now only a matter of time before the problems of tooling and setup would be corrected. The Durard Company had profited immensely from the long strike of its competitor because it was able to take business on a more selective basis and set up certain equipment to run continuously, day in and day out. One-shift operations were expanded to two shifts, and the work week was extended to 45 hours. Sales and profits soared—somewhat relieving a serious shortage of working capital.

THE TEN COMMANDMENTS FOR PROFITABLE EXPANSION

Norm felt that the pictorial diary of problems experienced by the Durard Company, which are depicted in Exhibit 1, could serve a twofold purpose:

1. It would provide a history of past events and demonstrate their effect on operations.
2. The availability of this type of data would be helpful at management meetings to reinforce the need for solid planning.

It seemed that the previous two general managers moved too quickly to fulfil the company's desire for growth—with the result that the company's working capital became seriously impaired. As a result of this and the other observations made by Norm, the following "ten commandments for expansion" were established:

1. Expand in your own field of expertise. Competition is tough enough without giving your competitors a built-in advantage.
2. Evaluate the market potential before expanding. Check the life cycle of your products to assure that you don't find yourself making a horse-and-buggy product in the automotive age.
3. Check possible monopoly restrictions. There is no point in expanding and then going through divestiture proceedings.
4. Evaluate your financial resources. Determine the potential effect on working capital if things don't go according to plan.
5. Check what your competitors are doing. If they have already embarked on a major expansion program, you may want to take a different course to avoid a large investment in excess facilities of that particular product.
6. Don't expand just for the sake of size. Nothing is to be gained by increasing sales at the sacrifice of profits.
7. Coordinate engineering and production activities. Make certain that bills of material and process specifications are documented rather than being kept in someone's head. This applies to nonmanufacturing activities with equal force.
8. If the design of a product is changed, modify the tooling immediately. Waiting until the order is processed can mean expensive delays and problems in scheduling.
9. Don't expand beyond the limits of available skills. Hold expansion within the limits of the skills that can be made available in the foreseeable future, otherwise efficiency and utilization of equipment will suffer.
10. Transfer the required skills—hourly as well as salaried. If some employees are reluctant to relocate, ask them to stay on for an additional six-month period to train employees at the new location. The extra travel and living expenses will be far cheaper in the long run.

The company recognized that its policies emphasizing growth had been taken too literally by past general managers. To avoid a recurrence, the ten commandments were summarized in the form of a policy letter to all members of management. All subsequent plans for expansion were reviewed by a committee headed by the executive vice-president and made up of representatives of the following divisions: operations, engineering, sales, and finance. This group met once a month to evaluate plans for future expansion and to review progress on current moves. The results of these meetings were summarized and presented to the officers of the company for review.

Establishment of the ten commandments and the monthly reviews had a salutory effect. The rate of growth for the balance of the 10-year period was not as great as the company had hoped for originally. However, the rate did exceed the growth pace of the first five-year period. The growth of profits, however, tripled the rate of the first five years.

The experience of the Durard Company provides an object lesson for other companies intent on rapid growth. The question they should ask is: "Am I interested in rapid expansion of sales volume or am I interested in more profits?" It may be more judicious, for reasons outlined in this chapter, to slow down the rate of sales growth in order to maximize profits.

"Past history contains a wealth of information on past errors in judgment, which should be considered carefully in future planning to avoid repetition."   *Thomas S. Dudick*

KEEPING SCORE:
HOW ARE WE DOING?

CHAPTER 22

ARE YOU PLANNING WISE AND PERFORMANCE FOOLISH?

FRANK J. TANZOLA

"Whatever the background of the excutives responsible for profit planning may be, it is important that the results of their efforts be quantified in the accounting procedures."

Anyone familiar with the history of U.S. Industries knows that it has been one of substantial growth. The sales and earnings growth was from acquisition of businesses, from internal growth of the pre-1965 companies, and from internal growth of the added companies subsequent to acquisition. In fact, USI acquired approximately 100 companies during that period, most of them in the five years 1965 through 1969.

Understandably, assimilation of these companies into the organization required a management approach that was flexible and adaptable to growth. Also, USI was determined to provide an operating atmosphere that blended the latitudes and agility of an entrepreneurship with the disciplines and strengths of a large public company.

Outside observers interested in knowing how USI functions invariably ask the same two questions, "How do you manage so many diverse businesses?", and "How do you motivate the people running the businesses (many of whom are independently wealthy by virtue of having sold their businesses to USI)?" The answer to both questions is—in many ways. It goes to organization structure, comprehensive planning and accountability in the form of budgeting and monthly reporting, pooling expertise and business acumen, financial and other incentives (the carrot), and at times, unfortunately, downright toughness (the stick). The USI incentives for good performance have been fairly broad in that they have included contingency arrangements whereby the total consideration paid for acquired businesses was dependent on profits during a number of years subsequent to acquisition, a bonus system based on profits after a return on the corporation's investment, a stock option plan, base salary levels commensurate with position, responsibilities, and achievement, and a preference for internal promotion to staff higher level positions. Nevertheless, during in-depth discussions of the many ramifications of these areas, one technique—one tool—when described, never fails to excite the questioners' interest and curiosity for more specifics. With these experiences in mind, I thought the technique would be of general interest to management executives and, hence, the purpose of this chapter.

DIVISION PERFORMANCE RATING

At USI, we refer to it as our achievement of objectives system, or performance rating system. As more fully described below, it is a quantification of progress against preset and agreed upon standards, those being good, prudent business measures of operating results. The rating system has been in use at USI for more than ten years, predating the acquisition period mentioned earlier, but it proved to be easily adaptable to a growing number of diverse businesses. Each year the group operating executives solicited the ideas of their division managements regarding appropriate measurement standards, and then common standards were adopted by agreement of the group executives and corporate management. The system is flexible in that points are assigned to standards according to wherever management decides to focus attention and emphasis. Moreover, either the point weighting or the standards themselves can be varied with changing priorities.

BASIS FOR MEASUREMENT

The standards and point assignments are part of USI's Management Guide, which sets forth the corporation's policies and objectives. It is distributed to all of the top executives throughout the corporation. It therefore provides all managers with a clear understanding of the challenge presented to their operation. The latest point system is outlined below.

Doing Better Than Last Year
  Pretax dollar profit
    exceeds same period prior year   1 Point
    exceeds same period prior year by 15% or more   1 Point
    exceeds same period prior year by 25% or more   1 Point
  Pretax Profit Percentage on Sales
    exceeds same period prior year   1 Point
  Return on Average Investment
    exceeds same period prior year   1 Point

Planning Realistically
  Pretax dollar profit for period
    not less than 90% nor more than 125% of budget   1 Point
  Pretax percent profit on sales for the period
    equals or exceeds budget   1 Point
  Return on average capital employed for period
    not less than 90% of budget   1 Point

Managing Cash and Capital
  Investment criteria
    number of months' sales in receivables equals or less than
      budget[a]   1 Point
    number of months' cost of sales in inventory equals or less
      than budget[a]   1 Point
  Cash transfers to headquarters
    at least 75% of prior 12 months' pretax profits   1 Point
    equals or exceeds year-to-date budgeted transfers   2 Points

                               Maximum per period   13 Points[b]

[a] Provided return on capital employed is better than prior year.
[b] 12 Points achieves standard of excellence.

As can be seen from the above, the measure of performance is in three broad areas:

- Profits are compared to prior year, as to absolute dollars, margins, and return on investment. The investment community applies these yardsticks in total company evaluation.
- Profits are compared to budget. Note that a point is lost for dollars of profit either too far below or *too far above* the amount budgeted. This is one way of discouraging divisional budgets that are either too cozy or too aggressive. Realistic divisional budgets serve as a norm to identify during the year good or poor performers or shifts in business condi-

tions. They also provide the required firm basis for overall corporate planning.

- Managing cash and capital. The emphasis here is on good management of inventory and receivables. Sales turnover ratios are used to allow for better or worse than expected business conditions and to measure management reaction in controllable areas to the changed conditions. Cash, of course, is the ultimate end product of business activity, and its emphasis here needs no rationale other than to provide incentive to produce it so that it can be kept at work in the overall corporate structure.

It should be noted that this approach also affords a better performance evaluation of the management of a business operating in a market that has become depressed. While admittedly, through no fault of their own, they may not be able to earn the points based on profit comparisons to the prior year, they could nevertheless earn the points for good management of cash and capital and, to the extent they had the foresight, the points based on budgeted amounts. Thus, the management of such a business would not be rated as poorly as they might be if they were to be judged solely on comparative profit results.

THE PERFORMANCE REPORT

Each quarter, every division rates itself on a form devised and provided for that purpose and with reference to the Management Guide point standards. These forms are forwarded to corporate headquarters where they are reviewed and the divisions ranked, according to points earned, among all divisions in the company. Where divisions have earned the same number of points, ranking in the quarterly report is according to the percent improvement of dollars profits over the prior year period. A sample of the quarterly rating form is shown as Exhibit 1.

GIVING VISIBILITY TO PERFORMANCE

When this information has been assembled and divisions ranked at corporate headquarters, a performance standing report is prepared and distributed throughout the company to all Management Guide holders during the third week following each quarter. A sample of a performance standing report is shown below. The names used are not the actual USI divisions nor are the points shown necessarily indicative of ratings on any actual USI quarterly report (see Exhibit 2).

In practice, this same system is applied to the four USI operating groups and they too are rated and ranked, but separately among themselves.

To provide increased visibility for performance and additional incentives, and to foster the competitive spirit implicit in the system, twelve pointers have been presented excellence awards in the form of "E" flags each quarter. The division and group with the highest cumulative points for the year has each received the annual first place award—a bronze plaque. Also, a quarterly "Performance Awards" brochure has been distributed. A full page has been devoted to each of the winning organizations with photos of the key executives together with an announcement of the award and a write-up of their division or group. The first page of this brochure has been a letter of congratulations from the chairman and president. In short, it isn't enough to merely tabulate performance statistics. The results must be widely publicized, and the system must have the interest and support of top management. Additional importance is attached to it when high point achievement is given weight in annual bonus considerations.

HAS IT BEEN EFFECTIVE?

Managing a giant corporation from the top can be a very lonely and at times, a frustrating and thankless job. The question of how best to get line management to function most effectively in areas of corporate concern and benefit has no easy answer. The fields of employee motivation and management science are broad. Their volumes and practitioners offer many varied approaches adaptable to particular circumstances. At USI we employ many of the usual approaches, but the rating system that I have described has contributed surprisingly well among our motivational tools. I say surprisingly because at first blush it may seem schoolboyish and unlikely to interest the sophisticated, successful businessmen. On the contrary, however, we have witnessed that extra effort, that special attention to achieving goals by both our professional managers and entrepreneurs to come away with the honors of the awards for their divisions or to gain a respectable ranking among all di-

Exhibit 1. Performance Measurement Report

PERFORMANCE MEASUREMENT REPORT

COMPANY _____

GROUP _____   (SUBSIDIARY/DIVISION)   (DATE)

(Dollars Amounts In Thousands)

	This Year Actual	This Year Budget	Last Year's Actual	This Year % of Budget	This Year vs. Last % Incr.	Points Current Quarter	Points Year to Date
PROFIT OBJECTIVES							
Pretax Profit (A)							
Current Quarter	$____	$____	$____	____%	____%	☐	
Year to Date	$____	$____	$____	____%	____%		☐
Net Sales							
Current Quarter	$____	$____	$____				
Year to Date	$____	$____	$____				
Pretax Profit % (B)							
Current Quarter	____%	____%	____%			☐	
Year to Date	____%	____%	____%				☐
Average Investment (C)	$____	$____	$____				
Return on Average Investment	____%	____%	____%			☐	☐

340

INVESTMENT CRITERIA (D)

Receivables

Average Sales–Last 3 Months $ _____

Number of Months Sales in Receivables $ _____ _____

Inventories

Average Cost of Sales–Last 3 Months $ _____

Number of Months Cost of Sales in Inventory $ _____ _____

CASH TRANSFERS (E)

Pure Cash Transfers Equal to Budget-Year
To Date $ _____

12 Mos. Cash	12 Mos. Equiv.	12 Mos. Total	12 Mos. PTP	12 Mos. Percent

Pure Cash Transfers and Equivalents[a]
as % of most recent 12 months'
pretax profits:

$ _____ $ _____ $ _____ $ _____   _____ %

Total Performance Points _____

[a] Includes any direct payments for income taxes or debt.

Exhibit 2. Performance Standing Report

THREE MONTH ENDED MARCH 31, 19xx
RANKED IN ACCORDANCE WITH USI MANAGEMENT GUIDE NO. P-11

TOP 25%		SECOND 25%		THIRD 25%		FOURTH 25%	
RANK	DIVISION (AND POINTS)	RANK	DIVISION (AND POINTS)	RANK	DIVISION (AND POINTS)	RANK	DIVISION (AND POINTS)
1	Apex (12)	29	Scatter Chain (9)	57	Ramco (5)	85	Tool Steel Products (2)
2	Durel (12)	30	Boggs Ewell (9)	58	Runarko (5)	86	Grand Junction (2)
3	A E Wire & Cable (12)	31	West-Link (9)	59	Regale (5)	87	Hamiltonian (2)
4	Nashville (12)	32	Duralee (9)	60	Prosper-Gordon (4)	88	Georgia Belle (2)
5	Rolled Steel Products (12)	33	Specto (9)	61	Relco (4)	89	Transparo Pack (2)
6	Daly Baking (12)	34	Riviera (9)	62	Decorel (4)	90	Tacoma (2)
7	Hudson Chemical (12)	35	Tacco (9)	63	Levivo (4)	91	Meropo (2)
8	Super Automatic (12)	36	Springdale (9)	64	Beverly (4)	92	Bow-Tel (2)
9	Bevy Products (12)	37	Dusco (9)	65	Covia (4)	93	Valiant (2)
10	Lingus Linens (12)	38	Bulleg-Art (9)	66	Records Devices (3)	94	Reducto (2)
11	Minute Foods (12)	39	Greenco (9)	67	Global-Reliance (3)	95	El-Con (2)
12	Harvey Fasteners (12)	40	Halfield (8)	68	Xenia (3)	96	Karpo (2)
13	Burkey's (12)	41	Relayne (8)	69	Charleston (3)	97	BelTone (2)
14	Atwell (12)	42	Dubuque (8)	70	Llewellyn (3)	98	Brookings (2)
15	Ginter Products (12)	43	Relyan (8)	71	Denver (3)	99	Konsor (2)
16	Agrol (11)	44	Bellows Falls (8)	72	Phoenix (3)	100	Gurney (2)
17	Mann's Supply (11)	45	Drymouth (7)	73	Car-Cote (3)	101	El Paso (2)
18	Hyko (11)	46	Girken (7)	74	Desmond-Reed (3)	102	Holsum Kraft (2)
19	Remson (11)	47	Ledeaux (7)	75	Tallisman (3)	103	Centrex Leasing (2)
20	Warston (10)	48	Lindenhayn (7)	76	Midway (3)	104	D & W Fixtures (2)
21	Phillipsburg (10)	49	Krotulis (7)	77	San Miguel (3)	105	National Abrading (2)
22	Hartwell (10)	50	Kelly (7)	78	Temper-Tone (3)	106	Thompson (2)
23	Prince Charming (10)	51	Duchess (6)	79	Real-Time (3)	107	Portland (2)
24	Eastern Window (10)	52	Danny (6)	80	Iron-Bilt (3)	108	Southwest Reduction (2)
25	Royal (10)	53	Green Kalto (6)	81	Reading (3)	109	Revolvo (2)
26	Keystone (10)	54	Leghorn (5)	82	Pueblo (3)	110	Timer Tones (2)
27	Southern Aire (10)	55	Recycle Products (5)	83	Ark-Tire (3)	111	Halgren (2)
28	Brown Company (9)	56	Reota (5)	84	Harken's (3)	112	Culver (2)

visions. It reaffirms for us that pride and the competitive spirit are potent human drives. A motivational or incentive package that ignores or underrates them is missing a fundamental.

SIDE BENEFITS

At the risk of claiming too much for the system, it is important to list some of its secondary benefits. Starting out with the premise that the agreed upon standards are good prudent business measures of operating results, it follows that:

- Management can see by a glance at the performance standing report which divisions are performing well and which not so well.
- The lost points act as red flags directing management's attention to those areas.
- Among the required agenda items for monthly division executive meetings is a discussion of the areas where points were lost, the reasons, and corrective actions taken. This often leads to in-depth discussion of business conditions and/or operating problems. Minutes of these meetings are forwarded to group and corporate headquarters where they are read by all key executives.
- Included in the internal audit review scope is a procedure where the auditor satisfies himself as to the stated reasons for the division's lost points. This can lead the auditor to important findings that might otherwise escape his attention.

ONCE MORE ON FLEXIBILITY

I mentioned earlier that the system has inherent flexibility in regard to shifting management emphasis. In closing, it should be added that it is also flexible as to its application to organizational units other than the operating division. The group organization at USI has already been mentioned but it could likewise be applied to smaller or larger units such as departments or even business segments.

In fact, a good example of adapting it for both shifting emphasis and different organization units is currently underway at USI. Management has determined that with post acquisition earnout periods largely past, and for reasons related to concentrating business expertise and operating efficiencies, the company would now be better served if it were to reorganize divisions into much fewer but larger operating units along product lines. Added benefits expected from the more simplified structure are better investor understanding of the company and better market identification. This necessitates a complete revision of the rating system to adapt it to the new structure. Nevertheless, we fully expect that when we enter the new year, the revised system will be fully operational and will be serving us as well in the future as it has in the past.

"It isn't enough to merely tabulate performance statistics. They must be given proper visibility and the procedure must have the interest and backing of top management."   Frank J. Tanzola

INDEX